COMMUNITY COLLEGES OF TENNESSEE

Volume 2

The Tennessee Series

COMMUNITY COLLEGES OF TENNESSEE

The Founding and Early Years

edited by
Roy S. Nicks

Memphis State University Press
Memphis, Tennessee

Copyright © 1979 by
Memphis State University Press

All rights reserved. No part of this book may be reproduced or utilized in
any form or by any means, electronic or mechanical, including photocopy-
ing and recording, or by any information storage and retrieval system,
without permission from the publisher.

Manufactured in the United States of America

ISBN 0-87870-054-4

TABLE OF CONTENTS

To the memory of Frank G. Clement, a great governor, who possessed the foresight and ability to lead the development of the first community colleges and who gave this writer, as a young man, an opportunity to serve.

Photograph by George W. Hornal, courtesy Tennessee Department of Transportation.

To J. Howard Warf, a tenacious commissioner of education, who midwifed and then nurtured the first community colleges into viable components of higher education in Tennessee.

Photograph courtesy Tennessee State Board of Education.

THE EDITOR

Roy S. Nicks, chancellor of the State University and Community College System of Tennessee since 1975, is a native of Chapel Hill, Tennessee, and received the Ed.D. from Memphis State University. At the time of his selection as system chancellor, he was serving as chancellor of the University of Tennessee at Nashville and as vice-president for Urban and Public Affairs of the University of Tennessee System.

Photograph courtesy State Board of Regents.

CONTRIBUTORS

CHARLES W. BRANCH, the president of Chattanooga State Technical Community College since 1974, was born in Gaffney, South Carolina. He earned the Ed.D. at the University of Alabama and was serving as the assistant executive secretary of the Commission on Colleges of the Southern Association of Colleges and Schools at the time of his appointment at Chattanooga State.

JACK E. CAMPBELL has been president of Walters State Community College since 1974. A native of Johnson City, Tennessee, he received the Ed.D. from the University of Mississippi. He was the dean of instruction at Calhoun State Technical Junior College in Alabama prior to coming to Walters State.

CUYLER A. DUNBAR, founding president of Roane State Community College, was born in Nashville, Tennessee. He was awarded the Ed.D. at Auburn University. At the time of his appointment to Roane State, he was serving as the dean of student personnel at Columbia State Community College.

EDWARD B. ELLER, the founding president of Dyersburg State Community College, was born in Spencer, North Carolina, and earned the Ed.D. at the University of Tennessee. He was the assistant state education commissioner for instruction prior to his appointment at Dyersburg State.

L. QUENTIN LANE, president of Cleveland State Community College since 1978, is a native of Birchwood, Tennessee. He received the Ed.D. from the University of Tennessee and was dean of academic affairs at Cleveland State at the time of his appointment as president.

WALTER L. NELMS, the president of Jackson State Community College since 1976, was born in Memphis, Tennessee. He earned the Ed.D. at the University of Mississippi. Prior to being selected as president, he served as dean of the college at Jackson State.

JESS H. PARRISH, founding president of Shelby State Community College, was born in Ballinger, Texas, and earned the Ed.D. at Texas Technological University. He served as vice-president for student affairs at Memphis State University prior to his appointment at Shelby State. DONALD M. MIKULA is dean of planning and development at Shelby State Community College.

HAROLD S. PRYOR, the first president of Columbia State Community College, is a native of Livingston, Tennessee. He received the Ed.D. from the University of Tennessee and was director of teacher education at Austin Peay State University at the time of his appointment to Columbia State.

HAL R. RAMER, the founding president of Volunteer State Community College, was born in Kenton, Tennessee, and awarded the Ph.D. from Ohio State University. He was assistant state education commissioner for higher education at the time of his appointment to Volunteer State.

RICHARD G. RHODA, the assistant to the chancellor of the State University and Community College System of Tennessee, was born in Allentown, Pennsylvania, and is a Ph.D. candidate at George Peabody College. He served as a research associate in the system staff prior to his assuming his current position.

HARRY D. WAGNER, president of Motlow State Community College since 1975, is a native of Dunlap, Tennessee. He earned the Ed.D. at George Peabody College and was vice-president for student affairs at Middle Tennessee State University prior to coming to Motlow State.

PREFACE
by Roy S. Nicks

*T*he most important development in Tennessee public higher education—since the establishment of the normal schools in 1909—has been an endeavor that has changed the entire character and complexion of higher education in the state. Beginning in 1963 and continuing through graduated initiations between 1965 and 1973, Tennessee developed a unified network of 10 dynamic community colleges that were geographically dispersed throughout the state in urban, suburban, and rural locales. The services provided by community colleges and the progress they have realized in a relatively brief period have surpassed all expectations. As of 1978-1979, Tennessee community colleges collectively have enrolled more than 29,000 degree-credit students, employed some 600 full-time faculty, maintained campuses exceeding $92.6 million in plant value, and operated with annual budgets totaling $47.9 million.

The community college concept was clearly an idea whose time had come to Tennessee by the mid-1960s. The 1950s and early 1960s were periods of overall change and transition for the state. The economy and population were rapidly moving away from a primarily agrarian dependence toward a diversity that comes with industrial growth. These changes gave rise to overwhelming demands for improving and extending the public education system. The community college, as an institution, was established in studied response to these changes and the confluence of at least four resulting factors: tremendous enrollment increases had been experienced and more were anticipated in Tennessee's colleges and universities; the existing institutions were pushed to capacity; there was a determined need for types of postsecondary programs sorely lacking in Tennessee higher education; and increasing student accessibility to postsecondary education was a paramount concern.

The purpose of this book is to chronicle the origins and developments to date of Tennessee's community colleges. It attempts to present these colleges' development in a manner that accurately reflects the dynamics and realities of their evolution from concept to their current stature as viable institutions. Further, it attempts to describe the establishment of the partnership between statewide initiative and local impetus in community college education. This book is intended for the readership of educators and students, as well as those with general interests in community colleges, educational planning, and organizational development.

The emergence of community colleges in Tennessee adds a vital dimension to state and local history. Throughout their founding and early years, the colleges developed as continuums of successful efforts by communities, educators, and the state administration and legislature working in partnership to tailor the institutions to local and regional needs. The particular sequence of events shaping the individual colleges' growth has varied with the diversity and uniqueness of their settings. At the same time, the progress of each college has been directed by the commonalities incumbent of a statewide undertaking of such great magnitude.

The founding and early years of the community colleges—from the mid-1960s through the close of the 1970s—represent a definitive period in their individual and collective development. It is a period of activities and impact that will never again be experienced in Tennessee higher education, nor will the colleges themselves ever repeat such adventures and growth in their institutional life cycles.

The founding years of the community colleges occurred during a period of major change within the entire Tennessee higher education community. In response to the same pressures for growth and expansion that spurred the establishment of the colleges, and within the same time frame, the current structure of state-supported higher education was molded. Between the years of 1963 and 1973, other key changes occurred: Each of the remaining four senior regional colleges advanced to university status; the University of Tennessee assumed control of a private institution and reorganized as a system with five campuses; a network of postsecondary technical institutes and area vocational-technical schools was established; the Tennessee Higher Education Commission was created as the coordinating agency for higher education; and the State University and Community College System of Tennessee was established with the State Board of Regents as the governing body. The impact of these changes and the development of the community college program have been interrelated and significant. Such issues as the governance, support, and role and scope of the colleges were initially and have been continually addressed in consideration of the total development of Tennessee higher education.

In purpose and practice, Tennessee's community colleges have developed to fulfill the state's commitment to ensuring student access to a comprehensive range of one-year and two-year quality postsecondary education programs and to lifelong learning.

This book is composed of 10 chapters, introduction, summary, and appendix. The introduction provides an overview of the conceptualization and initiation of the Tennessee community college program from the statewide perspective. In this introductory chapter, the major considerations and events leading up to and through the colleges' founding have been reconstructed, not only in a chronological sense, but also in terms of the topical and environmental aspects of the times which impacted the implementation and character of the colleges. Chapters one through 10 are the histories of the individual colleges. Appearing in the order of the institution's date of founding, each chapter is authored by the current college president. In keeping with the unique nature of each community college, these chapters reflect and enhance the presentation of the colleges' great diversity. The summary presents a brief overview of the colleges' development, from their foundings through these early years, highlighting and drawing into perspective the more dominant features, trends, and issues which have characterized Tennessee's community college program. Finally, the summary offers a prospectus for the future of the colleges as they enter the stage of maturing institutions. The appendix contains tables which support and supplement the narrative of the various chapters and which summarize the colleges' enrollment and fiscal development since inception. The tables are also intended to serve as a ready reference to the comparative and aggregate growth of the colleges.

COMMUNITY COLLEGES
TENNESSEE

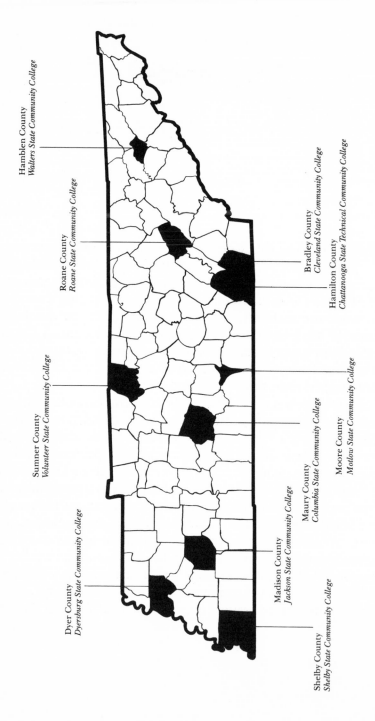

Hamblen County
Walters State Community College

Bradley County
Cleveland State Community College

Hamilton County
Chattanooga State Technical Community College

Roane County
Roane State Community College

Sumner County
Volunteer State Community College

Maury County
Columbia State Community College

Moore County
Motlow State Community College

Madison County
Jackson State Community College

Dyer County
Dyersburg State Community College

Shelby County
Shelby State Community College

ACKNOWLEDGMENTS

On behalf of the State Board of Regents and others who have personal and professional interests in Tennessee's community colleges, we wish to express our sincere appreciation to the Memphis State University Press for encouraging the writing of this book and including it as the second volume in the Tennessee Series—a truly inspired undertaking documenting significant aspects of the state's heritage and culture. We are grateful to have the early history of the community colleges preserved as a part of this distinguished collection.

We also wish to acknowledge those who contributed valuable information and insight to the writing of this book. One of the most striking features of the founding of Tennessee's community colleges was the influence imparted by a number of prominent leaders in state education. Many of these "pioneers" continue to serve Tennessee higher education today; in fact, four of the current college presidents have provided leadership in that capacity since the creation of their institutions. To these and other individuals we offer our sincere thanks for sharing with us their time, records, and recollections. We especially want to thank J. Howard Warf, presently a member of the State Board of Regents and widely regarded as a principal figure in the development of the community colleges while serving as the state commissioner of education from 1963 to 1971, and Dr. Hal R.

Ramer, the founding and current president of Volunteer State Community College, who served as assistant commissioner for higher education from 1963 to 1970.

Roy S. Nicks

Nashville, Tennessee
September 6, 1979

INTRODUCTION
by Richard G. Rhoda

*T*ennessee is a state of bountiful natural and man-made resources. Located in the Ohio Valley region of the nation, Tennessee has a colorful history uniquely significant in its geographical and cultural diversities, spanning from the Great Smoky Mountains in the east to the Mississippi River in the west. Progress and development of this state have been hallmarked by populism, individuals and actions of courage and vision, and human industry responsive to the ever-changing needs and dreams of its people. A proud legacy of progressive statewide programs has continually enhanced individual and community well-being and opportunity.

In many respects, Tennessee community colleges manifest the inherent qualities of the state for developing resources. The colleges were established in response to recognized needs for improving and expanding higher educational opportunities. By concept and design, the colleges were initiated in key locations throughout the state as a community-oriented program for making postsecondary education and services more accessible to all Tennesseans. The role and scope of the individual colleges with time have diversified and developed to accommodate both unique local characteristics and statewide considerations.

The successful initiation and subsequent development of the community colleges are attributable to strong leadership and support on state and local levels. Growing from the wisdom and practical abilities of responsive individuals and governmental bodies, the colleges, as educational, social, and cultural centers, have captured and embodied the imagination of thousands of Tennesseans.

While the precise origins and historical antecedents of the community colleges are subject to debate, the findings and recommendations of a study, *Public Higher Education in Tennessee,* initiated in 1955 and concluded in 1957 by the legislative council of the Tennessee General Assembly, are widely regarded as the cornerstone of this movement in Tennessee. The purpose of this study, conducted under the primary direction of Dr. Truman Pierce and Dr. A. D. Albright, was twofold: "(1) to point up possible improvements in current programs of public higher education in Tennessee with present resources, and (2) to provide a design for intelligent planning to meet future needs." Significant needs for expanding Tennessee's existing public higher education programs, identified in the Pierce-Albright Report, were predicated upon the fundamental changes that had occurred and were foreseen in the state's economy and population. The more pertinent economic and social findings stated that

> Tennessee's wealth was increasing rapidly; industrial development was proceeding at an excellerated pace; new industry tended to concentrate in and around metropolitan areas; agriculture was declining in relative importance; overall population was increasing and shifting from the rural to metropolitan areas; in-state birthrate would continue to increase; therefore, college-age population would likewise increase; the number of high school and other students seeking college educations would increase, and the number of veterans eligible for education benefits after the Korean War was significant.

Based on these and other study findings, including the expressed convictions of the citizenry that education was a means of achieving maximum individual and social growth and that the responsibility of providing needed educational programs rested with the state, the report recommendations provided, in part, that

> all persons who can profit from it should have the opportunity of receiving a college education; provisions should be made for a larger percentage of the bright and more able students to attend colleges and universities; the program of higher education should be of significant variety and comprehensiveness; the program of higher education should include extensive services

to people who are not formally enrolled in courses offered on
the campus; higher education opportunities should be readily
accessible to the youth of the state.

Flowing from the latter recommendation, the report noted that
the seven state-supported colleges and universities existing at that
time—all four-year institutions—were "distributed geographically
so that a substantial part of the state is located within a radius of 50
miles of one or more of the institutions." Glaring exceptions to that
finding cited by the report were the Chattanooga area, a large metropolitan trade center in the southeastern corner of the state; the
Pulaski-Columbia area, a large geographical section of south-central
Tennessee; and the Jackson area, a well-populated commerce center
in West Tennessee. New state colleges were, therefore, recommended for those three unserved areas. While it is clear that the
report's recommendation envisioned the establishment of new
four-year state colleges, the concept of accessibility was paramount,
for "the distribution of colleges thus assured would mean that each
could serve the function of a community college as well as such other
functions as are desired and feasible."

The Pierce-Albright Report generated great interest for expanding the Tennessee higher education program. Reflective of the report's findings and recommendations and those of ensuing studies
on the state, regional, and national levels, a public mandate emerged
toward establishing new state colleges. Community groups began to
solicit advice as to how they could secure new institutions for their
localities, and over the next few years all elements in the state responsible for educational policy and planning were deeply involved
in deliberations as to what type of institution and how many should
be established, how they should be governed and financed, and
where and under what criteria they should be located.

An undercurrent of consideration for two-year institutions ran
through the thoughts of this period. Posed against the clearly defined educational needs of the state, there was considerable sentiment that the junior or community college was a possible alternative
to additional free-standing four-year institutions. Reflecting this belief, on various occasions State Education Commissioner Joe Morgan suggested that some form of two-year postsecondary
institutions—making accessible the first two years of a four-year col-

lege program, offering comprehensive vocational-technical education programs, and serving full-time/ part-time college age and adult
students—could alleviate the needs and fill the voids in the state's
education program. At this time, however, the two-year junior or
community college was regarded as little more than an abstract alternative; the community college concept was still relatively vague
and nebulous to Tennesseans.

A change in the state administration marked the turning point in
this period of search for the most feasible answers to the question of
new colleges. Early in 1963, recently reelected Governor Frank G.
Clement consulted with his new state education commissioner, J.
Howard Warf, concerning the status of the ongoing deliberations.
Convinced that the time was right to set in motion formal authorization to pursue development of new institutions, Governor Clement
and Commissioner Warf met with the leadership of the Tennessee
General Assembly, and ultimately an agreement to proceed was
reached and embodied in legislation. Chapter 379 of the 1963 Public
Acts, Section four, Item 43, read as follows:

> There is hereby appropriated the sum of One Hundred
> Thousand ($100,000.00) Dollars, per annum, to the State Board
> of Education, in addition to the appropriations used and dis-
> bursed for the purpose of preliminary planning and the estab-
> lishment of additional, regional-type institutions of higher
> learning in Tennessee as recommended by the 1957 report on
> public higher education in Tennessee, and the Legislative Coun-
> cil Committee report of the Eightieth General Assembly of the
> State of Tennessee.

Three aspects of this authorization are of great significance to
the character of the colleges which emerged. First, the fundamental
responsibility for preliminary planning and establishment of the colleges was steered away from the political arena of the General Assembly and directed to the State Board of Education, the governing
body for the state colleges and universities and public elementary,
secondary, and special schools. Second, the legislation spoke in terms
of "additional, regional-type institutions of higher learning," which
reflected support for the general concept of need-based expansion,
rather than authorizing the development of specific institutions.
The third aspect of importance in this act was the direct reference
and reliance upon the recommendations of the 1957 Pierce-
Albright Report. This acknowledgment signified a commitment by

the General Assembly to the findings of fact and rationale for en-
hancing the reach of public education in the state.

To proceed with the implementation of this legislation, the State
Board of Education adopted a resolution at its meeting on August 9,
1963, which authorized the chairman, Commissioner Warf,

> to appoint five members of this board to make preliminary plans
> for a state college in the south-central area of Tennessee, to con-
> fer with interested citizens and public officials in that area on this
> matter, to ascertain what contributions to the establishment of a
> state college local governments in the area are prepared to
> make, to visit possible sites, and to make a report with recom-
> mendations as to the site and the method of establishing a new
> college . . . .

The singular reference in the board's action to a state college in
the south-central area of the state was significant. While the 1957
study identified two other major areas in need of public higher education services, the need for a state-supported institution in the
Chattanooga region had been addressed three months earlier by the
board with the establishment of a postsecondary regional technical
training school there. The Jackson area was still considered to be in
substantial need of services; however, the press for a college in the
Pulaski-Columbia (south-central) area was considered principal and
significant of popular, long-standing concerns in that area for a
higher education institution, dating back to the early 1900s when the
General Education Act established the state normal colleges.

Pursuant to the resolution, Commissioner Warf appointed a
committee composed of T. M. Divine of Kingsport, Dale F. Glover of
Obion, Mrs. B. A. McDermott of Nashville, J. Frank Taylor of Huntingdon, with Edward L. Jennings of Liberty as chairman. During
the next six months, the south-central college committee dutifully
attacked its charge, joined by Commissioner Warf and such principal
members of the State Department of Education staff as T. Wesley
Pickel, assistant commissioner for special services, and Dr. Hal R.
Ramer, assistant commissioner for higher education. At the February 7, 1964, meeting, the State Board of Education adopted a progress report from the committee—now known as the Committee for a
Junior College in South-Central Tennessee. The committee reported that its members had visited a number of sites in the general
area and met with citizens "relative to the possible establishment of a

Junior College in that region." It further noted that "Careful consideration has led us to the conclusion that a multi-purpose college is needed in that area . . . ." Avoiding definite recommendations pending specific determination of such matters as cost factors, physical facilities, and curriculum for the new college, the report requested the commissioner to proceed with measures necessary to expedite the committee's final recommendation to the board.

The junior college recommendation which surfaced in the committee's report may be attributed to a number of considerations. Ever since the determination had been made to pursue the establishment of new public colleges, the existing four-year colleges and universities had exerted considerable pressure at the state level to discourage the development of new, competing four-year institutions. Complementing this reality, impetus for thought toward two-year institutions was enhanced by the advent of funding under the 1963 Higher Education Facilities Act. This federal legislation authorized a special grant program for financing the construction of two-year colleges. In addition, the committee's conclusion regarding a multi-purpose college was significant of the progress that had been made in conceptualizing a two-year institution which would offer senior college transfer programs, including pre-professional and general education and liberal arts; vocational-technical programs designed to meet local needs; and programs of community services, as well as continuing adult education.

It was for these reasons that the junior college emerged as a generic concept, with the specifics to be developed by the commissioner and the Department of Education staff. As a result of this emphasis on further exploring the prospects of the new type of institution, the initial charge of the committee concerning the selection of a location for a south-central college would not be fulfilled for another 16 months.

Over the next several months, Commissioner Warf and his staff engaged in the complex planning, study, and operations essential to an orderly and qualitative development of the new college. The scope of their activities was also extended beyond the south-central region to include other areas of the state where needs for expanded postsecondary services were identified. Their studies took into consideration the operations of two-year public colleges in other states, notably Florida, Texas, California, and Mississippi. Assisted by an update of the 1957 study, in depth analyses were also made of the current and anticipated enrollment increases and trends throughout Tennessee and the capacities of the 47 existing public and private colleges and universities in the state. Central to planning and study was the determination to increase the number and percentage of high school graduates attending college, which sorely lagged behind national averages, and those factors known to enhance accessibility to higher education.

The principal findings and recommendations of these efforts were then considered by the committee on community-junior colleges, which in a called session on December 17, 1964, adopted a landmark resolution for the establishment of three community-junior colleges. Reflective of the state's needs, the resolution asserted the belief that

> The establishment of a select number of State community-junior colleges, strategically located, can assist in relieving enrollment pressures on existing institutions and, at the same time, can provide additional educational opportunities closer to students' homes, as amply demonstrated by many other states of our nation . . . .

It further expressed the need to initiate definite measures by stating

> It is the considered judgment of this Committee that three such State community-junior colleges will need to be established in the 1965-67 biennium (one in each Grand Division of Tennessee), that prototype plans should be promulgated, and that the experience of other states has shown that the factors of location of these colleges and their services in cooperation with existing public higher education institutions are of utmost importance . . . and requiring adequate appropriations, continued planning involving institutional service areas, curricular offerings, accreditation and credit-transfer agreements, and similar questions. . . .

While not adopted by the full State Board of Education until its February 5, 1965, regular quarterly session, the committee's recommendation was submitted for incorporation in Governor Clement's 1965-1966 budget. Having the full support of the governor and key legislative leaders, the 84th General Assembly authorized $100,000 for fiscal year 1965-1966, and $500,000 for fiscal year 1966-1967 to the board for the operation, maintenance, and control of the first three community-junior colleges. An additional four-million-dollar capital outlay was authorized for the construction of the colleges. The state senate also expressed interest in the locations of the new colleges during the 1965 legislative session with adoption of Senate Resolution No. 25, which suggested

> That in order to accomplish the greatest good for the largest number of Tennessee citizens, that these institutions be located at the most accessible point nearest the center of the area in each Grand Division of the State which is now over 50 miles from any State Supported Institution of Higher Learning . . . .

With the authorization of the General Assembly, the momentum which had been mounting over the past two years for initiating a statewide program of two-year colleges was soon to be realized. Renewed campaigns were waged by numerous community groups, and the continuing studies for locating the colleges assumed a quickened cadence, as did the planning of the colleges' operational and programmatic aspects. All of these efforts reached a point of fruition at a called session of the State Board of Education on June 22, 1965. It was during that meeting that the community-junior college committee made its report, recommending the location of the first three of the new colleges, and that other important action by the board was transacted, shaping the destiny of other colleges yet to be founded.

Prefacing the reading of the report, Chairman Jennings offered the following statement:

> I wish to thank each member of the committee who has worked hard and long in order to reach our present decisions and recommendations. I also wish to thank all those officials and representatives from the 22 communities who have sought these institutions of higher learning—their presentations and information furnished have been outstanding and we, who have served on this committee, have received a liberal education in the fields of Tennessee economics and geography, and our only regret is that we do not have a junior college to allocate to each of them. Our report is in harmony with recent studies of the needs of public higher education in Tennessee, including the Pierce-Albright Report of 1957. The report that we bring is not a unanimous one, in that the three selections that I am about to read are not the first choices of each of us; in fact, they are not all

my first choices, but the report is a consensus report of the committee and is signed by each member of the committee.

The board then unanimously adopted the committee's report which, in the form of a resolution, established the Cleveland area adjacent to Chattanooga, the Columbia area in south-central Tennessee, and the Jackson area in West Tennessee as the locations of the first three community-junior colleges, with the exact sites to be selected by the board chairman. The board further authorized and empowered the chairman, Commissioner Warf, to "do all things necessary in expediting the establishment of each said institution." In addition, the board resolved that six additional colleges, two in each Grand Division of the state, be established as soon as possible.

During the discussion related to this action, Commissioner Warf noted that the 22 community delegations proposing location of the colleges were represented by a myriad of private citizens, civic and professional groups and associations, city and county officials, legislators, and development district staffs. They came, he said, from across the state, armed with surveys, maps, and signed petitions, all with the common purpose of securing a junior-community college for their localities. He recounted that the committee had heard all of the delegation presentations in a two-day session and had deliberated at length before making its most difficult decisions. He also pointed out that the recommendation for additional colleges would surely become a reality within a few years, giving other communities the opportunity to be the site of one of these institutions.

It was at this same meeting that the board adopted a position on the requisite local contributions toward the establishment of the community-junior colleges. Based on the firm belief that the colleges should not be placed on the "auction block" but that an adequate and uniform amount of money and property should be required from the local area, it was decided that the county or city where a college would be located must contribute $250,000 for construction of the campus and land in the amount of 100 acres or more with all utilities, to the site. This policy, which remained intact as the standard for all of the yet-to-be-established colleges, set forth the fundamental relationship between local and state support of the colleges—a partnership predicated on local commitment and investment in the colleges' development.

One other key element of the new colleges' character—institutional autonomy—was established at the June 22, 1965, State Board of Education meeting. At the recommendation of Commissioner Warf, the board adopted a resolution that the new colleges

> ... which are to be established shall be operated on the same bases as the colleges and universities which are now under the jurisdiction of this Board.... This shall include, but not be limited to, the employment of personnel, the purchasing of supplies and equipment, the expenditures of operating funds, and accounting and budgeting procedures.

This action signified the board's intent to assign the new colleges the same degree of delegated authority enjoyed by the existing four-year institutions. It was felt that this operational flexibility would be essential in the founding phases of the new colleges, fostering initiatives and expediting the implementation of board policies and guidelines by the campus presidents and their staffs.

Pursuant to these directives, over the course of the next several months, Commissioner Warf and his staff proceeded with the charge to select specific campus sites and develop the overall programmatic designs and educational specifications for the form and structure for these new institutions. Timing was urgent. The college in the Columbia area was designated to serve as the prototype, and it was essential for the Department of Education to formulate basic principles and transit the new colleges from concept to reality.

Building upon earlier studies, contemporary theory, and models in other states, major policy decisions were reached which would influence profoundly the character and quality of Tennessee's two-year public colleges. The colleges would be state-controlled and state-supported, with relatively modest student fees, and, except for initial cash and land contributions, the continuing financial support of local governments would not be required. This position was taken in deference to the level of local support required for Tennessee's public elementary and secondary schools.

Community colleges also were to be teaching institutions and offer comprehensive programs of high quality appropriate to an accredited two-year collegiate format, under the standards of the Commission on Colleges of the Southern Association of Colleges and Schools. They would award associate degrees and certificates, employ regular faculty with at least a master's degree in the teaching discipline, operate day and night on a year-round quarter-term calendar, and draw students of all ages on an "open-admissions" basis. The comprehensive program approach was definitive and multi-purpose. It included the two-year university parallel curriculum for transfer to senior institutions; the strong emphasis on career-vocational-technical education of collegiate character and tailored to existing and projected occupational needs and opportunities; and, importantly, adult continuing education courses and community service activities.

All of these curricula would be augmented by sound counseling and guidance services. Clearly, this approach was a distinct departure from the old "junior" college concept, nationally, which solely emphasized two-year liberal arts instruction. Consensus was readily achieved, therefore, that this new type of state college for Tennessee would be called "community," rather than "junior," to reflect a partnership of state and local initiatives in comprehensive educational programming with a strong base of community participation. The new colleges were to be regional in nature and serve a commuting public within a driving radius of approximately 40 miles, although no plans were made, statutory or otherwise, to formally "district" the state with rigid college service areas. First-class buildings and equipment would be provided for all college operations. However, no college-operated dormitories were envisaged.

Organization of the college administrative structure, positions authorized, and a salary schedule were crucial decisions. Principal officers of the college included the president, dean of instruction, dean of students, business manager, and director of public information and field services. The traditional rank system for faculty was adopted, but instruction would be organized and delivered through broad curricular groupings, such as divisions, rather than myriad disciplinary departments. Although some institutional variations would be developed, a typical divisional format consisted of humanities, social science and education, career-technical and continuing education, sciences and mathematics, and library services. To tie in voluntary community support and involvement, and to utilize specialized talent, the creation of local college advisory councils, technical advisory committees, and foundations were authorized.

Original presidents of the first nine community colleges and the higher education staff of the State Department of Education. *Standing, left to right:* Hal R. Ramer, Volunteer State Community College; David F. Adkisson, Cleveland State Community College; Cuyler A. Dunbar, Roane State Community College; John H. M. Smith, provost for academic services; Francis E. Wright, Jackson State Community College; Jess H. Parrish, Shelby State Community College; James W. Clark, Walters State Community College; Edward B. Eller, Dyersburg State Community College; Jerry L. Jones, provost for fiscal services; and George M. Roberts, executive dean for community colleges; *seated:* Harold S. Pryor, Columbia State Community College; T. Wesley Pickel, assistant commissioner for special services; J. Howard Warf, commissioner; and Sam H. Ingram, Motlow State Community College.

Concurrent with the formulation of these comprehensive concepts, the initiation of Tennessee's community college program was launched with tremendous velocity. Driven by public demand and the support of the legislature, between 1965 and 1969 nine of the 10 colleges were authorized and established. And, by 1974, all of the colleges had opened their doors, enrolling a total of nearly 18,400 students.

Throughout this founding period, a similar sequence of events characterized each institution. Upon authorization by the General Assembly, the campus location, site, architect, and contractor were selected, the local contribution and property deed were received, application was made for federal construction funds, and the president and key staff were appointed. Then on the campus level, the arduous process of becoming operational entailed academic and support staffing, program planning, and the use of temporary facilities while the physical plant was constructed. On average, the period from authorization to starting classes was 26 months. Slight to extreme variations in this course and period of founding occurred among the institutions due to their unique circumstances and extenuating considerations. Overall, however, the sound procedures of the State Board of Education and the experience gained from the development of the prototype college in Columbia enabled the swift and effective implementation of the statewide community college program. A base relief of the colleges' founding demonstrates the determined and deliberate course toward this end.

Of the three colleges authorized in 1965—subsequently named Columbia State Community College, Cleveland State Community College, and Jackson State Community College—Columbia State assumed the lead in commencing operations. After its site was selected in July of 1965, Commissioner Warf and Dr. Archie Rushton, the department of education's first executive dean of community colleges, guided the critical path toward full operation. In the fall of 1966, Tennessee's first community college students, numbering 393, started classes at Columbia State, with Dr. James W. Clark as the college's acting chief administrator.

The development of Cleveland State Community College and Jackson State Community College proceeded close behind that of Columbia State. Site selections for both campuses were determined by the early fall of 1965. The activities necessary to the opening of the colleges in fall of 1967 were directed by their first presidents. Dr. David F. Adkisson assumed the presidency of Cleveland State in January of 1967 and Dr. F. E. Wright was named to the presidency of Jackson State Community College that following February.

In 1967, the 85th General Assembly provided significant legislation and support for the community colleges. Chapter 294 of the 1967 Public Acts formally amended the statutory authority of the State Board of Education by specifically including the three existing community colleges and "such state community-junior colleges as shall hereinafter be established," under the maintenance and control of the board. The legislature also appropriated adequate operating support for the three colleges and bond funding to the board for capital improvements of "existing or newly created Junior Colleges." Although a particular number of new colleges was not specified, it was understood that, based on the recommendation on June 22, 1965, of the board for additional colleges, it was the intent of the legislature and the new administration of Governor Buford Ellington to establish three more community colleges, one in each Grand Division of the state.

In accordance with this authorization enabling the establishment of the new colleges, the State Board of Education immediately proceeded with the selection of locations. Drawing primarily on the studies and proposals submitted earlier in 1965, at its meeting of June 13, 1967, the board adopted the recommendations of the committee on community colleges to locate new colleges in the Dyersburg area in the northwest corner of the state and in the Tullahoma area in the heart of Middle Tennessee. Commissioner Warf also moved quickly with the selection of sites for these two colleges, later named Dyersburg State Community College and Motlow State Community College—the latter being named in honor of the family who donated the land for the college. In December of 1968, the presidents for both campuses were appointed: Dr. Edward B. Eller was named president of Dyersburg State, and Dr. Sam H. Ingram was selected as president of Motlow State. Both campuses first enrolled students in the fall of 1969.

The location for the third of this second group of colleges authorized in 1967 was determined by the newly created Tennessee Higher Education Commission. Established by the 85th General Assembly as the coordinating agency for public higher education, the commission's purview included the responsibility previously held by the State Board of Education for selecting the locations of new institutions. The commission became operational in the fall of 1967, and in late 1968, using essentially the same criteria adopted by the State Board of Education, it designated Hamblen County in northeast Tennessee as the college's location. The specific site in Morristown was selected soon thereafter by Commissioner Warf. Dr. James W. Clark was appointed as the college's first president in the fall of 1969. Later named Walters State Community College in honor of U.S. Senator Herbert S. Walters from that area, the institution opened its doors to students in the fall of 1970.

In the 1969 legislative session, the 86th General Assembly appropriated operating funds for the six community colleges and again provided capital outlay for the existing and newly created colleges. In preparation for this authorization, the Higher Education Commission and the Department of Education had proceeded with plans for establishment of the remaining three additional community colleges recommended four years earlier by the State Board of Education. Based on previous and updated surveys and the commission's criteria for the location of new colleges, which included a factor of projected enrollment, it was determined that this final group of institutions would be developed in Roane County, in the Cumberland Plateau region of East Tennessee; in Shelby County, encompassing the city of Memphis in the extreme southwest corner of the state; and in Sumner County, in the north-central part of the state. By the spring of 1970, specific sites in Harriman and Gallatin had been selected for the Roane and Sumner County colleges, subsequently named Roane State Community College and Volunteer State Community College. In May of 1970, Dr. Cuyler A. Dunbar was named president of Roane State, and Dr. Hal R. Ramer was selected as the first president of Volunteer State. Both colleges admitted their first classes of students in the fall of 1971.

The third college of this last group, named Shelby State Community College, differed in initial concept from the other colleges. Located in Memphis, the state's largest city with a population of nearly 750,000, Shelby State was designated to serve as a multi-campus institution. In May of 1970, Dr. Jess H. Parrish was named president, and in the fall of 1972, Shelby State admitted its first students.

The establishment of the state's 10th community college came about quite differently than that of the preceding nine. As a result of the combination of unmet needs and legislative interest, studies and hearings were conducted early in 1972 by the Higher Education Commission to assess the best ways of providing a community college program in the Chattanooga metropolitan area. Based on their findings, the 88th General Assembly enacted legislation which elevated the status of the existing Chattanooga State Technical Institute to that of a comprehensive community college. Chapter 80 of the 1973 Public Acts also transferred governance of the college from the State Board of Education to the State Board of Regents, governing body of the new State University and Community College System of

Tennessee established by the legislature in 1972. Chattanooga State Technical Community College enrolled its first class of community college students in the fall of 1974, and in January of 1974, Dr. Charles W. Branch was appointed as the college's first president.

The rapid and cyclical drive by which the colleges were established represents by far the greatest undertaking of widespread activity and impact in Tennessee higher education since the foundings of the state normal colleges in the early 1900s. While not without deterrents and disputes, the cooperative and successive actions by the legislature and officials at the state level were unprecedented for a particular educational program. This progress is all the more impressive in light of the overall changes and major developments that occurred throughout state higher education concurrent with the emergence of the community colleges.

In response to the same demands for expansion which contributed to the establishment of the new colleges, and as a result of the ensuing impetus for upgrading the coordination and control of public higher education, the current structure of Tennessee postsecondary education evolved between 1963 and 1973. During this 10-year time frame, several developments occurred.

A network of three technical institutes and 26 area vocational-technical schools was authorized in 1963 to provide non-collegiate, postsecondary training opportunities throughout the state, and by 1973, these institutions were enrolling some 40,000 students. University status was achieved by East Tennessee State University in 1963, by Tennessee Technological University and Middle Tennessee State University in 1965, and by Austin Peay State University in 1967. This action made all six of the senior institutions then governed by the State Board of Education, including Memphis State University and Tennessee State University, graduate degree granting institutions. From 1963 to 1973, the combined enrollments of the universities grew from 27,900 to 55,000.

The Tennessee Higher Education Commission was created in 1967 as the coordinating agency for public higher education with such responsibilities as the development and maintenance of a funding formula, master planning, and program review of the colleges and universities. The University of Tennessee reorganized as a multi-campus system in 1968 and assumed control of the University of Chattanooga in 1969 to complete its statewide network of five campuses, which by 1973 enrolled nearly 43,400 students. In 1972, the State University and Community College System of Tennessee was established with the State Board of Regents as the governing body for the state universities and community colleges previously under the control of the State Board of Education. The relationship between these developments and the foundings of the community colleges threaded through this period of massive changes in Tennessee higher education was significant to the extent that the colleges were respected and fostered as a vital dimension and complement of programming and services not within the role and scope of all other branches of the total higher education community.

In the overall developments of that period, at least four factors were responsible for maintaining the foundings of the community colleges on a steady and determined course. First, the program's aggressive initiation was largely attributable to strength and continuity in state leadership committed to the community college concept. The combined and alternating terms of only two governors ran the length of 1953 to 1971. It was under the direction of Frank G. Clement during his first stay in office, from 1953 to 1959, that the need for the colleges was studied and documented, and it was during his 1963 to 1967 term that he boldly led the movement for their authorization. Buford Ellington, whose dedication to improving statewide programs complemented that of Frank Clement's, served as governor from 1959 to 1963 and again from 1967 to 1971. It was during his terms that much of the conceptualization, as well as realization, of the community college program, was culminated. The ardent determination of both Governors Clement and Ellington, their persuasive relations with the legislature, and the non-partisan nature of the community college program assured the swift establishment of the institutions.

Second, the leadership of the State Board of Education was of tantamount importance to the community colleges' successful initiation. A lay body composed of active and dedicated citizens from across the state, the board had long established its capacities to govern public education effectively and to accommodate change as well as invoke innovation. These characteristics were personified in J. Howard Warf who, serving as state commissioner of education from 1963 to 1971 under the administrations of Governors Clement and Ellington, vigorously pursued the community college program with both personal and professional conviction.

As commissioner, Warf also chaired the State Board of Education

Members of the State Board of Education in 1968. *Left to right, back row:* J. Frank Taylor, Edwin H. Kennedy, James Williams, Dale F. Glover, Ernest C. Ball, Dr. D. M. Spotwood, James H. Jones, Jr., and Thornton Strang; *front row:* Edward L. Jennings, Mrs. Sam Wilson, Commissioner J. Howard Warf, Mrs. B. A. McDermott, and Thomas M. Divine.

during the crucial founding years of the community colleges. An educator and administrator of proven ability, he drew on his prior experience as a member of the board to enhance a firm grasp of the realities involved in implementing a statewide undertaking of the magnitude of the community colleges. Politically astute and administratively forceful, he worked masterfully in handling the tremendous responsibilities vested in the chairman of the board for making the colleges operational, including the critical selections of the colleges' locations and chief administrators.

As a third factor in the colleges' realization, the political aspect relative to their prospective locations was in itself significant to the total program's success in the legislature. Authorization of the new colleges on the basis of the state's three Grand Divisions was typical of the traditional approach taken by the General Assembly toward major statewide programs and policy issues. Within these bounds and among the areas determined by geographical, demographical, and logistical factors, the locations of the new institutions represented political appeal and considerations of no little consequence.

While the responsibility for selecting these locations clearly rested with the State Board of Education and later with the Tennessee Higher Education Commission, the ramifications of these decisions for the legislature were apparent. State legislators and delegations from the 22 communities that initially submitted proposals for the colleges, as well as those from other areas throughout the state, were acutely aware of the educational and economic benefits to be derived by their constituents from a community college in their home or neighboring districts. This factor fueled the fire of support for the program, and the achievement of channeling overall legislative support essential for the authorization of the total program, while maintaining and balancing studied need in the selection of the colleges' locations with key legislative backing, was due to the tact and prowess of Commissioner Warf.

A fourth factor in the colleges' rapid founding was the availability and receipt of federal funding for initial campus construction. Federal support, principally through the Higher Education Facilities Act, posed an added incentive for the fiscally conservative legislature to authorize the institutions while it was possible to take advantage of this matching grant program. In this regard, the services of Gordon W. Sweet, executive director of the Commission on Colleges of the Southern Association of Colleges and Schools, were invaluable. Sweet's frequent consultations with Commissioner Warf, numerous visits to Tennessee, and assessments of programmatic and campus facility plans on an expedited basis enabled the colleges to qualify for the federal building and equipment funding essential to their scheduled establishments.

It was during the founding period of the colleges that the major sphere and focus of action shifted from the state to the local level. Once the individual institutions were established, and after the initial groundwork and selection of campus administrators were accomplished, the primary thrust of the State Board of Education's role became more supportive than directive in the colleges' development. The exciting and challenging tasks of introducing and actualizing the community college concept in their local settings were seized by the institutions.

As their first governing board, the State Board of Education, through Commissioner Warf, continually sought and secured adequate operating and capital support from the legislature and provided the necessary actions and supportive services to maintain the fledgling colleges on even keel. While in their staggered stages of early development, the colleges were guided full stride into the mainstream of higher education by the policy decisions of the board and the administrative directives of Commissioner Warf and his staff. Accountability and effectiveness in the institutions' fiscal affairs were assured by the board's committee on budgets chaired by James H. Jones, Jr., of Mt. Pleasant.

The general operations of the colleges were coordinated at the state department level by Dr. Archie Rushton, followed by Dr. George M. Roberts serving as executive dean of the community colleges. From the outset of the first college's establishment, the board amended its policies affecting the senior colleges and universities, where appropriate, to include the community colleges. New higher education policies also incorporated provisions for the two-year colleges. In addition, policies and uniform procedures addressing the specific concerns of the community colleges were adopted. In each case, the original concepts of the colleges and campus integrity were first and foremost considerations in enabling the colleges to assume their role in the overall state higher education program.

The success of the colleges in building upon their foundations to actualize these original community-oriented, low-cost, open-access concepts has been overwhelming. Since their beginnings, the colleges have tailored their programs—university parallel, career-oriented, continuing education, and public service—with the same spirit of imagination and responsiveness to local need that led to the statewide establishment of the institutions themselves. From the first days they opened their doors, the colleges have attracted the variety of students they were conceived to serve: the commuter student for whom the first two years of a four-year college education away from home is undesirable or impossible for any of a number of reasons; the part-time working student; adults; those preferring the environment of a smaller college; the academic "late-bloomer;" those desiring a two-year career-oriented degree for immediate entry into the job market; and people of all ages who seek continuing education for personal enrichment.

The dramatic progress of Tennessee's community colleges, the wide range of positive and problematic challenges they have each experienced, and the dedicated services of faculty and staff that have been integral to their emergence as viable, dynamic institutions are evident and well reflected in each of the college's founding and early years as detailed in the 10 chapters that follow.

COLUMBIA STATE COMMUNITY COLLEGE
by Harold S. Pryor

*T*he dreams and aspirations of the people of Maury County for a local college really began more than 60 years ago when James Finney, editor and publisher of the *Columbia Daily Herald* and member of the board of trustees of the University of Tennessee, led a campaign to establish an institution in Columbia. While the legislature agreed on the need for a new college in Middle Tennessee, it chose Murfreesboro as the site for what is now a regional university. Led by Colonel J. S. Chapman, president of the local chamber of commerce, another attempt to establish a state institution was launched in 1928-1929. However, legislative approval again eluded the committee formed to bring state-supported higher education to Maury County.

Interest was rekindled in the late 1950s when the Pierce-Albright Report recommended establishing three new state colleges. This led to the organization of a local citizens' committee of 600 advocates promoting Maury County as the site for a college. The committee was headed by John Finney, son of the original leader in the quest for a college and member of the State Board of Education, and Hardin Hill, a local engineer and civic leader. The Maury County Quarterly Court quickly pledged one million dollars for the development of the college if it was established within 12 miles of the courthouse. The citizens' committee promptly published a brochure promoting Columbia as the site for the new college.

The years of commitment and work were rewarded on June 22, 1965, when the State Board of Education unanimously approved Columbia as the site of the Middle Tennessee college. The *Columbia*

Daily Herald proclaimed the news that day in a huge red headline, and the editorial was entitled "A Day To Rejoice—School Bells Ring For Us."

Commissioner J. Howard Warf personally toured prospective sites for the college and selected the 204-acre Hickman farm just west of the city as the best available location. On July 12 the Maury County Quarterly Court unanimously approved a resolution to purchase the property and pledged an additional $250,000 toward construction costs of the new campus. Governor Frank Clement and Commissioner Warf broke ground for the construction in ceremonies enthusiastically applauded by local citizens on October 20— just four short months after approval of the new college. Planning was rushed by the architectural firm of Yearwood and Johnson. Melson Contractors, Incorporated, was awarded a contract for the $2,750,000 project in February of 1966, with completion scheduled for the fall of 1967.

Dr. Archie Rushton, the first executive dean of community colleges in Tennessee, joined Commissioner Warf in providing guidance for the critical first years of the college. Dr. Rushton emphasized that Tennessee's community colleges were to be "second to none" in providing quality education and directed the development of broad-based institutions which would serve career and adult educational needs, as well as transfer students destined for senior colleges and universities. His philosophy that a community college should be an institution of higher education and not an extension of high school has directed the development of Columbia State. The faculty continues to be selected from a wide geographical and educational base.

The commissioner and his staff moved quickly to initiate the academic program of this first of the new community colleges in the state. Dr. James Wesley Clark, from Auburn, Alabama, was appointed dean of instruction on March 29, 1966, with directions to open the college by the fall of that year. He was to provide the leadership as chief administrative officer until a permanent president could be selected. By the following month, the initial staff of nine administrators and 21 faculty members had begun to form. The community responded to the needs of the fledgling institution, and by September facilities were available for the initial student body of 393 students. Administrative offices for the "all-over-the-place-

President Harold S. Pryor. *Photograph courtesy Columbia State Community College.*

campus" were located in a converted residence on West Seventh Street, and classes were scheduled in almost a dozen locations, including the First Baptist Church, an old post office, and a science lab on the Columbia Military Academy campus. The first applications were taken by W. O. Johnson, admissions director, and John Thomas, business manager, sitting on the sidewalk outside the temporary administration building—the office furniture had not yet arrived.

On September 26, 1966, the first college convocation was held at the Polk Theatre in downtown Columbia. Members of the State Board of Education attended, and one of their members, James H. Jones, Jr., acted as master of ceremonies. Commissioner Warf introduced Governor Clement as the principal speaker. The governor emphasized the importance of the occasion by saying, "Because of this school, young people who otherwise would have to terminate their academic career at the high school level will here find a way into the world of higher education." Enrollment climbed to 538 for the winter quarter as news of the college spread through the service area and as the permanent campus began to take shape along Highway 99.

Excitement filled the air in Columbia as Lyndon Johnson's visit—the first by an American president in 150 years—approached. The dedication of the campus was scheduled for March 15, which was proclaimed "CSCC Dedication Day" by Mayor James Dowdy and County Judge John Stanton. Mrs. Lyndon Johnson, the First Lady, officially dedicated the new campus and called Columbia State the "new beat and rhythm of our land." She also said that "when a Columbia Community College rises from a once empty field, the country expands not outward, but upward.... I am honored to dedicate this college—to dedicate it forever to the service of the people and the progress of our nation." More than 8000 delighted supporters of the college braved the cold March wind as they watched her unveil the dedication plaque and present the library with two gifts—a volume of Shakespeare and the film, *I, Leonardo*.

Mrs. Johnson's dedication was preceded by remarks by Governor Buford Ellington and John Gardner, secretary of health, education, and welfare. The governor introduced President Johnson who said that he could not resist coming to Columbia to add his congratulations to the people who had worked so hard to

Left to right: State Senator Joe Thomas Kelley, Governor Frank G. Clement, and State Education Commissioner J. Howard Warf at Columbia State groundbreaking ceremony. *Photograph courtesy Columbia State Community College.*

develop the college: "What you are doing here in Columbia is closer to my heart than anything else I deal with within the whole range of national policy."

The original campus, consisting of administration building, library, classroom building, student center, gymnasium, and power building, was completed for the opening of classes in September of 1967. In October the library was dedicated to John W. Finney who had worked many years to bring the institution into being. He had died only six months before his dream was officially realized. Con-

Left to right: Mrs. Lyndon B. Johnson, Governor Buford Ellington, Dean James W. Clark, and President Lyndon B. Johnson at dedication ceremony for the new campus. *Photograph courtesy Columbia State Community College.*

current with the opening of the campus, the promise to provide classes for all people in the service area was fulfilled. A series of steadily growing extension programs, begun in Lawrenceburg, expanded to 10 locations during the intervening years.

On February 9, 1968, Commissioner Warf announced that the State Board of Education had selected Dr. Harold Pryor, director of teacher education at Austin Peay State University, as the first president of Columbia State. Dr. Pryor, a native Tennessean, also had served on the faculties of East Tennessee State University, the University of Tennessee, and George Peabody College for Teachers. The new president was a widely traveled geographer and educator and prominent in civic activities in the Clarksville area of northern Tennessee.

On June 7, the first 44 graduates of the new institution marched into the gymnasium to hear the commencement address of Commissioner Warf. President Pryor also read a letter of congratulations from President Johnson, who remembered his visit to the fledgling campus. The crowning achievement of the opening phase of the college followed in December of 1968 when initial accreditation was awarded the institution by the Southern Association of Colleges and Schools in the shortest time allowable for such accreditation.

Early development was in keeping with the purpose of the college: to provide two years of university parallel courses, to provide

Aerial view of the campus. *Photograph courtesy Columbia State Community College.*

technological and preprofessional courses for those preparing to enter the work force, and to offer a program of continuing education for those primarily earning a living or making a home.

By the fall of 1969 college enrollment was more than 1300 students, mostly from the nine-county service area of the institution. Nursing education assumed a prominent part in the Columbia State curriculum. The Class of 1969 included the first 30 graduates of the nursing program, which has continued to grow over the years.

On March 4, 1971, the secretary of state granted a charter which provided for a foundation to accept financial contributions to the institution. The college president, serving as foundation president, is assisted by a board of trustees composed of prominent citizens of the region. The foundation has grown to provide significant aid to college development each year, offering approximately $5000 in scholarships and a revolving loan fund for students, a distinguished professor award, and funds for a speakers' series to enrich the extracurricular life of the campus.

Recognizing the need for organization and compilation of internal data in a period of rapid growth, the president obtained permission to establish an office of institutional research in 1971. In Sep-

Columbia State's first graduating class. *Photograph courtesy Columbia State Community College.*

tember, Dr. Richard Cooper, a Clarksville native, became the first director. The office of administrative affairs evolved as further growth required a broader range of services.

In spite of careful planning, physical facilities of the new campus were insufficient to serve the growing student body. A baseball field was added in 1968, and a second classroom building, designed to serve humanities and social science disciplines, was completed in 1969. In 1970 a maintenance building and a track enclosing a playing field were added to the campus, while landscaping and beautification projects continued. The second phase of campus construction was completed in 1972 when an addition to the student center and a new expanded library were finished.

A committee from the Southern Association of Colleges and Schools visited the campus in April of 1972, and the college received full accreditation by SACS at its annual meeting the following December. On June 26, 1972, a special program of commemoration and dedication was held on the campus. Dr. John Folger, a director of the Tennessee Higher Education Commission, gave the principal address. The humanities building was named for former governor Frank Clement, the original classroom building designated the J. Howard Warf Science Building, and the new library rededicated to the memory of James W. Finney. The original library had been converted into a nursing education building.

Another phase of educational commitment began in 1972 when the college responded to local demand for upper division and graduate work, especially in the area of teacher certification. Negotiations with Middle Tennessee State University resulted in the appointment of Dr. Uriah Clemmer as coordinator for advanced work on the CSCC campus and for the enrollment of 95 advanced students in the fall quarter of 1972. Expansion of the program in 1974 created an upper division and graduate education center at Columbia State which serves not only MTSU, but also Tennessee State University and the University of Tennessee's campuses at Knoxville and Nashville.

Reorganization became a dominant factor in 1972-1974. The State University and Community College System was formed under the State Board of Regents, and campus growth in the offerings of business called for creation of a new division composed of business administration, marketing and distribution, and secretarial science, all formerly housed in the career education division. Increased demand for off-campus courses led to the appointment of a director of field services under the umbrella of administrative services, for which an office was created under the supervision of a new dean to incorporate the functions of institutional research, field services, public information, computer operations, printing, and affirmative action.

Another milestone in professional development occurred in 1974 when the associate degree nursing program received accreditation from the National League of Nursing. Health occupations programs continued to grow as new career education programs were added in related fields which included animal hospital technology, respiratory therapy, radiologic technology, and optometrics. A new allied health building, completed in 1977, helped satisfy the need for expansion of facilities. The radiologic technician program achieved professional recognition in 1978 when it was accredited by the American Medical Association.

The college celebrated its 10th anniversary of growth and service in 1976 and became one of five community colleges in Tennessee designated official bicentennial campuses. Activities included a colonial arts festival and a day on which students, dressed in styles of

Original faculty and staff as they look today. *Left to right, seated:* Carolyn Allred, Dr. Paul Sands, and Ava Eaton; *left to right, standing:* Edward Durham, Fred Behrens, Dr. Lewis Moore, W. O. Johnson, and George Watson. (Not pictured is Monte Bayless). *Photograph courtesy Columbia State Community College.*

the 17th and 18th centuries, participated in social and sporting events of that period. The highlight of the year was the presentation of an original bicentennial play entitled *Light Across the Water.* A fictional account of early Middle Tennessee inhabitants, the play was written by Timothy Yeager, a Columbia musician and writer, and directed by Jim Spresser, drama instructor of the college.

The anniversary also marked the beginning of increased emphasis on long-range planning and administrative efficiency. Steps included the development of a long-range master plan in cooperation with the State Board of Regents, a management by objectives system, a formal evaluation process for faculty and staff, and the upgrading of the computer system to support both academic and administrative functions of the college.

The faculty has grown proportionally to the student body over the years since the first class began. Nine of the original staff remain. Known locally as the "Antediluvians," they occupy key faculty and staff positions throughout the college. Present faculty and administrators hold graduate degrees from 32 colleges and universities in 21 different states.

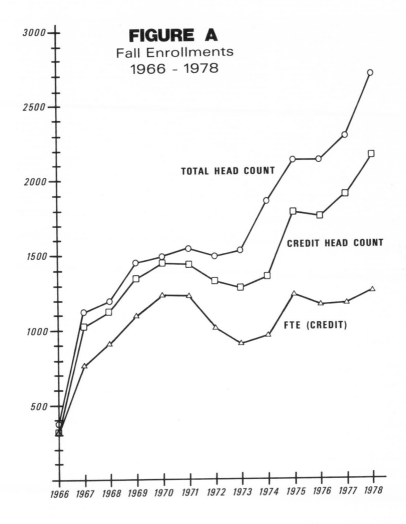

FIGURE A
Fall Enrollments
1966 - 1978

TOTAL HEAD COUNT

CREDIT HEAD COUNT

FTE (CREDIT)

Patterns of student enrollment are shown in Figure A, which reflects spectacular growth in the first few years, a downturn in 1972-1974, and renewed growth thereafter. The most significant factor—increased emphasis on the part-time student—follows national trends. While the early years of development show a relatively small difference between full-time equivalent (FTE) students and total students served, patterns in the middle to late 1970s depict this trend clearly.

During the five-year period from 1973 to 1978, credit hours

earned by part-time students increased steadily from 20 to 30 percent of all credit awarded. Following the end of the military draft, the student body composition also changed to show a majority of female students.

Students found courses of study in 13 areas largely traditional in nature. Six were "pre" types of programs, designed to facilitate transfer to four-year institutions in liberal arts (associate of arts or science options), business, engineering, medical arts, and education; they still remain the most popular transfer programs. Original career education courses of study centered around the disciplines of engineering technology, electronics, food service, nursing, and secretarial science. The latter two remain important facets of the CSCC curriculum. The electronics and engineering programs were revised and adjusted over the years, and food service technology was eliminated due to lack of demand and placement opportunities.

Several programs which developed during the 12-year span of operation were eliminated when anticipated demand failed to materialize or the market for graduates disappeared. Examples of such programs include electronic computer engineering, library technology, pre-industrial arts education, public administration, mental health technology, and teacher aide training.

Current students may choose from more than 40 associate degree programs in technical and transfer areas. Health programs are particularly attractive to occupationally oriented students, and the also popular business division has expanded its offerings to include degree programs in marketing-retailing and accounting technology. The associate programs failed to meet the needs of some students who desired a shorter course of study. Since 1969 the college has responded to these needs by adding certificate programs of one year or less in such diverse fields as drafting technology, data processing, real estate, insurance underwriting, industrial technology, electronics, and clerical studies.

Institutional leadership is an indistinct characteristic—yet one typified by the number of "firsts" credited to Columbia State. It was one of the first three community colleges to be approved, the first to open its doors, and the first to achieve accreditation. The first Tennessean elected a national officer in Phi Beta Lambda, the national business fraternity, was a Columbia State student.

In curricular affairs, the college led the way in offering associate degrees in computer science, animal hospital technology, and optometric technology. Adoption of the Library of Congress cataloging system provided further opportunity for exercising leadership; George Watson, director of the library, developed a cataloging program on the CSCC campus for use by two other community colleges until they could install their own systems. The computer center and learning resource center have consistently been called on to provide assistance in upgrading capabilities of other colleges in the system.

Long-range planning made it possible for Columbia State to accept handicapped students before federal guidelines mandated such action. Wheelchair ramps, elevators, curb cuts, handicapped parking, and special restroom facilities were part of the natural development of the college. The 1977-1978 student body president was an armless thalidomide victim confined to a wheelchair.

Integration always has been a way of life at Columbia State. The goals set for full-time minority students have been met. Nondiscrimination has been evidenced by the election of two black homecoming queens and a black student body president in 1978-1979.

The college also has provided leadership personnel for other community colleges in the system. CSCC staff members have become presidents of two other colleges, an academic dean and a business manager at still others. President Pryor served as president of the Tennessee College Association in 1974-1975—the only state community college president to be so honored.

In many colleges, preoccupation with management techniques, athletics, career counseling, and occupations (or vocationalism) have crowded out appreciation of the arts and sciences, but not at Columbia State. The college has recognized the importance of a strong liberal arts base in both curricular and extracurricular fields.

Innovation and recognition have highlighted the recent past at Columbia State. Inspired by a grant from the National Endowment for the Humanities, the college instituted a humanities tutorial program for full-time freshmen in 1978. The required series of one-credit courses carries students through the classical ages of Greece and Rome, the middle ages of Northern Europe, and the Renaissance. The college concurrently received, on a permanent loan basis, 13 plaster statuary casts from the Metropolitan Museum of Art in New York. The collection of four statues, six busts, and three bas-reliefs provides a decorative as well as educational tone to the library.

Dramatic productions have sought to establish a cultural base, rather than to present popular and light fare. From examples of social commentary in the late 1960s to classics such as *Spoon River Anthology* and *The Man Who Came to Dinner,* the small drama department has focused on filling the cultural void common in small communities. The 1978 tutorial program and statuary gift prompted production of the classic Greek tragedy, *Antigone.* The drama department spawned a community theatre organization.

The lyceum committee of the college has concentrated on bringing dramatic and musical presentations to the campus. Musical presentations by students and faculty have included Christmas concerts, a community chorus, and recitals. These programs have received assistance from the Tennessee Arts Commission and the Maury County Creative Arts Guild. The campus also has responded to concerts by Nashville and Chattanooga symphonies, jazz greats from Memphis, and the National Opera Company.

In 1976 the college began sponsoring an annual Outlook Speakers Series. Funded by the Columbia State Foundation, the series has enabled staff, students, and the community to hear nationally known individuals from business, politics, news media, and the arts speak on topics relevant to the current national scene. The humanities division instituted a spring arts festival in 1971, and the annual program has become an important part of the cultural aspects of the college.

The Columbia State mathematics and science division is an innovative force on the campus. Its graduates have been highly successful in obtaining appointments to professional schools throughout Tennessee. Adaptation of a national auto-tutorial system with open laboratories in biology led to on-campus development of an auto-tutorial approach to the teaching of chemistry. Other instructors have developed their own computerized, self-paced instructional units as a supplement to mathematics class requirements and have instituted video-taped lecture units for physics. Carolyn Allred, a member of the original faculty, has published a mathematics text. In addition to offering courses for science preprofessional students for general education requirements, the division has filled an important need in support of the allied health programs in career education.

The Tennessee Junior College Athletic Association, formed in 1968 at a meeting on the Columbia State campus, has grown to a membership of 15 colleges. The college provided early leadership in the organization, with Paul Sands, CSCC athletic director, serving as the first president. Dr. Sands later became dean of instruction at Columbia State.

In 10 years of participation in the TJCAA and National Junior College Athletic Association, the Charger teams have won 31 championships at the state, regional, and district levels and have earned a place in national tournaments on eight occasions. Columbia State coaches have been honored with 15 Coach-of-the-Year Awards. Dave Hall, the second athletic director for the college, also served as president of the TJCAA.

A stellar year, 1977-1978 is unparalleled in Tennessee junior college athletics. CSCC fielded five intercollegiate teams which won 10 conference, regional, and district championships and qualified four teams for NJCAA national tournaments. The baseball team has never had a losing season, compiling a 342-74 record since 1967. It has earned two third-place and two fourth-place finishes in the national tournament. Fourteen players have been selected first or second team All-Americans and one was named "Most Valuable Player" in the 1970 national tournament. Numerous players have won conference, district, or regional honors, and many have earned scholarships to senior institutions or been drafted into professional baseball. Two players now serve as coaches of other TJCAA colleges.

Winning basketball became a reality in 1970, a record of 202-47 having been compiled since that time. The Chargers have claimed three TJCAA titles, two Region VII NJCAA championships, and participated in three national tournaments, earning as high as a sixth-place finish. Six players have been named first or second team All-Americans or All-National Tournament players, and two have been selected for the East-West NJCAA All-American games. The Lady Chargers, while relatively new to intercollegiate competition, have won two Western Division championships in the TJCAA.

Conference championships in golf (1970) and men's tennis (1969) have brought further recognition to Columbia State. The women's tennis team has won two TJCAA titles, the first Region VII NJCAA championship won by a Tennessee team, and a place in the 1978 national tournament.

The 1978 championship Charger team. *Photograph courtesy Columbia State Community College.*

Hayward Bond, the first director of continuing education activities of the college, continually emphasized that "Education is a life-long process." He used the symbol for infinity on publications of his office.

Community service courses have been an integral part of the total program of the college almost from its inception. In the second quarter of college operations, three non-credit courses were offered—interior decorating, genealogy, and flower arranging. Initially they were called "short courses," then "special interest courses," and, by the spring quarter of 1967, "community service courses"— the current title.

These courses carry continuing education credit (CEUs): records of courses taken are maintained, but no credit is allowed toward a college degree. From the first three offerings in 1967, the program expanded to include 32 popular courses in 1978. Some are serious in nature, some occupationally oriented, and some are just for entertainment. They have run the gamut from cybernetics to needlepoint, from guitar to expectant motherhood, from belly dancing to scuba diving. Some professional courses, workshops, and seminars are offered through the continuing education operation—especially in the areas of health occupations and business management. Other courses, such as real estate, banking, and medical office procedures, originally offered on a non-credit basis, have earned their way into regular credit offerings of the college.

Special statewide service was provided in 1975 and 1976, when the continuing education division organized video-taped courses in pharmacology and ocular pharmacology for optometrists in Knoxville, Kingsport, and Chattanooga—areas normally far beyond the scope of the Columbia State service area. Because Columbia State had developed a unique program in optometric technology, professional courses, directed toward working technicians who lacked formal training, were offered at Tullahoma, Cleveland, Morristown, and Nashville in 1977-1978. The Cleveland program maintained the level of enrollment considered necessary for continuation of the classes in 1978-1979, and a new cycle was begun at Jackson. Cooperation with business, industry, and community agencies provides special courses on an "in-plant" basis as needed.

The field service component of the college has been responsible for off-campus classes. Beginning with two courses in Lawrenceburg in 1967, the program had expanded by the fall of 1978 to offer 48 credit classes in 10 locations. The broadened service area included Centerville, Franklin, Hohenwald, Lawrenceburg, Lewisburg, Linden, Pulaski, Savannah, Turney Center, and Waynesboro. Non-credit courses also are offered at these locations on demand. The field services office also schedules events on campus initiated by outside organizations, or college-sponsored events to which the public is invited. The impact of such community service is difficult to measure, but the increase in public support and participation is evident. In 1977-1978 an estimated 33,000 visitors were drawn to the campus for 170 events or meetings.

Early in the evolvement of the college, a study was requested by community agencies to chart past progress and to project the potential of economic growth in Maury County. The study, directed by Dr. Lewis Moore, of Columbia State, was published in 1970 and is used as a guideline for economic development in the area.

Commitment to the non-traditional student became an important factor in 1972. Responding to a demonstrated need in the county and funded by an HEW grant, a three-year "right to read" program was developed. As a result of the program, more than 500 adults received training necessary to pass the general educational development (GED) examination and attain their high school equivalency diplomas. Many continued their educations on the college level. Materials developed in the program are used in GED preparation courses offered each quarter.

The CSCC computer center has had a positive effect on the community. By contract arrangements, computer services have been offered to local government agencies, school systems, and private agencies since 1970. The greatest impact has been within Maury County where busing, attendance reporting, and payroll applications for the county school system originate in the computer center. The cities of Columbia and Mount Pleasant utilize the accounting services available, and classroom scheduling is prepared for Mount Pleasant High School.

Adherents of higher education in Columbia 60 years ago would be justifiably proud if they could see the modern campus that rose from the rolling hills of the Hickman farm and could measure the impact of the college on the educational, cultural, and social life of Maury County and south-central Tennessee. The growing pains have eased; the student unrest of the 1960s, the muddy campus and parking problems, and the uncertainties of any new venture seem far behind. Twelve years of progress are relegated to the history of Columbia State; the future promises continued success and growth.

2

CLEVELAND STATE
COMMUNITY COLLEGE
by L. Quentin Lane

*T*he story of Cleveland State Community College is a powerful and inspiring record of hope, accomplishment, challenge, and mastery. It is an account of men and women with vision who worked together to open the doors of education to southeast Tennessee and to bring to the people of the area the great gifts of freedom of opportunity and the chance to enrich their lives. This story of progress can and should serve as a model to new educational institutions of outstanding involvement and support.

From the time the college was born to the presentation of its 10th graduation class in 1979, the history of Cleveland State records the names of those citizens who first forged the way, carried their dreams of building a college in Cleveland, and molded them into reality. Frank Manly, Eugene Callaway, William Fillauer, Hallman Bell, John Dunlap, Ernest Guffey, Nelom Jackson, Grover Ashe, Kenneth Tinsley, W. A. Jones, H. M. Fulbright, John Clayton, and many others devoted their time and skills, surmounted political encumbrances, skepticism, competition, and sometimes rigid opposition until the goal was reached in June of 1965, when the State Board of Education officially named Cleveland as the site for the establishment of one of the state's first three colleges.

Because the concept of the community college was relatively new to the area, no precedents existed for this type of institution in Tennessee. Many wondered if it would be another junior college; in fact the newspaper headlines labeled it as such. Some questioned the credentials of the community college and wondered if the credits earned there would be acceptable at a university. Still others predicted it would be nothing more than a "glorified high school." Many, however, were eagerly awaiting to view it firsthand, to sample the public higher education offered within such a short distance of their homes, and then to make their judgments.

Cleveland State Community College received its official name in February of 1966, after the State Board of Education decided that the names of the state's three new community colleges should contain the name of the community in which each institution would be located. Contracts were let on July 20, 1966, for construction of five red brick and crab orchard stone buildings to contain 130,000 square feet and to accommodate a projected enrollment of 500 to 750 students. The initial cost of construction, including equipment, was $2,494,000. In September of 1966, a groundbreaking ceremony was held on the 105-acre tract of woodland located beyond the northwest boundaries of the city and north of the Georgetown Road interchange of Interstate 75, which then was only a trail scraped in red clay.

Dr. D. F. Adkisson became the college's first employee after he assumed the presidency of the college on January 1, 1967. A native of Ashland City, Dr. Adkisson previously served as an elementary and high school teacher, principal, school superintendent, State Board of Education high school supervisor for 34 East Tennessee counties, director of instruction for the Knox County School System, and instructor at the University of Tennessee at Knoxville. He received an associate degree from Austin Peay Normal, a bachelor's degree from Middle Tennessee State University, a master's degree from George Peabody College, and a doctorate from the University of Tennessee.

As president, Dr. Adkisson recruited Dr. George L. Mathis, principal of Brainerd High School, to become the dean of students. In March of 1967, temporary administrative offices were opened at 623 Broad Street in a converted residence.

By the time classes began, another group of dedicated people were at the helm. Their guidance, determination, and enthusiasm ensured the college's strong and healthy development. D. F. Adkisson, George Mathis, F. Dean Banta, Roy G. Lillard, James Cigliano, Ozane Adams, Tom Boles, Joe Guest, John Bradley, Jere Chumley, Irene Millsaps, Josephine Pritchett, and John Smeltzer were among

President L. Quentin Lane. *Photograph courtesy Cleveland State Community College.*

Dr. D. F. Adkisson, former president of Cleveland State. *Photograph courtesy Cleveland State Community College.*

charter members of the fledgling college's administration and faculty.

The task of recruiting the first class soon began. Without physical facilities, without fancy literature, without firsthand information of the characteristics of the college, without equipment for the classrooms, and without a faculty, Dr. Mathis began a monumental sales task. He went from high school to high school to recruit, singling out those who had no previous plans to attend college. His message was the same wherever he went: "If you want to go to college, see me, and I'll see that you have the opportunity to get an education at Cleveland State." The success of that sales drive is history. It is written many times over in the lives of those who responded to the call.

In August of 1967, the first college catalog was published. Associate degree programs were offered in 17 fields of study in both the day program and the evening division of the continuing education program. Ninety-eight quarter hours of credit, including physical education, were required to obtain an associate degree. A number of certificate programs in concentrated areas of study were available: a total of 30 credit hours of course work was required to obtain a certificate of proficiency. An adult education program was offered "for personal enrichment, general cultural benefits to comply with business or industrial opportunities or requirements for specific information." An extensive summer program of course work and a community service program, which included lectures, concerts, a fine arts festival, and special workshops, also were announced.

For full-time students who were residents of Tennessee, costs were $50 for tuition and five dollars a quarter for registration. A non-resident, full-time student paid $145 in registration and tuition fees for a quarter. Despite nationwide inflationary trends, tuition has remained low thereby fulfilling the State Legislature's intent to "place an institution of higher education within commuting distance of every college-age person in Tennessee with low-cost tuition." In 1978, the fee for Cleveland State students taking 12 or more hours was $84 per quarter; for part-time students, it was seven dollars per quarter-hour credit.

The purposes and objectives of the college were recorded in the first section of the 72-page catalog:

> Cleveland State Community College is dedicated to the ideal of providing continuing educational opportunities for all. Continuing education offers opportunities in academic, professional and technological personal enrichment.
>
> The faculty and staff of Cleveland State continually strive to make it an institution through which the entire area will receive cooperation, help, and encouragement in individual and community development.
>
> Specifically, Cleveland State Community College devotes its energies to achieving the following objectives:

1. To provide an academic program that will prepare students to transfer two years of collegiate work to four-year colleges and universities.
2. To provide programs of technological and pre-professional work for those students preparing to enter industry, business and the professions within a two or three year period and who need a marketable skill that can be acquired through a degree.
3. To offer a program of continuing education for those who are primarily occupied with making a living. This work may be taken for either credit or non-credit with the objective of professional growth or personal enrichment.
4. To provide counseling and guidance services to students and members of the community, according to personal, occupational, and academic needs.
5. To create a cultural atmosphere and make the facilities of the college available to the community in order to promote better citizenship and a profitable use of leisure time.

Cleveland State accepts each student as a worthy individual with unique abilities and capacities and endeavors to provide leadership which will enable each individual to develop and mature toward the realization of his potentialities.

From an enrollment of 681 students in its opening quarter of 1967, the student body has grown steadily, exceeding its projected growth rate year after year, until it reached a total head count of more than 4500 students during the 1978-1979 academic year. From an initial faculty and administrative staff of 34, the college staff had expanded to 212 by 1978. During the first quarter, five hundred students were enrolled in the day division and 191 students in the evening division. Classes were held during this quarter in the educational building of the North Cleveland Baptist Church while campus construction was being completed. "Without the assistance of the church, the school could not have opened until January," wrote Judy Johnston in a Cleveland State student newspaper editorial thanking members of the church. Off-campus courses are offered in Athens, Copperhill, Dayton, Benton, Sweetwater, Calhoun, Charleston, Chattanooga, Riceville, Spring City, Etowah, and in homes, churches, and businesses as the college continually concentrates efforts to bring education to the people.

Despite crowded conditions in the temporary quarters, the new students elected student body officers, published a newspaper, produced a prize-winning float for the annual Cleveland Christmas parade, formed a college chorus, made plans for the formation of campus organizations, supported the Cougar basketball team, and selected cheerleaders. "Cleveland State is a new school with no past," Bill Sander thoughtfully commented in a sports editorial in the first edition of the college newspaper. "In the years to come," he added, "many will leave their mark . . . but none will have so profound an effect upon this school's basic policies as we, its first student body."

Throughout its history, the college has received unwavering, enthusiastic support from the community it serves. At the very outset, the acreage on which the college was to be built was donated by Bradley County, and the sum of $250,000, required by the state to aid in construction, was supplied by the local city and county governments. From the start, financial assistance has been provided by local firms and individuals to prospective students for whom the college's tuition, low-cost as it was, remained a prohibitive factor. The community went even further in 1977 when the college completed its most comprehensive fund-raising drive; the successful effort resulted in a scholarship endowment fund. The total of $225,000 in donations —$25,000 over the goal—enabled 45 full scholarships to be awarded each year to deserving students.

During Christmas vacation in 1967, 34 students in the college work-study program assisted in moving equipment and materials from the church to the new campus. The administration building, science building, student center, and library were completed, and the gymnasium was near completion. The winter quarter began on January 31, 1968, at the new campus with enrollment increasing to 766 students—a gain of 85 students over the first quarter.

The official dedication ceremony of Cleveland State Community College was held April 29, 1968. Governor Buford Ellington and State Education Commissioner J. H. Warf, local and state dignitaries, and a crowd estimated at 2500 attended the ceremony, which was followed by an open house. U. S. Senators Howard Baker and Albert Gore and State Senator Calvin Cannon were among those who sent congratulations.

Summer bids were opened for paving parking lots, and construction was scheduled for a new parking area near the gym. A sports field was under construction. In September construction of

Original five campus buildings, occupied in January of 1968, three months after classes had begun in 1967. *Photograph courtesy Cleveland State Community College.*

the sixth campus structure, the humanities building, was begun. Since the groundbreaking ceremony in 1966, the tranquil and beautifully wooded campus has been the site of continual construction to accommodate expanded enrollments and academic offerings. The 10th building, to house community services and continuing education, was completed in 1978 and contains a 394-seat auditorium available for both college and community events.

Sixty-nine degrees were awarded during the college's first graduation ceremony in 1969. Elizabeth Jane Anstey received the first degree, and Walter Presswood was presented the first faculty award. In 1978, 359 degrees were awarded. Since that year 2369 students have graduated from Cleveland State, and more than 80,000 registrants (duplicated enrollment) have augmented their education within its doors, serving primarily students from a 13-county area.

A well-defined pattern for the future path of Cleveland State became apparent during the 1969-1970 academic year. In a brief time the college had become a major force in the community. Students were coming to its doors in increased numbers each quarter. New course offerings and degree programs were being added to meet the needs of students and area business and industry. Highly competent instructors were drawn to the challenges of a new concept of higher education. The strength of the school's administrative staff was obvious. The college was developing on a rock-solid foundation. Clearly, its flourishing course was set. Cleveland State received accreditation by the Southern Association of Colleges and Schools.

Diplomas were awarded to 69 students on June 6, 1970, and another 300 students were reported to be transferring course work to senior colleges and universities. Dr. Joe Morgan, president of Austin Peay College, was commencement speaker. A letter to the 1970 graduating class from U. S. President Richard Nixon was reprinted in the college newspaper. "I look to you with greater confidence," the 37th president wrote, "because I know of the exceptional qualifications you bring to the exceptional demands of our time."

An astonishing growth rate continued during 1970-1971 as enrollment records again were set each quarter. Physical facilities were expanded, the faculty was increased, and new courses were added. In 1967, the operating budget of the college was $621,750 with a state expenditure of $725 per student. By 1970, the college operating budget had grown to $1,061,065 and the yearly per-student expenditure was $838.

On the nationwide scene, demonstrations took place against the Vietnam War. Scant attention was afforded the divisive war by students in the college newspaper, however. Jubilation was expressed in a special eight-page publication released by the public relations office in recognition of the moon rock exhibit. The Apollo 12 lunar sample, which was displayed at Cleveland State for four days in March, drew more than 15,000 viewers. "It is fitting," Dr. Adkisson commented, "that Cleveland State have this privilege of sponsoring the moon rock exhibit . . . . It will further strengthen the college recruiting theme, 'Footsteps to Further Education.'"

As fall quarter began, construction was underway for a $30,000 parking lot that would provide more than one hundred additional parking spaces on the three-million-dollar campus. Two expansion projects were expected to begin which would double the sizes of the library and student center at an estimated cost of one million dollars. Funds from the Department of Health, Education and Welfare, the Appalachian Regional Planning Commission, and the state would finance the new construction. Equipment that included oscilloscopes, carrels with projectors and listening devices, had been installed during the summer and was valued at $75,000. Degrees were awarded to 106 students when, on June 12, 1971, Tennessee Education Commissioner E. C. Stimbert gave the commencement address.

Another enrollment milestone was recorded in the fall quarter of 1971, as the 2000 mark was surpassed. Building expansions continued, and state funds were already earmarked for construction of a technology building. Instructional equipment in campus classrooms had reached a value of $800,000. The faculty was increased to give an instructor-student ratio of one-to-18. The operating budget for the year was $2,533,933 with a per-student expenditure of $1057. The total annual payroll was $1,441,169, an increase of $380,104 over the previous year. Area industry and citizens continued contributing funds for scholarships, and a foundation was created in 1971 to oversee the scholarship fund.

Degrees were awarded to 173 students at the June 10, 1972, commencement. Dr. Andrew Holt, president of the University of Tennessee at Knoxville, gave the address. In a letter to the graduating class, President Nixon wrote, "You are the best educated generation in history."

Another prosperous year was realized at the college during 1972-1973. New academic innovations, supplemented by versatile equipment and newly developed instructional aids, gave students a wide range of opportunity. New degree programs and additional courses were offered. Construction continued along with plans for future expansion. Enrollment reached a plateau for the first time as 2167 students from 31 counties and two foreign countries enrolled for the fall quarter. The freshman class had 1567 students; the sophomore class, 569; and others were registered in non-credit or GED refresher courses. Only students who had been enrolled full-time prior to June 1, 1972, continued to be eligible for deferment from the military draft. The one-million-dollar expansion of the student center and library had been completed, final confirmation for construction of the technology building had been received, and bids also had been let for a new $110,000 maintenance building. The new media center housed equipment with a capacity to produce college-originated instructional material, and a complete offset print shop had been opened.

In an interview on May 11, State Representative Ben Longley

said, "Indications are that the prime building site for a vocational-technical school is the area adjacent to the Cleveland State campus." Longley had co-sponsored a bill aimed at establishing a statewide vocational-technical school system at a reported cost of $180 million. An earlier survey had shown Bradley County "fourth in need of a center" with "an estimated 2276 people here who need such a school." The school would open, according to Longley, in 1975.

Enrollment records were set again during 1973-1974. Construction had begun on the $1,087,000 career education building, the $105,900 maintenance building was occupied, and a paved student parking lot was completed at a cost of $64,261. Investment in permanent facilities totaled $5,876,810, and instructional equipment was valued at $1,290,650. A learning skills center was opened to provide special assistance to students in strengthening academic skills in specific courses, and a cooperative education program was initiated which would give students the opportunity to work in their fields of study while earning on-the-job experience, academic credits, and salaries. Following an evaluation, Cleveland State received reaccreditation for the standard 10-year period from the Southern Association of Colleges and Schools.

Dr. L. Quentin Lane was named dean of instruction when Dr. F. Dean Banta resigned from that position to become director of the division of education, health, physical education and recreation, and psychology. Dr. Lane formerly had held the position of director of institutional research.

By February of 1974, a $9000 color video camera had been installed in the media center. All campus buildings had been wired with the center so that closed circuit television, with the capacity for producing and broadcasting live video-taped programs, became a reality across the campus. On June 8 of that year, degrees were awarded to 278 graduates at commencement. Mildred E. Doyle, superintendent of Knox County schools, was the speaker.

An astonishing year of progress was apparent during 1974-1975 at Cleveland State. A record enrollment was set as 2832 students registered in credit courses and another 143 in non-credit courses. Enrollment soared to an all-time high when 3184 students registered for the winter quarter. The increases were particularly noteworthy in light of the fact that Chattanooga State Technical Community College had just begun operation only 25 miles away.

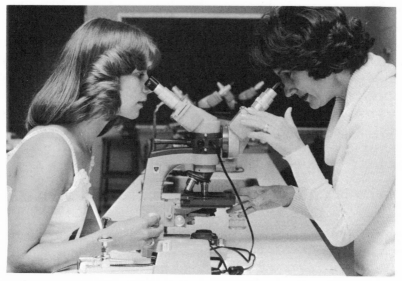

Microscopic examinations in biology laboratory. *Photograph courtesy Cleveland State Community College.*

Sophisticated instructional equipment was in operation in a variety of fields, giving students almost unlimited opportunity to fulfill their chosen educational goals. Continued construction became a hallmark of the young college's growth as new buildings rose on the campus and proposals for expansion accelerated.

The new instructional television studio was able to telecast four different programs simultaneously through 40 color television monitors, and one informational channel was available for transmitting messages throughout the campus via 14 black and white monitors. Dr. Adkisson called the system "an important step toward individualizing instruction."

Construction was scheduled to begin in February of 1975 on a $15,000 observatory to be equipped with a $7000 Schmitt-Cassegrain telescope; according to Buford Guy, physics instructor, the observatory would be "one of the largest in the state." An anonymous donor had provided $7500 toward building the observatory.

A significant study was completed by Director of Admissions James Cigliano which showed that 50.1 percent of the 325 students graduating from Cleveland State in June planned to transfer to a senior institution of higher education, contrary to the then-popular concept that most community college students planned to seek immediate employment following their two-year education. Slightly more than 22 percent stated their intention to pursue one or two years of graduate study. The majority of the students surveyed said that their most important goal in attending college was "to secure vocational or professional training;" this response was followed closely by "to develop my mind and intellectual abilities." Despite a tight labor market at the time of the study, only three percent named "earning a higher income" as their most important goal.

Degrees were awarded in 1975 to a record number of 332 graduates. J. A. Barksdale, former state commissioner of education, addressed the commencement audience on June 6, and a letter of congratulations to the class from U. S. President Gerald Ford was reprinted in the *Cherokee Signal.*

While community college enrollments peaked in 1975, state appropriations were cut by 20 percent, causing serious financial problems. President Adkisson appealed "to all citizens of Tennessee" to ". . . encourage your legislators to place more emphasis on education and provide the necessary funding, before it is too late." By spring, the situation was alleviated when legislation was passed for a one-cent sales tax increase.

The phenomenal growth of Cleveland State continued during the fall-quarter enrollment. Registers for day classes carried 1239 students, evening students numbered 1685, and 336 students enrolled in both. Two hundred ninety-three registered for non-credit courses.

Dean of Students Mathis announced his retirement, ending a 35-year career in education. Students and faculty responded with an outpouring of tributes. President Adkisson said, "It is impossible for me to realize what it's going to be like when he is gone." Director of Admissions Cigliano said, " . . . I don't think a lot of things would ever have gotten off the ground without Dr. Mathis." Carl Wright, news editor of the *Signal,* wrote, "Dr. Mathis' presence at Cleveland State has left an irrepressible sensation of compassion among everyone he has dealt with at the school in administrative and academic affairs." The State Board of Regents named the student center in his honor.

The year 1976-1977 was highlighted by an event of extraordinary significance: the naming of the D. F. Adkisson Administration Building in honor of Dr. Adkisson, who had served as Cleveland State's first president and in the educational field for 44 years. Representative Longley had, in response to requests, recommended in an open letter of August 25, 1976, that the State Board of Regents allow the building to be named for Dr. Adkisson: " . . . It is not only the need for the building that is important. It most particularly is the recognition of the excellent performance of the staff, faculty, and administration of Cleveland State under the direction of President D. F. Adkisson that is so richly deserved and noteworthy." On September 24, 1976, the Board of Regents voted to name the building in honor of Dr. Adkisson; they expressed appreciation "for his guidance and direction in making Cleveland State one of the finest institutions in Tennessee . . . ."

The 1976 fall-quarter enrollment peaked at 3710, with those registering for credit course work numbering 3067. The college operating budget for the year was $4,295,130. Full-time employees at the college numbered 205. James M. Cigliano was named dean of student personnel services. Frances Layne, a member of the counseling staff, was named director of admissions, and David E. Watts was named to the new position of assistant to the dean of academic affairs. The cooperative education and job placement programs were combined and Rosemary Den Uyl named coordinator.

Cleveland State's general education development (GED) program tested 682 persons in 1977. According to a report on the success of the testing program, "A majority passed . . . and a large number, equivalent to another high school graduating class, enrolled at Cleveland State and are now pursuing a college education." During that year, Cleveland State, one of eight GED testing centers, reportedly "tested almost 200 more persons" than any of the other community college centers.

In a public statement in February of 1977, director of student activities, development, and alumni affairs, Walter Presswood, explained the need for a scholarship endowment program:

> While the Cleveland State Foundation, established in 1971, to provide scholarships for academically deserving students, students needing financial aid and students needing an interest-free emergency loan was basically a sound program there were some disadvantages. First, there was always a possibility that the

college would not receive enough donations in a given year. Second, the donors could die or discontinue giving for some reason .... The college was constantly looking for a new source of revenue for the foundation. Realizing these problems, the college came up with an alternate solution: the establishment of the Cleveland State Endowment Fund .... The Cleveland State Foundation will continue to administer the endowment fund.

An editorial in the *Cleveland Daily Banner* proclaimed:

This community is being handed a challenge .... It is being challenged to invest in the lives of its own offspring, for they are the ones who will directly benefit from the endowment. Bradley County is one of the leading areas of the state in growth and progress. Many factors have made it so. But the decision to locate Cleveland State in this community is perhaps the most important single development in its illustrious history. Its impact on the city and county is much more profound than the location of any industry here. Its presence, in fact, is a drawing card—and a powerful one—for new plants.

The first donation was made in February by the faculty and staff of Cleveland State in honor of Dr. Adkisson, with the provision that it be awarded annually as the "Dr. D. F. Adkisson Scholarship."

Plans were announced during the winter quarter of 1977 for development of a historical museum to be housed in the college library. Roy Lillard, division head of business and social sciences, was named director of the project. Following his formal retirement from that post, Lillard returned to his former position as an instructor of history and political science. Four students also were appointed to the museum committee: Karen Higgins, Frances Kimbrough, Robert Ramsey, and Marvin Kelley.

By 1977 the total operating budget was $4.6 million with the state expenditure per full-time student at $1404. Several changes in division scopes and administration were announced for the 1977-1978 academic year: accounting was slated to become a part of the mathematics-science division, headed by Dr. Irene Millsaps; general business was to become a part of the career education division, headed by Dr. Matt Reiser; and the social sciences division was to become a part of the humanities and social sciences division, headed by Mary Barker.

The first 10-year service awards were presented to President

Adkisson, George Mathis, Roy Lillard, Norma Davis, F. Dean Banta, Tom Boles, Jim Cigliano, Jere Chumley, Joe Guest, Janie Arms, and Mollie Smith.

Associate degrees were awarded to 320 graduates at the college's ninth commencement held June 10, 1977. In that ceremony, the college awarded its two thousandth associate degree. Dr. C. C. Bond, assistant superintendent for Chattanooga City Schools and a member of the State Board of Regents, was graduation speaker.

The year 1977-1978 was a time for both reflection and resolution. The announcement of Dr. Adkisson's retirement was met first with sadness, then with awe as his accomplishments were reviewed, and finally with hope for a future patterned from a decade of strong, imaginative leadership. When Dr. Adkisson arrived at Cleveland State in 1967, the population of Cleveland was 20,000 and slightly more than 38,000 persons resided in Bradley County. The campus of the college was lovely Tennessee woodland. No staff awaited the president; no conference rooms held procedural outlines for program development; and the concept of the community college was new in the state. By 1978, Cleveland's population had grown to an estimated 30,100, and Bradley County was the home of more than 63,000 people. The college employed 212 professional and supportive personnel whose salaries amounted to almost three million dollars. Enrollment figures had surpassed the 4000 mark, and the total budget exceeded $4.5 million. Associate of science, associate of arts, and associate of applied science degrees were being offered in more than 30 fields. In answer to a request by area residents, the Tennessee State House of Representatives and Senate passed a joint resolution ". . . that we honor Dr. Adkisson on his retirement as president of Cleveland State Community College and express our appreciation to him for spending 45 years educating the future leaders of Tennessee."

As Cleveland State entered its second decade, the challenges were readily apparent. Despite increased appropriations, budgets were beginning to tighten due to rising costs of fuels, services, and supplies. Added to the problems caused by inflation was a concern about declining enrollments nationwide. Adkisson, however, viewed Cleveland State's position as "enviable." He stated, "We are flexible and more attuned to the needs of the community. The growth is going to be with part-time students. If we provide the programs that

Aerial view of expanded campus in 1978. *Photograph courtesy Cleveland State Community College.*

they want and need, there is a possibility of growth, as we are seeing this quarter. Any institutions that are willing to accommodate the working people in the types of courses they offer and at the times they offer these courses can continue to make progress and grow." The State Board of Regents accepted Dr. Adkisson's request for retirement status on October 7, 1977, and expressed "appreciation for his many years of outstanding service to Cleveland . . . and all of Tennessee public education." They also provided for his being named president emeritus of Cleveland State upon leaving active service. President and Mrs. Adkisson were honored at a retirement reception on June 30, 1978, his last day as president, with an outpouring of affection from the members of the community and the staff.

Following an extensive search, Dr. L. Quentin Lane was selected by the State Board of Regents to become the college's second president. Dr. Lane, who was officially to assume his new position July 1, 1978, stated, "My main motive will be to strengthen what we presently have rather than seeking a number of changes." On April 26, he announced the appointment of Dr. McBride as the new dean of academic affairs.

Cleveland State began its 11th year of operation with a total enrollment of more than 3263. The recommended operating budget was $4,742,852, providing for a five percent inflation factor in general operating expenses and an additional $88,000 in salary improvements. Records for the scholarship endowment fund—the largest scholarship program among the state's 10 community colleges—showed a total of $224,366.80 in contributions and pledges. The following new foundation officers were elected: Dr. Adkisson, president; Eugene Callaway, vice-president; Henry Barkley, treasurer; Frank Manly, secretary; and W. K. Fillauer, executive committee member-at-large.

Ten-year service awards were presented to Ozane Adams, Jim Allen, Paul Boynton, Kay Graham, Dianne Harrison, Beverly Evans, Alleyna Ellis, Buford Guy, Renate Hufft, Fred Anderson, James Passmore, Marilyn Fillers, T. P. Mathai, Irene Millsaps, John Bradley, Larry Speight, Wanda Cartwright, and Nancy Boyd.

Representative Longley announced that he had negotiated an agreement whereby the State Vocational Technical Center, located on the Cleveland State campus, would become the property of the college at the close of the 1978-1979 academic year. More than a million dollars would be spent to build additional classrooms at Cleveland High and at Polk County High to house vo-tech students, he said.

An administrative reorganization to become effective July 1, 1978, was announced by President-Elect Lane. Instead of the original six divisions, the college would be represented by three academic areas: arts and sciences, career education, and continuing education and community services. Dr. Mary Barker was named to head arts and sciences; Dr. Matt Reiser was to continue as head of career education; and Al Fine was to remain as head of continuing education and community services. Arts and sciences department heads included, math and science, Dr. Irene Millsaps; education, psychology, and physical education, Dr. F. Dean Banta; humanities, Renate Hufft; and social sciences, Dr. Spencer Culbreth. Career education department heads were, nursing, Shelby Millsaps; allied health, Joe Semak; industrial technology, Jan Evans; and, business and office careers, Dr. Frank McKenzie. Dr. James M. Stubbs was designated as director of affirmative action/personnel services in an expansion of his duties and services to the institution.

As a by-product of its educational services, Cleveland State provides East Tennessee with a yearly boost of five million dollars to the economy. With a $4.5 million operational budget and a capital expenditures budget of $750,000, the college's total budget for the 1977 fiscal year exceeded five million dollars, and almost all of it was spent in East Tennessee. More than half of the money originates in other parts of the state, according to James Morris, business manager of the college. Added to the community's existing money flow, it produces a subsidizing effect which is not felt when money is merely recirculated.

Of Cleveland State's expenditures, salaries comprise the largest portion, amounting to $2.8 million in 1978-1979. A sizeable percentage of college employees are hired from within the area. For both established and new industry, Cleveland State offers training for potential employees, special short-term courses geared to industrial needs, and consultation and educational opportunities for workers and their families—all reap untold economic benefits. While most students are residents of the immediate area, many from other areas are attracted to the college, creating yet another source of consumer revenue. Finally, increasing numbers of campus visitors contribute to the area economy. In 1977-1978 alone, 1500 individuals attended conferences and forums, and several hundred others participated in various non-credit offerings averaging four weeks in duration.

President Walter L. Nelms. *Photograph courtesy Jackson State Community College.*

3

JACKSON STATE COMMUNITY COLLEGE
by Walter L. Nelms

While it is difficult to identify an exact date to mark Jackson State Community College's beginning, perhaps June 22, 1965, is the most appropriate choice. Although much preliminary work was done before the summer of 1965, this date is significant because of action taken then by the Tennessee State Board of Education in selecting Jackson as one of three Tennessee cities where community colleges would be established. This selection was based on work begun in the middle 1950s, as well as on work by a Tennessee State Board of Education ad hoc committee charged with the responsibility of selecting cities where community colleges would be constructed. Several cities in West Tennessee lobbied for the location of a community college within their boundaries. The committee, headed by Edward L. Jennings, reviewed the applications of these cities and selected Jackson as the site for the West Tennessee community college—primarily because Jackson, in Madison County, and its surrounding counties had the population necessary to support a community college and to assure its success based on potential student enrollment.

Location of a community college in Jackson was the result of work on the parts of individuals too numerous to list here. However, an article appearing in the *Jackson Sun* on June 22, 1965, identified several local people who were instrumental in procuring the institution: George Smith, the mayor of Jackson; Ben Langford, Jackson commissioner of education; Baxter Smith, president of the Jackson Area Chamber of Commerce; Madison County Judge Leroy Pope; Chancellor Brooks McLemore; and E. L. Morgan, a Jackson businessman. In addition to these local men, Governor Frank G. Clement and State Education Commissioner J. Howard Warf were principal figures in the undertaking.

Responsibility for selecting a specific site for construction of the college was assigned to Commissioner Warf. During the selection process, he visited Jackson on several occasions and looked at nine prospective tracts. Potential choices were not publicized, primarily to prevent the possibility of escalating land costs. On August 20, 1965, T. W. Pickel, assistant commissioner of education for special services, announced Commissioner Warf's choice for the community college site. Options for purchase of the 103.5 acres, located on Highway 70 East, were taken at a cost of $1000 per acre for a 78.4-acre tract owned by Mr. and Mrs. Paul Carter and a 25.1-acre tract owned by Mr. and Mrs. F. H. Dyer. Following this action, the city commission and the Madison County Court voted to exercise the options and proceed with the purchase of the land. In addition to the site purchase, the county and city each agreed to provide $125,000 toward construction, equipment for facilities, and utilities. Construction of the college facilities was anticipated to begin in February of 1966 at a cost of approximately 2.5 to three million dollars. State Board of Education personnel did not anticipate that the college would be operative by the fall of 1966.

The Jackson architectural firm of Thomas, Ross, Stanfill, and Associates, Incorporated, was employed to develop the plans for college facilities, and the J. A. Jones Construction Company of Charlotte, North Carolina, won the bid for construction. The actual construction of campus facilities began in the summer of 1966 at a contract price of $2,008,018. Contingency plans were made as the possibility was explored of opening Jackson State Community College in temporary quarters during the fall of 1966; however, these plans proved unfeasible and the first classes were not held at the new institution until the fall of 1967.

Francis Everett Wright was named to the presidency of the college on February 17, 1967. At that time Dr. Wright was president of Union University, also located in Jackson, Tennessee. The 51-year-old educator had held that position since 1963 and had served as the university's academic dean for nine years prior to that time. He also had been dean of men at Baylor University and for two years had served as personnel counselor at Northwestern State College in

Dr. Francis E. Wright, first president of Jackson State. *Photograph courtesy Jackson State Community College.*

Louisiana. A native of DeQueen, Arkansas, Dr. Wright had lived in Waco, Texas, for many years. Having received his bachelor's degree from Baylor University and having spent three years in the United States Air Force during World War II, he later received master's and doctoral degrees from George Peabody College in Nashville, Tennessee. Dr. Wright returned from the Nashville meeting where he had been named president of Jackson State Community College carrying a pasteboard box which, containing numerous applications for positions at the institution, represented the entire college at that time. Dr. Wright was to assume responsibilities as president on March 15, 1967. Among his early primary tasks was the assemblage of an administrative staff. Included in that staff were Dr. Walter L. Nelms, dean of instruction; Dr. James E. Toomey, dean of student affairs; and Sam Burns, business manager. Chester Parham was selected to be in charge of public relations and field services; Mary

First registration, held fall quarter of 1967. *Photograph courtesy Jackson State Community College.*

Craig was chosen to serve as director of admissions; Dr. Homer Lawrence became director of continuing education; Joe Pierce became superintendent of buildings and grounds; R. C. Rumfelt was selected director of the student union building; Marsh Goodson was employed as instructor of physical education and coach of basketball and baseball; Dr. Ray A. Palmer was selected chairman of the division of mathematics and science; Joe Pentecost was employed as instructor of marketing and distribution technology; and Clyde Fugate was chosen to serve as a counselor. Employed to assist these staff members in accomplishing their tasks were Jackie Bobbitt, secretary to the president; Anne Crossnoe, secretary to the dean of instruction; Virginia Snipes, secretary to the director of admissions; Suzanne Tipton, secretary to the director of public relations and field services; and Joe Riddle, accounting clerk.

In temporary offices established in a rented house at 279 Airways Boulevard, President Wright and his staff worked diligently during the summer of 1967 to accomplish the tasks necessary for the anticipated opening of the institution in the fall of 1967. This work included the employment of a faculty and staff, the procurement of physical equipment for the educational programs of the institution, the development of a college catalog, the publication of college policies, and the obtaining of textbooks and other teaching aids.

It long had been anticipated that approximately 400 students would enroll initially; however, registration on September 27 and 28, 1967, produced an enrollment of 640 students, representing the 21 West Tennessee counties. The higher-than-expected enrollment indicated the early popularity of the college.

The faculty and staff employed by the college were carefully selected in keeping with qualifications deemed requisite to the efficient operation of a community college. Key among those qualifications was the employees' commitment to a student-oriented and community-conscious institution. Throughout its history, Jackson State has worked toward developing educational programs and methods to meet the needs of the students and the community, offering the following services:

1. An academic program to provide the student with two years of higher education that might be transferred to four-year institutions toward the completion of a baccalaureate degree.

2. A technical program to provide the student an opportunity to develop a marketable skill upon the completion of a two-year program of study.

3. A continuing education program designed to provide the student with an educational opportunity for personal enrichment or professional improvement.

4. A program of personal, academic, and occupational guidance and counseling services provided to assist individual students or members of the community better to understand themselves and their potential.

5. A service program for research, cultural enrichment, and entertainment to afford more profitable use of leisure to the entire community.

The institution has always maintained an open-door policy, accepting all qualified students who desired to improve themselves through education. A concerted effort has been made to lead and direct all students to the fulfillment of their personal goals and aspirations.

In the beginning, six buildings were constructed on the campus: an administration building, a classroom building, library, physical education/music building, student center and maintenance building. These and additional buildings were funded by approximately 60 percent general obligation bonds and 40 percent federal grants. Construction began on August 8, 1966. The administration building was occupied September 5, 1967, and classes began October 2, 1967. When the construction contracts were originally bid, it was anticipated that an over-run of contract funds would exist; thus, there would not be enough funds available to complete the campus as designed. Therefore, several alternates were written into the bid specifications which were later deducted from the original contract. As a result of these deductions, Jackson State initially did not have paved parking lots, storm drains, curbs, or lighting for parking areas. Another alternate that was deducted from the original contract was air conditioning for the major classroom building. During the summers of 1968 and 1969, classes were held in a building without air conditioning; although designed for air conditioning, installation did not take place until late August of 1969.

A science building was completed during the fiscal year 1968-1969, providing a second classroom facility and greatly relieving utilization of the major classroom building, especially in the area of laboratory classes. In September of 1973, an addition to the student center and an addition to the library were completed at a total cost of $755,000. With these additions, the campus consisted of approximately 200,000 square feet of building area. Spaces in these additions provided guidance and testing, financial aid, and other student personnel offices which enabled the college to supply better service to the students. An addition to the maintenance building was completed in January of 1975, providing approximately 6600 square feet of additional storage and work facilities for the operation and maintenance of the physical plant. During the fiscal year 1974-1975, $20,033 became available for Jackson State to make campus improvements. Approximately 4500 feet of curbs and gutters were installed with these funds. By 1979 the college had expanded to approximately 210,000 square feet of physical facilities and employed approximately 30 full-time and part-time maintenance staff.

Left to right: Dale Glover, representing the State Board of Education; Commissioner J. Howard Warf; President Francis E. Wright; and Governor Buford Ellington at groundbreaking ceremony for the science building in 1968. *Photograph courtesy Jackson State Community College.*

In May of 1976, Dr. Wright, founding president of Jackson State Community College, died. In December of 1976, the Tennessee State Board of Regents honored Dr. Wright by naming the administration building the F. E. Wright Administration Building; it was the first structure to be given a formal name.

During the latter part of 1977, the college contracted with Burkhalter-Hickerson, Associates, Incorporated, to design a master plan for the development of physical facilities and grounds based on anticipated growth at the institution. This completed master plan is a planning tool for future expansion of buildings, utilities, streets, parking areas, recreational and athletic facilities, and other types of developments that come with institutional growth.

Academic year 1967-1968 was the inaugural year for Jackson State Community College and the first in which all educational programs were offered. The second year of instruction began with the summer quarter of 1968 and offered two basic transfer programs, associate of science general and associate of arts general. The associate of science degree was offered in the areas of prebusiness, preengineering, premedical technician, and preteaching; the associate of arts degree was offered in the areas of prelaw, premedicine, predentistry, and prepharmacy.

Six technological programs, designed to enable the student to develop a marketable skill immediately upon graduation from the institution, were offered beginning with the 1967-1968 academic year. Each program was unique in its requirements which were based on competencies needed in each of the vocational fields. One of the original technology programs was in agricultural technology with a business option. It was designed to meet the increasing need for trained personnel to work in grain, feed, seed, farm supply, and other farm-related industries. Another technology program offered at the time was in the area of construction technology, designed to prepare students for jobs in the construction industry. A program in engineering graphic technology also was offered in the effort to provide instruction and training in drafting techniques. Related courses were developed to provide training in planning and production methods for construction, industrial manufacturing, and engineering. Also among the original technology programs at Jackson State was a program in marketing and distribution technology which was designed to provide the trainee with the educational background required for entry into an occupation in marketing at the mid-management level. Secretarial science also was offered during the college's initial year. This program was designed to develop a well-trained professional secretary for business or industry. A program in electronic communication technology, designed to meet the increasing need for electronic personnel in the production, operation, and service of electronic equipment, was never fully implemented by the college.

Beginning with the 1968-1969 academic year, Jackson State Community College offered a number of additional transfer programs in addition to associate of science general and associate of arts general. New majors were available in general agriculture, fine arts, business, English, home economics, journalism, mathematics, music, science, elementary education, health and physical education, social science general, history, geography, political science, and sociology. A new program in electronic data processing was added for the 1968-1969 academic year to the two-year technical programs.

Development of the data processing program in 1968 set in motion a series of events that have led over the years to an expanding utilization of the computer—not only in the instructional area, but also in administrative and academic support and in community-oriented services and projects. In 1968 the college acquired a computer system with appropriate unit record equipment backup. The computer hardware has been continually updated since that year. In 1974 and 1975, the college developed on-line data processing systems for registration and student records and a partial system for the library. In 1977 the college installed another computer system, which is a time-sharing system used primarily to support terminals. In 1979 computer-assisted instruction programs were either underway or being developed in several instructional divisions of the college.

A new audio-tutorial system was implemented in the area of biology in the fall quarter of 1969. Representatives of the college had reviewed the original audio-tutorial system at Purdue University in Indiana before pioneering its implementation in Tennessee and surrounding areas. The program continued intact until the fall quarter of 1976 when a modified version of the system was implemented to allow a more flexible scheduling approach and to blend the audio-tutorial system with a more traditional approach to teaching.

During the academic year 1970-1971, three new technical programs were fully implemented at the college. The first, a two-year medical laboratory technician program, was designed to enable students to attain associate of science degrees in that field, thus qualifying them to take national and state examinations to gain licensure. A second program developed that year was radiologic technology, designed to prepare students for employment as X-ray technologists by dividing their time between the college and Jackson-Madison County General Hospital. The third medical technology program implemented during the 1970-1971 academic year was inhalation therapy. It was designed to lead to an associate of science degree and to qualify the graduate for the American Registry examination in inhalation therapy. All three programs operated on a cooperative basis with the local hospital.

During the years 1970-1972, development and implementation occurred in the area of general technical education (basic studies) in the division of technology. This program was designed to assist students primarily in the area of technical communication skills by developing courses and procedures to provide students with placement advisement based largely on ACT scores. Although most of these programs had been in existence prior to 1970, the division of humanities supported the effort through its courses in basic writing skills, as did the division of social studies and education through its courses in reading. By the 1976-1977 academic year, a new general developmental education program had been implemented with much of it housed in the division of social studies and education. A voluntary placement testing program was begun; developmental courses were available in mathematics, English, human relations, listening skills, reading improvement, and study skills improvement. The college continues to update and improve this program each year.

Two new technology programs were implemented during the 1972-1973 academic year. The industrial management program was intended to prepare students for supervisory positions in the manufacturing industry. Offered for the first time in 1972-1973, machine design technology was developed to provide instruction and training in the design of machine tools and parts.

In the 1977-1978 academic year, a learning resources center was developed in the Jackson State Community College library building. This program was designed to assist all instructional areas with audio-visual services, tutoring facilities, and housing of much of the developmental program. The learning resources center was expanded during the 1978-1979 academic year and was renamed the instructional support center. In cooperation with various developmental programs of the college, the center offers services such as tutoring, individual writing assistance, study aids, classroom aids, term paper clinics, listening and study facilities, and audio-visual equipment.

Needs studies are currently being done for four new technology programs and one new transfer and career (occupational) program at the college. If planning is successful, these programs could be implemented in the fall of 1979: medical assistant technology, medical records technology, physical science technology, industrial laboratory technology, and criminal justice.

The various academic divisions of the college and their leaders have been instrumental in the development of various programs at Jackson State. The division of mathematics and science was one of the original academic divisions of the college. Dr. Ray A. Palmer has served as chairman of the division from the school's inception, except for a period of time from June of 1976 until July of 1978 when he served as acting dean of instruction and associate dean. The division of technology was also one of the original divisions of the college. Dr. James E. Coburn was employed as chairman of the division on August 15, 1967. In 1971 he was replaced by Joe M. Pentecost, who became acting chairman of the division. An original employee of the institution, Pentecost had been head of the department of marketing since 1969. His status was changed from acting chairman to chairman on March 21, 1972, and he remained in the position until July 1, 1978, when all technology programs were merged into other academic divisions of the college. At that time Pentecost became director of career education.

The division of humanities became an official entity of the college in the fall of 1968. Mildred Corley, who was employed as assistant professor of English on September 1, 1967, became acting chairman of the division. In the fall of 1969, C. D. Culver replaced Corley, who became involved in instructional television along with her English responsibilities. On March 21, 1972, Culver's title was changed from acting chairman to chairman.

The division of social studies and education officially began in the fall of 1968. Don E. Chevalia was employed at that time as acting chairman of the division and was elevated to full chairmanship in the fall of 1971. The department of business administration was a part of the social studies and education division from 1968, soon after the college was founded, until the fall of 1976, when it became part of the new division of business and data processing. The division of business and data processing was created and added to the college structure in the fall of 1976. Durward Denley became acting chairman of the new division on July 1, 1976, and was elevated to chairman on July 1, 1977. He had served as director of the computer center and head of the department of data processing at Jackson

State Community College prior to assuming the duties of the new chairmanship.

The office of continuing education began in 1967 with the birth of the college. The first course taught in the division was a non-credit course in sales training; it enrolled 156 students and lasted from July 5 until July 28, 1967. Sponsored jointly by the college, the Jackson Community Relations Council, and the Area Chamber of Commerce, the course was held at Jackson High School prior to the completion of the college's facilities. Other accomplishments during the period included courses in child care, flower arranging, decoupage, creative writing, GED, and both credit and non-credit programs in industry. The continuing education office was also active in the formation of the Harvest Years Club for senior citizens—a cooperative effort with the Dynamic Maturity Program of Jackson. Bentley Rawdon became director of the division in 1970 and served in that capacity until 1972. During this period, the off-campus program had its beginning with initial efforts in Savannah and Huntingdon. Other significant programs were started in real estate and business, and the agreement with the American Institute of Banking was formulated. In 1972 Gene Conyers was named director. He served until 1976, and it was during this period that the first major thrust for off-campus programs was initiated. Programs began in Selmer and Milan in 1973; Brownsville and Bolivar were added in 1974 and 1975, respectively. The college became more active in special interest non-credit courses, particularly in the area of art. The evening program, including both credit and non-credit programs, continued to expand. Dr. Marsh Goodson succeeded Conyers as director in 1976. Under his leadership the off-campus program has expanded further. Programs were initiated at Camden in 1977 and at Parsons in 1978. In 1979 more than 500 students were served at the college's off-campus centers.

The office of continuing education and evening programs has continued to expand its role in public service programs, non-credit programs, off-campus credit programs, and the direction of the evening program on campus. Examples of popular programs are a child abuse seminar, which attracted national attention, a "What's a Woman To Do?" workshop, on the state level, and the certified professional secretary review program. A night office has been created to better serve evening students. The off-campus and evening on-campus credit programs involve more than 300 students, with an additional 300 being involved in non-credit programs. In addition, the college serves more than 10,000 persons annually through meetings, workshops, and seminars.

The division of counseling services has provided a wide range of services for Jackson State Community College students. The center assists students in the areas of academic counseling, student advising, and personal counseling for night students. In addition the area provides services to the community. Among services rendered for the community are GED examinations; the state insurance examination; law enforcement candidate assessment program examinations; special testing sessions upon request; and Title I applicant testing, training, career guidance, and placement services for adults.

The Jackson State Community College library began operation in the fall of 1967. The objective of providing service was foremost in the library's role from the beginning. A committee was formed in October of 1967 to help formulate policies as they related to faculty and students, and the library's collection developed to support each facet of the college curriculum. Resources such as books, periodicals, multi-media materials, and other informational sources were ordered and made available. During the first year of operation, 618 items were checked out from the library. In July of 1968, Van H. Veatch was named head librarian. Ruth Gibbons became reference librarian in 1969 and, in 1972, acquisitions librarian. She remained with the library until her retirement in 1975.

With support from the college administration, the library was able to thrive in many innovative ways. President Wright encouraged library personnel to make use of the college's computer capabilities. The computer center cooperated with the library staff in converting many of the library's holdings data into machine-readable form. Print-outs of library materials by author, title, and classification number were developed, as were monthly updates. Another outgrowth of computer utilization was the *Jackson Area Union List of Periodicals,* which was begun in 1970. This list is published annually by the college library and is a record of the periodical holdings of many area college, public, and special libraries.

The library reached an important milestone in November of 1970, when it received its 20 thousandth volume, thus meeting standards for approval by the Southern Association of Colleges and

Schools and by the Association of College and Research Libraries. Several significant accomplishments were recorded in the intervening years. A materials loan arrangement was begun with area colleges, enabling a Jackson State student to check out materials at Bethel, Freed-Hardeman, Lane, Lambuth, Union, and the University of Tennessee at Martin. Students from these schools could also borrow materials from the Jackson State Library under the arrangement.

The library's resources also are available to members of the community, and many citizens make use of these materials. As a service to the community, the library became a regional resources center for the dissemination of materials from the educational resources information center in 1972. This program was in affiliation with the Tennessee research coordinating unit for vocational-technical education in Knoxville. When the research coordinating unit was phased out several years later, the center at Jackson State Community College was dissolved. In 1972 the library moved into its new and spacious addition, thus making its facilities more inviting for research and study. In the 1977-1978 school year, circulation of materials had reached 21,872, and the library's collection housed 45,825 volumes by June 30, 1978. In addition, it subscribed to 364 periodicals by that date. The library has remained a vital center for the seeking and recording of information necessary to the instructional process.

The intercollegiate athletic program began at Jackson State Community College in the fall of 1967, under the direction of Marsh Goodson. Varsity teams were fielded in men's basketball and baseball on a non-scholarship basis. Varsity sports for women did not begin officially until the fall of 1975, although the college did participate in an extramural program for women under the direction of Betty L. Watson.

The first intercollegiate contest at the college was a basketball game with Cumberland College on November 20, 1967. After operating on a non-scholarship basis for one year, a scholarship program was initiated in the fall of 1968; Edward Pollard of Ramer was the first scholarship athlete at Jackson State. Jim Swope, from the University of Tennessee at Martin, was hired to head the basketball program, and, the same year, the college became a charter member of the Tennessee Junior College Athletic Association, which was composed of all two-year public and private colleges in Tennessee.

Roger Jones attained all-conference recognition in basketball in 1968-1969, as did Charles Blanchard, Jerry Franklin, David Sikes, Ronnie Doss, and Ross Grimsley in baseball. Grimsley was named the most valuable player in the conference and signed a professional contract after the 1969 season. He went on to play with Cincinnati, Baltimore, and Montreal in the major leagues, attaining all-star status in 1978. The Jackson State Community College baseball team of 1968-1969, led by Grimsley, was co-champion of the Tennessee Junior College Athletic Association in its initial year.

Jack Martin from McMinnville, Tennessee, was employed in the fall of 1969 as baseball coach, with Marsh Goodson devoting full time to the direction of athletics and the physical education program. The baseball team qualified for the district play-offs in Columbia, Tennessee, in 1970, and Coach Martin was named TJCAA Baseball Coach of the Year. Basketball player Roger Jones was all-conference in 1969-1970, along with baseball players Charles Blanchard, David Glover, Barry Barnett, Ronnie Doss, and Ricky Sullivan. Blanchard, Doss, and Barnett were named to the all-eastern district team.

Jim Hart, who came to Jackson State Community College from Matthews, Missouri, was employed to replace Jim Swope as basketball coach in the summer of 1970. Swope returned to the University of Tennessee at Martin as an assistant coach. Calvin Bailey gained all-conference and all-regional basketball recognition in 1970-1971; all-conference baseball honors went to Troy Giles, David Glover, Danny Patterson, and James Gravenmier.

Gary Grisham in basketball and Gene Menees, Billy Ray Cox, George Sykes, and Mark Herring in baseball were named to the all-conference team in 1971-1972. Herring signed a professional contract with the Houston organization after the 1972 season. Jim Hart was named 1972-1973 TJCAA Basketball Co-Coach of the Year; Thomas Partee was all-conference in basketball, and Gene Menees, Don Hill, Steve McEwen, and Walter Glass were all-conference in baseball. Menees went on to become All-SEC at Vanderbilt and presently he is playing AAA professional ball in the American Association.

The basketball team qualified for the regional play-offs in the 1973-1974 season, and it led the conference in team defense. All-conference and all-regional honors went to Peter Pullen in basketball; Randy Mays, David Day, Steve McEwen, Walter Glass, and Henry Glass were all-conference in baseball. The 1974-1975 year was highlighted by the play of Larry Carter, who won all-conference and all-regional honors in basketball. He went on to star for two years with the University of Tennessee at Martin.

A varsity intercollegiate program for women officially began in basketball in the fall of 1975, on a non-scholarship basis. The first team was coached by Jim Hart, who continued to perform his duties as men's coach. Coach Hart was named TJCAA Co-Coach of the Year for his work with men's basketball. Scholarships for women were offered in basketball for the first time in 1976-1977, and Jeff Hopkins from Memphis, Tennessee, was hired to coach women's basketball and to assist in baseball. Jack Martin became athletic director replacing Marsh Goodson, who moved into administration. Preston Pearson was all-conference and all-regional in men's basketball, and Steve Lee, Tommy Blankenship, Chris Faulkner, and Keith Hegler were all-conference in baseball for 1976-1977.

All-conference and all-regional honors went to Jerry Robertson in men's basketball for 1977-1978. Tommy Blankenship and Dale Logan were all-conference in baseball. Jack Martin resigned as baseball coach in the summer of 1978 to devote full time to the direction of athletics and the physical education program. Jeff Hopkins became baseball coach and Marvin Williams, from Bolivar, became women's basketball coach, replacing Hopkins. Betty L. Watson, assistant professor of physical education and one of the original college faculty, resigned to continue her education.

Jackson State Community College officially became part of Tennessee's expanding education system on October 23, 1967, in a formal dedication held on the campus. In an address to students and visitors, Commissioner Warf dedicated the new junior college and delivered a charge "to service and to strength." Also attending the ceremonies were Mayor Bob Conger, Commissioner Ben Langford, County Judge Hugh Harvey, several members of the Madison County Quarterly Court, State Senator Lowell Thomas, State Representative Tommy McKnight, State Department of Education officials, and four members of the State Board of Education. Special guests included former Jackson resident Major George Smith and past County Judge Leroy Pope, who were instrumental in locating the new facility at Jackson. W. L. Barry, administrative aid to Governor Buford Ellington, represented the governor, who was attending the National Governors' Conference. Guided tours of the campus were conducted for the visitors, and students served as hostesses for the occasion. The Jackson State Choir, directed by music department head Donnie Adams, presented special music at the ceremonies.

On April 25, 1968, local Jackson residents paid tribute to the four institutions of higher learning in a "Salute to Higher Education Day." Local college presidents honored were Dr. Wright, Jackson State; Dr. C. A. Kirkendoll, Lane College; Dr. Robert E. Craig, Union University; and Dr. James S. Wilder, Lambuth College. The festivities began with a breakfast where Dr. Andrew P. Holt, president of the University of Tennessee, was principal speaker. Local and state government officials attended the dedication. The salute was hailed as one of the most ambitious and significant events ever undertaken in Jackson. Glenn Rainey, chairman of the college day salute, observed that few, if any, occasions have generated such enthusiasm among Jacksonians or created such a feeling of community pride.

An optimistic look at the future with no apologies for the present was the theme of the commencement address heard by the college's graduating class. Commissioner Warf addressed the 55 graduating students. Milton Armstrong of Bolivar was Jackson State's first graduate. Honored during the ceremony as the student who contributed the most to the college, he was named Mr. JSCC by students and served as their president. Also among the first graduating class were the college's first enrollees, twin sisters Wanda and Juanita Jernigan. The class presented Jackson State with a wrought iron sign to be located at the entrance of the school.

On December 4, 1969, local newspapers announced that the college had been accepted for membership in the Southern Association of Colleges and Schools. Dr. Wright said, "This is the earliest date our institution could have been accepted....When I was appointed president of Jackson State Community College, Mr. Warf gave me three directives. They were to get the college open, to get it established, and to get it accredited." Acceptance for membership in the association came to the college in fewer than three years after its organization. Jackson State's bold new approach to higher education at-

Graduation at Jackson State. *Photograph courtesy Jackson State Community College.*

tracted a record number of students. Its open-door admission policy, reasonable fees, high quality instruction, recognition by other colleges, and location were, and continue to be, features which appeal to students who might have by-passed a college career. Dr. Wright's three directives were achieved. Continued acceptance, quality education, growth, and service will remain objectives of Jackson State Community College. Jackson was selected one of two cities to welcome the 1970 spring drive-in conference, sponsored by the West Tennessee Education Association. The conference was held on campus, and about 1500 WTEA members attended. The theme of the conference was "Education 1970: Its Adventures and Challenges." Dr. Carl S. Winters, one of America's foremost inspirational speakers and humorists, delivered the morning address, and other speakers addressed the group of educators as well. Sectional meetings were held for elementary and secondary teachers, administrators, supervisors, and guidance personnel.

Open house at the college was held April 26, 1970. Staff, faculty, and student committees welcomed area citizens who were invited to visit the campus and discussed programs with them. Guests were directed on informal tours through the administration building, student center, science building, classroom building, physical education building, and library. The campus took on a natural beauty enhanced by blossoms of more than 12,000 tulip bulbs which had been planted that spring. The blooming azaleas were an additional attraction to the campus.

Aerial view of the campus. *Photograph courtesy Jackson State Community College.*

It was a proud moment for Bette J. Piercey and her six children when Mrs. Piercey, Jackson State's first full-time night graduate, received her associate of science degree cum laude. Cooperation from her family and co-workers enabled Mrs. Piercey to attend night school and maintain her home and office responsibilities. She planned to continue her education in one of Jackson's senior colleges, provided she could get night courses leading to a four-year degree. "Attendance at Jackson State Community College," she said, "has revealed to me that college instructors today are interested in their students. I was very much impressed with the quality of instruction and the interest which my instructors at Jackson State Community College showed in me and the other students."

Hollywood came to Jackson when Sherrod P. Sanders, custodial supervisor at Jackson State Community College, found himself a participant in the filming of *Walking Tall, Part II*. Reverend Sanders played the part of an elderly minister presiding over the funeral of Obra Eaker, the black deputy killed in the movie. Although many ministers were considered for the part, Sanders said he got it because of his gray hair. Sanders had other qualifications; in fact, he is the minister at the church where the funeral scene was filmed. "It's like a dream. It's just like a dream," Sanders said after the scene was filmed. If he was nervous, he did not show it. Nor did he lose his patience as the director, Earl Belamy, called for one retake after another. Sanders was a hero of the occasion. "I only had one dream when I was a little boy, and that was to fly in an airplane," he said, "but never in my life did I ever dream of being in a movie! I can't wait to see myself in it!"

Governor Ray Blanton, President Wright, the SGA, and students all honored W. L. Autry for the heroic deed of saving Juanita Campbell's life on November 5, 1975, when a near fatal accident caused her car to roll into one of the duck ponds on campus. Dr. Wright issued a presidential proclamation to all Jackson State Community College personnel, faculty, and students claiming Wednesday, December 3, 1975, as "W. L. Autry Day" on the campus. On that day, the SGA presented Autry an award in recognition of his heroic deed, and Dr. Wright recognized him with a special service award. In addition to recognition given Autry on campus, he received a citation from Governor Blanton for "outstanding service to mankind for rescuing a drowning person." Autry also received letters of commendation from U.S. Senators Bill Brock and Howard Baker.

Dr. Wright died Saturday afternoon, May 15, 1976, of a heart attack. He was 61 years old. Dr. Wright was pronounced dead on arrival at Jackson-Madison County General Hospital where he was taken after collapsing on the Jackson Golf and Country Club golf course about 4:30 p.m. Glenn Rainey of Jackson, higher education commission chairman and a close friend of Dr. Wright said, "His death is a tragic loss to the educational community and the citizens of Jackson." Rainey called Dr. Wright a "giant in the education circles of Tennessee. It's not often you rub shoulders with men the caliber of F. E. Wright."

During his latter years as president of the college, Dr. Wright suggested that a foundation be established to provide services that the college could not provide to the community and students through state appropriations. The foundation was not inaugurated during Dr. Wright's lifetime, but, at the time of his death, Glenn Rainey suggested that a service of this nature be initiated. Thus the F. E. Wright Memorial Foundation was formed to honor the late president, and friends of Dr. Wright were requested to contribute to the foundation in lieu of flowers or other tokens of esteem and affection. College faculty embraced the idea and contributed generously to the foundation, with donations reaching $11,600. A foundation board was formed to establish guidelines for implementing the program; it consisted of President Sam Watlington of Watlington Brothers; Vice-President Robert Caldwell, assistant trust officer for First National Bank; and Secretary-Treasurer Wayne Powers, dean of administrative and financial affairs for Jackson State. Other board members included Dr. Walter L. Nelms; Dr. Robert A. Harrell; J. Bentley Rawdon; Linda Theus, secretarial science instructor; George Kimes of Bowyer-Johnson-Kimes, Incorporated; James Buchanan, proprietor of Buchanan and Sons Exxon Service Station; and Neta McKnight, college instructor of allied health. Each year a scholarship is to be awarded in Jackson State's service area to a graduating senior high school student who excels in both leadership and academic work. The first was awarded to Lana Webb, a 1978 graduate of Maury City High School.

Shortly after the death of Dr. Wright, State Board of Regents Chancellor Roy Nicks named a three-person management team to head Jackson State Community College. Named chairman was Dr. Nelms, dean of JSCC; other members were Wayne Powers, business manager, and Bentley Rawdon, director of student affairs. The State Board of Regents met May 31, 1976, and appointed Dr. Nelms interim president. It authorized Chancellor Nicks to appoint a six-member advisory board and set the qualifications for a new president by August 1. Among the qualifications were an earned doctorate, five years' suitable administrative experience, leadership skills, commitment to the community college philosophy, and ability to work with the legislature, the students, and the faculty.

By mid-June, Chancellor Nicks had chosen the advisory committee. Using the membership formula the Regents had specified, he named Wayne Powers; William S. Hamilton, Jackson State Community College assistant professor of agriculture and president of the campus chapter of the Tennessee Education Association; Jack Warren, assistant professor of marketing information and faculty council chairman; Teri Braddy, immediate past president of the student government association; Larry D. Welch, executive vice-president of the Jackson Area Chamber of Commerce; and W. Wray Buchanan, vice-chancellor of the Board of Regents.

Advertisements in national education publications drew 117 applications for the presidential post. By July 8, Chancellor Nicks and the advisory committee had narrowed the list to four. The committee recommended and the board approved Dr. Nelms as Jackson State Community College's new president on July 21, 1976. Before joining the college staff, Dr. Nelms was associate professor of education in the department of educational administration and supervision at Memphis State University. A graduate assistant teacher in the school of education at the University of Mississippi from 1962 to 1964, his earlier employment included teaching and administrative positions on the secondary education level at facilities in Arkansas and West Tennessee. He was a Marine Corps veteran. Dr. Nelms received bachelor's and master's degrees from Harding College in Searcy, Arkansas, with majors in social studies and education. In 1964 he was awarded a doctorate in education and administration from the University of Mississippi. In comment to his appointment, Dr. Nelms said, "My goal in education has been to serve as the president of a community college; and in particular, Jackson State Community College, because I have had a significant role in its development."

One of the original employees of the college, Dr. Nelms was the institution's first academic dean. With some structural changes and reorganizations, he remained in that position until he was named interim president after the death of President Wright. Prior to Dr. Wright's death, Dr. Ray A. Palmer had been selected for a new position, associate dean of transfer programs. When Dr. Nelms became interim president on May 31, 1976, Dr. Palmer became acting dean of instruction. He served in that position during the selection process for a new dean, which began soon after Dr. Nelms was named president.

On the appointment of Dr. Nelms as president, a selection committee was established to receive applications for the deanship. Those serving on the committee were Jim Goodrich, college student government association president; David Favara, college counselor; Dr. Don Chevalia, representative of the division chairmen's committee; Wayne R. Powers; Linda Word, faculty representative of the college's unit of the United Teachers' Profession; Anne Crossnoe; and J. Bentley Rawdon. By the deadline, the committee had received 170 applications for the advertised position. In several marathon sessions, they narrowed the list of applicants to five. In the succeeding weeks, the final five applicants were interviewed by the committee. The selection process resulted in the appointment of the college's new dean of instruction.

Dr. Harrell came to the college from Pima County Community College in Tucson, Arizona. He had been the associate dean of instructional services and resource management there from 1973 until 1975 and dean of educational planning and services from 1975 until 1977. He began his duties at Jackson State on January 27, 1977.

Phi Theta Kappa was organized in 1971 on the college campus. The official name of the JSCC chapter was Chi Omicron. Varnell Rankin was asked by President Wright to be the institution's PTK sponsor, and Rankin asked Joy Nelms to assist him with this responsibility. He served in the sponsorship capacity until his retirement in 1977, when President Nelms appointed Jack Hadley to fill the vacancy and serve as co-sponsor for the organization. PTK was originally organized in 1918 to recognize academic excellence among community and junior college students. The organization provides opportunities for the development of leadership and service, an intellectual climate for exchange of ideas, lively fellowship for scholars, and stimulation of interest in continuing academic excellence. Local initiates must have completed one quarter of community college work, be judged to have good moral character, possess qualities of good citizenship, and have good academic ability. In the years that Jackson State has had a chapter, there have been approximately 320 members. Membership is by invitation only.

Graduation speakers at Jackson State have included these distinguished individuals: 1968-1969, Commissioner Warf; 1969-1970, Dr. C. C. Humphreys, president of Memphis State University; 1970-1971, Dr. E. C. Stimbert, State Commissioner of Education; 1972-1973, Dr. Archie R. Dykes, president-elect of Kansas State University and former chancellor of the University of Tennessee, Martin; 1973-1974, Dr. Billy M. Jones, president of Memphis State University; 1974-1975, Chancellor Nicks; 1975-1976, Dr. Sam H. Ingram, State Commissioner of Education; 1976-1977, Dr. John W. Richardson, Jr., retired dean of the graduate school, Memphis State University; and 1977-1978, Dr. C. C. Bond, retired assistant superintendent for pupil personnel services and community relations, Chattanooga Public Schools.

These students have held the office of student government as-

Faculty and staff dinner at which Dr. and Mrs. Francis E. Wright were hosts in September of 1974. *Photograph courtesy Jackson State Community College.*

sociation president: 1967-1968, Denny Newson; 1968-1969, Milton Armstrong; 1969-1970, Vickey Little; 1970-1971, Jerry Gordon; 1971-1972, Walter David; 1972-1973, Ron Lollar; 1973-1974, Rocky Acuff; 1974-1975, Dixie Chapman: 1975-1976, Teri Braddy; 1976-1977, Jim Goodrich; 1977-1978, Danny Kail; and 1978-1979, David Henderson.

In 1972-1973, Karen Cooley won the title of Miss Jackson State Community College, tied for talent honors in the 1972 Miss Tennessee Pageant, and was named first runner-up to Miss Tennessee in the final competition. Others who have held the title of Miss Jackson State Community College are, in 1973-1974, Kathy Earnest; in 1974-1975, Luanne Little; in 1975-1976, Susan Swaim; in 1976-1977, Cheryl McKnight; and in 1978-1979, Linda McClain.

The music and drama departments of the college began presenting plays in 1973, which in 1976 began to be associated with dinner theatre: *Paint Your Wagon,* 1973; *Mame,* 1974; *Finian's Rainbow,* 1975; *See How They Run,* 1976; *Anything Goes,* 1977; and *Mousetrap,* 1978.

The first 10-year service awards were presented to faculty and staff who had been with the college for 10 consecutive years during an in-service banquet held in the fall of 1977. Honored were Otto Rahm, Donnie J. Adams, Glenn Lemons, Charles Dyer, Dr. E. Marsh Goodson, Beverly Hardin, George McHan, Betty Lee Watson, Joe

M. Pentecost, William Hamilton, Dr. Ray A. Palmer, Genevieve Brooks, Joy Nelms, Dorothy Clayton, R. C. Rumfelt, Dr. Walter L. Nelms, Anne B. Crossnoe, Joe Riddle, Mary Craig, Arthur Baird, Joe Pierce, Sherrod Sanders, Martha Harvey, and Dr. Orville R. Williams. The second 10-year service awards were presented to faculty and staff who had been with the college for 10 consecutive years during an in-service banquet in the fall of 1978. Honored were Durward Denley, Ouita Haltom, Jack Hadley, Dr. Don E. Chevalia, Anne B. Bright, C. B. M. Bright, Marion Smothers, Jack Warren, Van Veatch, Martha Wallis, Wayne Powers, Willie James, W. L. Autry, and Linda Mays.

Jackson State Community College continues to work actively and closely with the community it seeks to serve. Its decade of development and accomplishment has reflected the support of its community and the strength of its administration, faculty, and staff. The foundation of these early years, established through the leadership of Commissioner Warf and President Wright, will enable Jackson State to remain a vital component of the Tennessee Higher Education System.

President Edward B. Eller. *Photograph courtesy Dyersburg State Community College.*

4

DYERSBURG STATE COMMUNITY COLLEGE
by Edward B. Eller

o say that the community founded Dyersburg State Community College is no exaggeration. The earliest organized supporters of a college for Dyersburg were the Jaycees who, by October of 1959, had organized their membership for a vigorous information campaign. The Jaycees may be commended for their foresight and dedication and for their equally remarkable understanding of what a college should do for the Dyersburg area. In the college they saw a solution to the problem for those who could not attend a residential institution, a school for the working man, a cultural center, and a training resource and laboratory for industry. The term *community college* was used little in Tennessee in 1959, and, although the description was not couched in the language of educators, citizens clearly wanted a community college.

The Jaycees took their case to the Dyersburg Chamber of Commerce who formed a committee to assist the Jaycees in promoting a community college. Jaycees and several public officials visited State Education Commissioner Joe Morgan to relate their interest in locating a college in Dyer County. At the time of the visit, no college program existed, but the time was approaching when an ambitious program for postsecondary education would reach fruition. After Commissioner Morgan advised them of what would be required for the community to prepare its justification, they returned home and began work toward their dream.

Although the initial effort of interested citizens was unsuccessful, in 1965 support for the idea of a community college persisted and continued to gather supporters. The desire of many dedicated citizens was finally achieved on June 13, 1967, when the State Board of Education approved Dyersburg as a location for a community college.

A portion of Okeena Park, a golf course totaling 100 acres, was selected as the site for Dyersburg State Community College. On May 29, 1968, groundbreaking ceremonies took place. County, state, and civic leaders were present with five golden shovels, one of which is now on display in the historical room of the McIver Grant Public Library in Dyersburg. The architectural firm of Thomas, Ross, and Stanfill, of Jackson, Tennessee, designed the college under the supervision of T. Wesley Pickel, assistant commissioner of special services for the State Department of Education. In the summer of 1968, Forcum Lannom of Dyersburg was awarded the contract, and the first phase of construction began.

On December 18, 1968, Dr. Edward B. Eller was appointed president of Dyersburg State Community College. Dr. Eller came to the role from the position of assistant commissioner for instruction. His career in Tennessee education was rich and varied; he had served in a local school capacity as a principal, and in statewide capacities as a regional supervisor, director of curriculum and supervision, and coordinator of the division of instruction with the Tennessee State Department of Education. The work which faced the new president was enormous and challenging. His first major goals were to select an able staff for the college and to build academic programs.

Between March 26 and April 16, 1969, five administrative appointments were announced—an important step in the assembly of an administrative team to lead the initial development of the institution. A dean of instruction, a business manager, a dean of students, an administrative assistant, and a public information officer were hired. A few clerical appointments also were made. The initial administrative cadre reflected the work to be done, and it needed to be done quickly: setting up new programs and defining procedures for finance, admissions, and personnel. Other jobs were, in part, the presentation of the school to a hopeful community. It is sometimes easy to forget the turbulence of the 1960s and the ground swell of public resentment from which higher education has not yet recovered. At the time, the public needed assurance that the new kind of college was a part of the "American dream" and not a part of the new American revolution which was occurring. Efforts to inform the

Frame dwelling, located on Parr Avenue in Dyersburg, where college operations began. *Photograph courtesy Dyersburg State Community College.*

public and work with students were initiated by the college in its desire to develop fundamental school-community relationships.

In early May of 1969, the appointment of a coach was announced. The first full-time faculty member was appointed in late May. By August 16 new faculty members had been hired, although some appointments, particularly in technology, had not been made. A librarian, counselor, and an admissions officer also had been hired. The administrative operations were temporarily housed in a frame dwelling. Ten administrative officers were housed in the building; one contained the admissions officer and the librarian, another the dean of instruction and the social studies chairman, and yet another the dean of students, the administrative assistant, and the public information officer.

More was shared than mere office space. The frame house was pervaded by a sense of community, cooperation, and sharing. The newness was exciting. Each bit of new information about a prospective student, a way to perform an administrative task, or an academic

Charter faculty and staff. *Left to right, front row:* Robin Pierce, Mitchell Bennett, Mary McCauley, Loretta Bond, Oneida Johnson, Sandra Rockett, Ann Carter, Wanda Green, Wanda Lemonds, Florence Schultz, Jackie Clift, and Larry York; *second row:* Bob Espey, Tony Hinson, Helen Bell, Linda Chambers, Carol Feather, Betty Cagle, Charles Kendrick, Connie Apple, Rosella McClain, Anne Sain, and Robert Logue; *third row:* Robert McCormick, William Penrod, Phillip Winkler, Billy Williams, Eugene Byrd, John Wilkinson, and President Eller; *fourth row:* Casey Vinson, Henry Butler, Dan Weatherspoon, David Kelly, and Donald Holland. *Photograph courtesy Dyersburg State Community College.*

program or course was shared among the group members. The spirit was almost messianic. The group was convinced of the unique worthiness of creating a college in the area, for it would give the area a new level of cultural awareness and aspiration.

If newness was exhilarating, it also was filled with some uncertainty. The new faculty in correspondence with the dean wondered which topics were to be covered in various courses. New administrative roles had to be created. Programs yet to be approved formally were planned and justified. Students with a host of needs inquired about the new college. Members of the public wrote to find out where the administrative offices were located. Yet the uncertainty of newness did not prevent tasks from being accomplished on schedule. September of 1969 brought three important events—the collective gathering of the first faculty, the completion of two of the six buildings under construction, and the first entering class. A two-week orientation of faculty to the community college concept was conducted; for most it was their first exposure to work in a collegiate setting. However, it was not all work: A tea was held in the president's home for all faculty and staff; an informal meeting was scheduled for the press to learn more about what was available at Dyersburg State; and a picnic was held for faculty and staff to meet with community members. Therefore, the orientation provided the faculty an opportunity to get acquainted with one another and the community they would serve, as well as an opportunity to deal with their enormous educational challenge.

The most important event of the year, registration for the first classes, began September 29, 1969. A special registration for evening students was held October 6. When registration was complete, 588 students had enrolled. The first class included numerous multiple enrollments from the same family, a relatively high percentage of part-time students, and several prominent citizens and officials. The enrollment exceeded the college estimate of 500 students, with about four-fifths of the initial student body coming from Dyer County—a statistic that would change as word of the new college spread into adjacent counties.

The students having arrived, an activities program began immediately. Cheerleaders were elected in late October. Student government association officers were elected in late November although students had no permanent meeting place until the facilities were finished, and the freshman basketball team practiced for the first season. The basketball team played its first home game in the Dyersburg High School gymnasium on December 13, 1969. Victory did not come easily for the newly formed team, but the Saints (later changed to Chiefs) won their first game February 9, 1970, in competition with Southwestern freshmen. The delay in home games was caused by a slight delay in finishing the gymnasium. All buildings were completed, however, by January of 1970. A similar delay was experienced in some equipment acquisitions. For a brief period of time some students were required to sit on the floor in the library because all of the furniture had not arrived.

Although the school had only begun to develop, its major emphasis clearly emerged during the first year. Pretechnical studies, a forerunner to developmental studies, was offered the first year. This effort was initially an activity of the division of technology and, later, a joint activity with student personnel services. General education development (GED) classes were offered and the test administered during the first quarter of operation. Dyersburg State was designated a testing center for the GED program in February of 1970. GED graduates have accounted for from five to 10 percent of Dyersburg State students since the program began at the college.

Continuing education and public service began during the first year of operation. Eleven credit-free courses and 15 credit courses were offered during the first quarter. A program on drug abuse was offered and a community band organized. The first year of operation also was a time of building for the technology program. A technology director was hired for the first year, as were instructors in business and electronics. Early quarterly reports of the institution reflected the concern for expanding career horizons of students in the area. Programs in nursing, business administration, civil engineering, data processing, office careers, inhalation therapy, manufacturing, marketing, and agriculture were proposed during the first year of operation. Most of the programs offered at Dyersburg State flourished and grew as career education became more popular with students. Manufacturing technology, however, did not prosper and was eliminated although one of its elements, industrial management, later was revised and emerged as a popular option.

The basic mission of the college—accomplishment—was firmly established in the first year. Preparations for enrolling and teaching a group of students were completed in fewer than six months by a small staff who had no procedure or precedent to guide them. State Education Commissioner J. H. Warf expressed this sentiment in another way: "Somebody could say that this institution is a result of genius, but I would be more inclined to think it is more due to hard work."

The creation of the college did take hard work, no small amount of ingenuity, a shared belief by the staff in the worthiness of a goal, and a warmly supportive community. The strong community effort was clearly recognized in the dedication ceremony of the college on May 4, 1970. President Eller expressed appreciation to the community for its support. The Jaycees and the chamber of commerce were thanked for their pioneering efforts. The resolution of the Dyer County Court authorizing a payment of $250,000 toward construction of facilities and the City of Dyersburg's donation of land totaling 100 acres was recognized as evidence of the commitment of the citizenry to the new college. More than 1500 citizens attended the dedication ceremony which was followed by an open house.

Commissioner J. Howard Warf delivers the dedication address, May 4, 1970. *Photograph courtesy Dyersburg State Community College.*

The major address was delivered by the chairman of the State Board of Education, Commissioner Warf, who sounded a theme considered characteristic of the aims of the college: "We dedicate Dyersburg State Community College to the role of questing, teaching, and serving for this region's bright today and even brighter tomorrow." The dedication was a celebration of the beginning and a challenge to strive toward greater achievement.

The major events to occur during the 12 months following the dedication were the first summer school term, acceptance into membership of the Southern Association, strengthening of faculty in science and technology, and the first graduating class. The first summer school schedule offered more than 30 classes for students who wanted to gain 12 hours credit toward a degree at DSCC or for transfer. Three hundred four students attended the session.

Academic staffing goals for the second year were twofold. The science division did not yet have a full complement of staff, and a new position was opened in mathematics and physics. New career programs proposed in agriculture and data processing required new faculty.

A computer was acquired in August of 1970 to be used for the

First graduation ceremony, June 5, 1971. *Photograph courtesy Dyersburg State Community College.*

automation of college financial operations, heretofore processed at a sister school, and for the new instructional program in data processing. A programmer and an accountant were hired to strengthen administrative operations.

Tangible evidence of the rapid movement toward excellence in education came in November of 1970 when DSCC was accepted as a member of the Southern Association of Colleges and Schools. Numerous programs of student and community interest were offered. The series of lectures on drug abuse which began the first year was continued. Dyersburg State welcomed a science fair with participants from 38 high schools. "Student-Family Night" was held for one basketball game. Speakers from the George C. Marshall Space Flight Center and the Atomic Energy Commission visited the campus. Piano and choral concerts were held.

The first class graduated June 5, 1971, in the gymnasium. Ninety-three students from six counties received the first associate degrees granted by the college. More than 1000 people attended the ceremony. Commissioner E. C. Stimbert delivered the address which challenged the class to determine what they would do about the problems which faced society at the time. A few weeks after the graduation ceremony, three new programs were approved: agricultural business, police science, and computer science, thus completing the bulk of initial career program approvals. The ceremony itself represented some measure of closure to a cycle which was characterized by pervasive newness. The tasks to come were those of steady and solid development, refinement, and improvement.

The strengthening of science and technology areas was again the staffing priority for 1971-1972. New instructors in business and mathematics were employed. An effort to strengthen a foreign language program also was undertaken. Science and technology courses were ultimately to prove fruitful. Although one section would continue to be available, foreign language courses became a victim of the move by colleges away from foreign language requirements.

The first dramatic production, Tennessee Williams' *Cat on a Hot Tin Roof,* was offered in December of 1971. Later in the same academic year the drama club presented *The Wizard of Oz* on campus. Short skits from *Oz* were presented on local television and to classes of elementary school children. The mayor of Dyersburg proclaimed the week of March 6-11, 1972, as "Wizard of Oz Week."

The most significant event of 1971 was the accreditation of Dyersburg State by the Southern Association of Colleges and Schools. Attained in the minimum time permitted by the association, accreditation was granted on December 1, 1971, at the annual meeting held in Miami, Florida.

In the spring of 1972, a home for the president of Dyersburg State was acquired. The lovely Tudor style home is located on Troy Avenue in Dyersburg. The 1972 fiscal year began under the auspices of a new governing board, the Tennessee State Board of Regents, created by legislative act in 1972. The new board was to be responsible for the operation of six regional universities and nine (now 10) state community colleges.

In the fall of 1972, a full-time instructor for the police science program was hired. Police science was to become one of the fastest growing programs at Dyersburg State and later would serve as the model for structuring off-campus classes. The first off-campus classes were offered at Fort Pillow State Farm in the fall of 1972. A section of sociology and a section of psychology were taken to the prison as an experiment. The prisoners were found to be as eager to learn and to perform well as were the students on campus. The experiment was an unqualified success: Prisoners were provided an opportunity for a better way of life in the world beyond the prison, and Dyersburg State Community College was provided with an opportunity for service and a precedent, albeit unusual, for further efforts in off-campus education.

Formal reading classes, early indications of an eventual developmental reading program, were offered for the first time in 1972. In October of 1972, many Dyersburg State faculty and staff were involved in a program funded by the National Endowment for the Humanities. The purpose of the project was to make the humanities accessible to the general public. Three thematic programs were presented in 1972-1973 in churches, homes, schools, public buildings, and on campus. The programs were well-received by the public, with as many as 900 persons attending some of the sessions. Themes for the sessions were the common experience of humanity through the ages, the significance of language, and rags-to-riches as viewed through the various humanities and arts. The humanities series was unprecedented in the local area in the scope and variety of the project, community enthusiasm, and quality of the lecturers and performers.

An area which began to receive increasing attention in 1972 was the academic organization. It became clear that the division chairperson's role is quite critical to the nurturing of continuing innovation and to efficiency in routine requirements. No structural changes were made. The process was one of developing individuals in their roles and creating a team for academic administration, a process which evolved during the period of 1972-1974.

The success at Fort Pillow in 1972 spurred additional interest in off-campus classes. A community survey was conducted in Tipton County during March of 1973, and results were encouraging. A class in interior decorating was offered in the spring of 1973. Seventy-five persons enrolled, resulting in the addition of an extra section to the schedule. Covington became an off-campus location for credit and non-credit courses thereafter.

In the summer of 1973, classes were offered for the guards at Fort Pillow in police science and supporting areas. From this effort, in-service education for correctional employees became available on a continuing basis. The new police science program was further strengthened by a grant from the Tennessee Law Enforcement Planning Agency. In the fall of 1973, police science and other classes were offered in Trenton as well. A non-credit class in basic canvas work was offered in Ripley. A study of the feasibility of a legal secretary/legal assistance program was conducted in 1973. The results were favorable, and a proposal for the program was approved the same year.

Most of the basic programming efforts were complete by the fall of 1973, and attention was turned to new courses in such diverse fields as estate planning, income tax, Bible, pottery-making, orchestra, bridge, Tennessee history, and black literature. Faculty began to expand into additional academic areas and into a vocational interest.

In accordance with the guidelines of the Southern Association of Colleges and Schools, the institutional self-study process began in the fall of 1973 and was to occupy a good portion of the energy of the college for a two-year period. Although the time requirement was enormous to those who looked toward its completion, a clear consensus existed that the self study was a significant step. It led to immediate consideration of improvements, and, in some cases, improvements were made before the final report of the committee was submitted. In addition to allowing time for discussion and reflection about the future of the college and the activities which should be given priority for action, the study provided for a comprehensive sharing of information about all phases of the campus. One self-study recommendation was to house the continuing education activities in a single office on campus. An office of continuing education was created in 1974 and was the final step in building the academic administrative structure which began in 1972. Responsibility for the continuing education effort belonged first to the administrative assistant and later to the dean of instruction.

A general theme of the self study was the need to formalize procedures which related to a diverse group of topics. From the self study came a reconsideration and compilation of institutional policy, a job description effort, and a call for annual review of institutional purpose and master planning. A faculty evaluation system was devised and, following a trial run in the spring of 1974, became operational in the 1975-1976 academic year. These activities were the result of time to reflect made available through the self study. As a result of the institutional self study and a visit by a committee representing the Commission on Colleges, the accreditation was reaffirmed at the Southern Association's annual meeting held in December of 1975.

Special programs designed to serve the various publics in the Dyersburg State service area were offered by the college or in campus facilities during the 1974-1975 year. A consumer education grant allowed several workshops to be offered to area public school teachers. Faculty and staff wrote articles for local newspapers on drug abuse. A retired senior volunteer program (RSVP) was funded for Dyersburg State to benefit the senior citizens of the area. The college also cooperated with civic groups to bring programs of classical, country, and gospel music to the area, as well as to provide entertainment by students and staff.

One of the most important instructional accomplishments of the 1974-1975 year was the planning of a development studies program. Efforts in the past—pretechnical studies and the employment of a reading teacher—had been successful but were not comprehensive. Courses were planned in reading, communications (basic writing), elementary algebra, arithmetic, and motivational adjustment. The program utilized the existing campus faculty and student services personnel. Thus the fourth mission of the community college was given continuity in its operation. The program was a shared responsibility of instruction and student personnel services. The integration of the program into existing academic divisions and student services served to keep developmental studies in the mainstream of campus activity.

The office of student activities was created from a revised existing office; it was to be responsible for social and recreational opportunities for students and for creating activities which could attract the commuter student. The office also would chair the bicentennial activities committee.

Changes made in student personnel in 1974-1975 resulted in part from the transfer of most advisement responsibilities to the instructional division. It was a beneficial step which allowed the counseling staff to devote considerable energy to institutional development in student activities and developmental studies. A transfer from student services provided experienced coordination for the continuing education program.

In October of 1975 ambitious plans for a bicentennial observation were announced. Activities which were conducted included two tours, one to Williamsburg and one of Eastern cities of historical import; humanities courses in American composers, American playwrights, community orchestra, and American artists; social science courses and programs on West Tennessee history, heroes and villains in American history, religious utopias, and political parties; and the American First Ladies, a series on prominent American women which included a visit by Luci Johnson Nugent to speak about her mother, Lady Bird Johnson. Dyersburg State Community College was designated by the American Revolution Bicentennial Commission as a "bicentennial campus" in October of 1975. Planned activities were implemented throughout 1976 and were well-attended. More than 600 persons attended the speech by Mrs. Nugent.

The first year of implementation for the developmental studies program began in the fall quarter of 1975 and was highly successful. Only three of 44 students who enrolled in the program failed to return to school in the winter quarter of 1976. The program thus displayed considerable promise in ameliorating the problem of retention.

Continuing education operated as a separate organizational unit for the first full year in 1975-1976. The office sponsored many activities related to the bicentennial but also was involved in scheduling credit courses at six off-campus locations and in offering non-credit courses in diverse areas. The office proved successful as an operation to serve the community. The off-campus program at Fort Pillow produced the first of several graduates in 1976, clear evidence that the effort was proving worthwhile.

Events which would significantly improve the administrative services of the college began in the fall of 1976. The computer center was charged with the selection of an appropriate vendor for the improvement of computer hardware. An institutional research office was established in October of 1976. A new administrative unit, Administrative and Business Services, was created in June of 1977 to house five offices: business affairs, physical plant, institutional research, the computer center, and the office of administrative services, created in July of 1977. Leadership was provided by the dean of administration who was experienced in both administration and instruction. Each office was headed by a professional employee. Four of five had at least a master's degree; three of five had experience in teaching, as well as in administration. The professionalization of the administrative staff provided capability to meet emerging management activities and the various external needs and expectations of the college; it also made possible more significant assistance to the instructional program. The new unit was the "accountability" unit of the college.

The computer center was charged with beginning the process of selection for a suitable computer vendor. Personnel in the center worked with the staff of the Board of Regents and computer personnel in other colleges in the selection process. The computer was, after considerable study, purchased from a sister institution and was delivered in August of 1977. In late 1977 the conversion of most administrative operations was completed, and on-line registration was available for the following quarter.

In 1977 the first Outstanding Faculty-Staff Member Award was presented as a part of an awards banquet evening which included recognition of staff and students for their achievements and contributions. The award was established as an annual event to pay tribute to the many excellent efforts of the college staff.

A rather exhaustive study of small career programs at Dyersburg State Community College was conducted in 1977 as a part of a statewide review of small programs. The work involved citizens on advisory committees and individuals throughout the campus. Constructive plans for strengthening each affected program were developed and shared a common commitment to further outreach into the community. A result of the study was the consolidation of the degree program structure at Dyersburg State from one with 22 degree programs to one with three. It was also the beginning of a degree option in industrial supervision, which was tested as a series of non-credit courses for first-line supervisors and as a sequence of credit courses. It experienced tremendous success.

A science day, held on campus in October of 1977, was attended by 230 students and later evolved into a campus-wide activity. Its successor in 1978 involved approximately 330 students. The activity was so well-received that plans were made to hold a day for high school students each year.

Many projects which had originated during the self-study process were renewed in 1978. A new look at policy was begun as a part of a special 10th-year management program. A reconsideration of institutional mission was completed which set forth the statement of role and scope for the institution. A new look at faculty evaluation was begun in 1978 with the aim of reviewing, perhaps changing, the instruments used and incorporating the management-by-objectives concept. The year also was filled with a campus-wide interest in developing new programs. A proposal was prepared for a degree option in mathematics and computer science. Extensive campus effort was directed to proposals for a nursing program and for a computer maintenance program. Community support and interest of the proposed programs are gratifying. Contact with the community has been a significant element in the process of preparing proposals. Businesses, health care agencies, high school students, and the community-at-large have been contacted. These proposals may well become the most significant happenings of 1978 and 1979.

Development studies received additional support in 1978-1979 through Title III of the Federal Higher Education Act. Three positions were added to the program which considerably improved the capability of the college to engage in the intensive counseling, testing, teaching, and follow-up. Title III assistance also allowed rapid advancement in the processing and analyzing of a broad spectrum of institutional information. Plans called for Dyersburg State to have its first fully developed management information system by the end of 1979.

In reviewing the progress of Dyersburg State Community College from the vantage point of its 10th year of operation, several aspects of institutional development are striking. It is clear that the college intended to follow a carefully charted course. The basic elements of transfer education (1969-1970), career education (1971-1972), continuing education (1974-1975), and developmental education (1975-1976) were present in varying degrees during the first year of operation. Since the time of their establishment at near present capability, substantial qualitative improvements have been made in staffing and academic degree programs. No attempt was made to create a full program in all areas at once; when one was firmly rooted, another was begun with equal earnest.

The college has a full history of service to its community through special activities. The community to be served is often a particular, rather than a general, one. Although the number of events and par-

Aerial view of the campus. *Photograph courtesy Dyersburg State Community College.*

ticipants each year has varied, a clear record of efforts with senior citizens, children, high school students, disadvantaged students, inmates, businessmen, farmers, and others has been established. Programs of interest in humanities and the arts, education, social sciences, science and mathematics, and career areas have been consistently present throughout the 10-year span during which the college has been in operation. The college also has allowed community groups to use its facilities for a wide variety of activities. Advisory committees from the community have been used for career programs and a range of other matters. The various activities, examples of which have only been mentioned, have served as a primary means of contact with the community-at-large and with the student body. The community has been most supportive of DSCC throughout the institution's first 10 years.

Dyersburg State Community College is still developing. New aspirations, and some older ones not fulfilled, are a part of the fabric of daily life in the college and of every contact with the community. Although the college in 1979 is different from the college of 1969—little of the procedural novelty once present exists today, and new roles are justifiably fewer—the "new college" idea continues to have an impact in the institution and on the community. Ideas from staff and the community remain mutually supportive thus perpetuating the "venture in cooperation" which characterized the early days of Dyersburg State Community College.

President Harry D. Wagner. *Photograph courtesy Motlow State Community College.*

5

MOTLOW STATE COMMUNITY COLLEGE
by Harry D. Wagner

O n June 13, 1967, the State Board of Education voted to establish a community college in Moore County near Tullahoma; their action climaxed a concerted effort begun almost three years earlier by area citizens. The first attempt by the Tullahoma Chamber of Commerce to obtain a college for the area gathered some support from surrounding communities but was dropped to permit sponsoring organizations to focus their efforts on establishing the University of Tennessee Space Institute at Arnold Engineering Development Center. At a meeting of the chamber on November 5, 1964, immediately following the official opening of the institute, the movement was renewed.

Morris L. Simon, a local businessman and chairman of the Tullahoma-Manchester Chamber of Commerce liaison committee, recommended adoption of a project to obtain a state junior or senior college for Tullahoma. Simon pointed out that such an undergraduate institution would greatly benefit both the area and a number of students who could not go to college away from home. The University of Tennessee's evening class enrollment of 270 students at Tullahoma High School indicated interest among area residents in attending college classes.

A motion by A. H. Sanders, seconded by Newell Comer, to adopt the project was voted unanimously by the directors, who also authorized Chamber President A. C. Jennings to appoint a permanent committee to spearhead the project. Members appointed to the committee were Clifton R. Lewis, Morris L. Simon, W. H. Hawkersmith, L. B. Jennings, and Mayor Floyd Mitchell. The project grew into an area undertaking on February 10, 1965, when officials of the Upper Duck River Development Association and the Elk River Development Association invited Simon to discuss the proposed project with two groups. The result was adoption of a resolution to begin joint efforts for locating a junior college in the area served by the two associations.

At the initial session no specific site recommendation was made. The goal was to obtain "an institution of higher learning at a location that will best serve the interests of the people in the area encompassed by the associations." Theron A. Bracey of Shelbyville, president of the UDRDA, and W. A. Smith of Winchester, president of the ERDA, were authorized to name committees to survey potential students and to collect other data pertinent to site selection. When preliminary study showed Moore County to be the approximate center of the seven-county area, Simon approached State Senator Reagor Motlow of Lynchburg and asked if the Motlow family would be interested in donating land for the proposed college. Senator Motlow was receptive to the idea.

In early March of 1965, Bracey and Smith named citizens from each of the seven counties to serve on the joint committee of the Elk River and Upper Duck River Development Associations: Morris L. Simon, W. H. Hagan, and David W. Shields of Coffee County; Harry Logue and Ervin Thomas of Bedford County; J. O. Barnes and Thomas B. Green of Marshall County; Malcolm Fults and Glenn Bonner of Grundy County; Paul Rose and J. D. Massey of Franklin County; Dan Masters and Don Bobo of Moore County; E. C. Norman and J. C. King of Lincoln County. At a meeting of the group held in Lynchburg on March 26, 1965, members voted to ask the state to establish the junior college in Moore County, approximately four miles from Tullahoma, at the center of the two-watershed region. Plans were made to notify State Education Commissioner J. Howard Warf of their request, as well as county judges, mayors, congressional representatives, and interested private groups.

Support for the college continued to grow as legislators and city and county officials in the seven-county area pledged their support at a meeting held April 2, 1965, in offices of *The Tullahoma News*. The group also endorsed Moore County as the site for the proposed college and set a fund-raising goal of $250,000.

A special committee of area state legislators and representatives from each of the seven counties was named to present the case for the junior college to the State Board of Education. Named to the committee were Senator Motlow of Lynchburg; State Senator Ernest Crouch of McMinnville; State Representative Thomas Wiseman of Tullahoma; State Representative Pat Lynch of Winchester; State Representative W. R. Lowe of Lewisburg; State Representative Tyrus Cobb of Shelbyville; State Representative Thornton Taylor of Fayetteville; Morris L. Simon, Coffee County; W. A. Smith, Franklin County; Theron Bracey, Bedford County; Glenn Bonner, Grundy County; J. O. Barnes, Marshall County; E. C. Norman, Lincoln County; and Don Bobo, Moore County. An executive committee, consisting of Simon, Senator Crouch, Senator Motlow, and Nelson Forrester, was appointed to represent the full committee.

During the ensuing months, the executive committee met numerous times, first with State Education Commissioner Warf and Governor Frank Clement and, later, with Governor Buford Ellington. Persons close to the movement indicated that the executive committee practically "camped" on the doorsteps of state officials. While discussing the donation of land for the college at one of the meetings, Commissioner Warf asked Senator Motlow how much land he would provide. The senator's reply was, "How much do you want?"

One goal of the committee was to secure endorsements and pledges of assistance from city and county governments, as well as from civic and other interested groups throughout the seven-county area. More than 90 endorsements in solid support of the project were obtained. The first concrete pledge of financial support came on June 3, 1965, when the Tullahoma Board of Mayor and Aldermen pledged $150,000 toward the cost of establishing a junior college in the area. It was hoped that this and pledges from other cities and counties in the area would influence state officials to build four junior colleges, rather than the three previously planned, by using local funds to supplement the four million dollars voted by the 1956 State Legislature. It was later determined that a total of $400,000 would be required, $250,000 in cash plus a site. The Tullahoma Board of Mayor and Aldermen agreed to pledge $250,000, hoping they could get additional support from neighboring communities. Later contributions were received from Coffee County, $25,000; Franklin County, $10,000; Moore County, $2000; and Normandy, $500.

Although unsuccessful in the attempt to get an additional junior college authorized, the group continued their efforts and maintained close contact with state officials. In meetings between the executive committee and Commissioner Warf throughout the almost three-year period, the commissioner made note on more than one occasion of the tremendous unity shown among the seven counties; they were obviously trying to establish a college in an area central to all of them, instead of fighting over the location.

On May 22, during the gubernatorial campaign of 1966, former governor Buford Ellington spoke to Lynchburg residents of the need for a community college in the area. In March of 1967, Governor Ellington asked the state legislature for funds to build three more community colleges to further his goal of placing "every Tennessean within commuting distance of a state college." The special committee intensified its efforts for the Moore County location and met several times with Governor Ellington and Commissioner Warf. Senator Crouch felt the governor and legislature would be "sympathetic to a Moore County location." He added, however, that 22 other groups were trying to win support for a junior college in their respective areas.

On Friday, June 9, efforts toward obtaining the college reached a dramatic point. Representative Pat Lynch of Winchester, one of Governor Ellington's floor leaders, delivered a message to Simon from Governor Ellington and Commissioner Warf stating that a college could be established, provided a check for $250,000 could be delivered to the State Board of Education at its next meeting the following Tuesday. Simon and A. H. Sanders, then head of the utilities board, summoned Mayor Mitchell and aldermen to the newspaper office to discuss the situation. They decided to ask Hubert Crouch, president of First National Bank in Tullahoma, for a $250,000 loan. The bank agreed to loan the city the money, provided an opinion assuring its legality could be obtained from the city attorney. A favorable opinion secured, three required readings of the ordinance followed: the first two were accomplished at called meetings of the board of mayor and aldermen on Saturday and Sunday; the third reading and the vote came at the regular meeting of the board on Monday evening, June 12.

Mayor Pro Tempore O. B. Carroll and Morris Simon were designated to take the city's check to Nashville on Tuesday morning, the day the State Board of Education was to meet. Also in the delegation

Left to right: State Senator Reagor Motlow, Commissioner J. Howard Warf, Governor Buford Ellington, Chamber of Commerce President Clifton Lewis during groundbreaking ceremony. *Photograph courtesy Motlow State Community College.*

were Nelson Forrester, Representative Lynch, Senator Motlow, and Senator Crouch.

Governor Ellington and Commissioner Warf recommended that the college be named Motlow State Community College because of the Motlow family's generous donation of land and in recognition of Senator Reagor Motlow's numerous contributions to education in Tennessee. Joining him in the gift of land for the college site were his brothers, Connor, Robert, and D. E. Motlow; his mother, Mrs. Lem Motlow; his sister, Mrs. James Boyd; and his uncle, Tom Motlow.

Because the state did not have sufficient funds to complete the water supply system for the site, the Tullahoma Board of Mayor and Aldermen appropriated $50,000 and the Tullahoma Board of Public Utilities designated $110,000 for the project. Groundbreaking ceremonies for the college were held November 26, 1967, with Governor Ellington, Commissioner Warf, and approximately 250 persons from surrounding counties in attendance.

Martindale Brothers, a Murfreesboro firm, was awarded the

Dr. Sam H. Ingram, first president of Motlow State. *Photograph courtesy Motlow State Community College.*

contract for construction of the five original buildings: administration building, student center, classroom building and library, physical education building, and maintenance building with a total area of 139,131 square feet designed to accommodate 1200 students. Cost for the original facilities, designed by Yearwood and Johnson of Nashville, was approximately $2.7 million with $986,000 coming from a federal grant under the Higher Education Facilities Act of 1963 and the remainder from state and local sources.

Clearing of the site was begun in April of 1968, and construction proceeded immediately. The target date for opening the college was September of 1969. One tragic accident during construction resulted in the death of two workers. The two men were working on an aeration tank near the power and maintenance building when a crane boom fell, killing both of them.

In December of 1968, Sam H. Ingram, dean of the school of education at Middle Tennessee State University, was named president of Motlow State Community College; his appointment was effective February 1, 1969. Dr. Ingram's career in education also included eight years in the public schools as teacher and principal, three years in the State Department of Education, two as a professor of education at Memphis State University, and five as chairman of the department of education at MTSU.

The college opened temporary offices February 3 in rent-free space provided by the First Baptist Church in Tullahoma. In March Dr. Ingram announced the appointment of E. G. Boyd of Pulaski, business manager; Kenneth B. Slifer of Gadsden, Alabama, dean of instruction; and Dr. Don C. England of White County, dean of students. The first faculty members were hired in April, and the staff began to take shape as, during the summer of 1969, facilities neared completion and Motlow State Community College prepared to open its doors to citizens of Bedford, Coffee, Franklin, Grundy, Lincoln, Moore, and Warren counties. The college accepted as its purpose development of cultural, intellectual, physical, and vocational resources of people in its service area through quality teaching, professional counseling and guidance, and comprehensive services. Motlow State committed itself to an "access to all" concept with a multitude of entry points, both in time and place, for all elements of the community. The college would provide day and evening programs on campus and at several other locations throughout its service area, combining general and career education flexible enough to meet changing needs of the community. The program was to be threefold: (1) to serve those who wished to transfer and complete a four-year college education; (2) to serve those who wished to complete their formal education upon graduation from Motlow; and (3) to serve the community through adult and continuing education programs based on community needs and demands.

Motlow State accepted the philosophy that a community college was neither two more years of high school, the first two years of college, nor simply a vocational or technical institution. It was, in fact, all these entities and more. The doors of Motlow State Community College were opened to all who came seeking knowledge. It accepted each student as a worthy individual with unique abilities and capacities and endeavored to provide leadership which would enable each individual to develop and mature toward realization of his or her potential.

On September 22, 1969, after almost five years of planning and work by a group of dedicated citizens, a dream was realized as 551 students attended classes for the first time at Motlow State Community College. More than 100 classes were offered during the day, and 12 classes were offered at night the first quarter. Approximately 97 percent of the students enrolled the first year were from the seven-county service area. Almost 50 percent of them were residents of Coffee County.

Associate of arts and associate of science degrees were offered. General requirements included completion of at least 96 quarter hours of work while maintaining at least a "C" average. Students could choose from four associate of arts degree programs: liberal arts; music; preart; and premedicine, predentistry or prepharmacy. Six associate of science degree programs available were general, prebusiness, preengineering, premedical technology, preteaching, and secretarial science. Students enrolled in either associate of arts or associate of science general programs would meet the prelaw requirements of both Memphis State University and the University of Tennessee.

Planned for implementation during the following year were associate of science degree programs in agricultural-business technology, computer science technology, electronics engineering technology, and nursing education. Within these degree programs offered during the college's first year, a student could choose a discipline from one of the following: agriculture, art, biology, business, chemistry, economics, electronics, engineering technology, English and speech, French, geography, health, history, mathematics, music, nursing education technology, physical education, physics, psychology, sociology, and Spanish. The registration fee for students the first year was a low $55 per quarter, with the total cost to the student—including fees, books and transportation—less than $600.

From the beginning, Motlow State has stressed the importance of providing extracurricular activities for students. Offered the first year were a student government organization, a student newspaper, a yearbook, public programs, an extensive intramural program, and a system of student clubs.

Initially, 18 full-time faculty members were employed: four in English, three in science, two each in mathematics and social science, and one each in health, psychology, physical education, Spanish, music, art, and business education. There also were seven part-time members of the faculty.

In April of 1970, a five-member evaluation team from the Southern Association of Colleges and Schools visited Motlow State to determine whether the college would be eligible for accreditation by the regional accrediting body for educational institutions. Because Southern Association rules required that at least one year of operation precede full accreditation, the visit to Motlow was one step toward that goal.

Formal dedication ceremonies for the college were held April 19, 1970. In his dedicatory address, Commissioner Warf termed the occasion "only the end of the beginning" and dedicated the college to a "life-long career of service to those who dared to dream a dream." Commissioner Warf also related a story on the naming of the college. He said that Governor Ellington's reply to the suggestion that the college be named Motlow State Community College in recognition of the Motlow family's donation of land and Senator Reagor Motlow's efforts for education throughout the state was "That is what we are going to do." When Senator Motlow protested saying, "We don't want that, Governor. We're not giving the land for that," Governor Ellington said, "Well, you're not the governor, Senator, and we're going to name it Motlow whether you want it or not."

The college began its second full year with an increase in enrollment of more than 40 percent as 782 students registered for fall quarter classes. A corresponding increase was felt in faculty ranks as the teaching staff grew to more than 30. The instructional program was organized into four divisions: humanities, including English, foreign languages, music, art, and speech; social science, including psychology, economics, geography, history, political science, business, and health and physical education; science and mathematics, including mathematics, chemistry, physical science, and biology; and technology, including electronics, engineering technology, business technology, and computer science technology. Dr. Don England became dean of instruction, and Dr. Joe B. Johnson was named dean of students.

The library, a central feature of the college, also was growing. The total number of volumes rose from roughly 1200 the first year to approximately 4000 as the staff moved steadily toward a goal of 20,000 volumes to meet standards of the Southern Association of

Student seeks help in locating information in the college library. *Photograph courtesy Motlow State Community College.*

Colleges and Schools. The library also increased its collections of magazines, professional journals, and audio-visual aids.

Another area of service begun by the college was operation of a Neighborhood Youth Corps program in 10 area counties through a contract with the U.S. Department of Labor. The program called for young people 16 to 18 years of age to be placed in jobs with governmental or non-profit agencies and to take courses aimed toward helping them earn high school diplomas and becoming employable.

The college's first graduating class was presented at commencement exercises June 4, 1971, as 79 students were granted associate degrees. James M. Bomar, former lieutenant governor, speaker of the State House of Representatives for many years, and a native of the Raus Community near Motlow College, delivered the commencement address.

Continued growth in programs and students characterized the college's third year as 861 students enrolled for the fall quarter. Three new technology programs were started, including marketing technology, industrial technology, and accounting technology, bringing the total technology programs offered at Motlow to seven.

A coordinator of the evening division was named in the fall quarter of 1971, the first supervisory appointment specifically for evening classes at the college. Forty-seven classes were offered at night as special attention began to be given to the evening instructional program.

Motlow also expanded its community service activities by accepting responsibility for administration of the Federal Emergency Employment Act program in the 13-county south-central region of Tennessee. More than $350,000 was allocated for the program to pay first-year salaries for 118 new jobs in the area.

A milestone for the college came in December of 1971 when it received full accreditation by the Southern Association of Colleges and Schools at the accrediting body's annual meeting in Miami. Motlow received the accreditation within the minimum period required.

In June of 1972, final approval was given by the Tennessee Higher Education Commission for Motlow State Community College and Middle Tennessee State University to begin a joint two-year nursing program. Approval of the program culminated a major effort initiated in early 1971 when the South Central Comprehensive Health Council adopted a resolution endorsing such a program. The need for a nursing program was also endorsed by the Nathan Bedford Forrest Chapter of the Tennessee Academy of General Practice, an 11-county medical group. The major obstacle was a regulation of the Tennessee Higher Education Commission which required participation from at least 100 students and provisions for clinical training in a cooperating hospital. The commission also took the position that a training program for nurses at Motlow was not feasible, financially or otherwise—a view which clashed with an extensive college study showing increasing need for registered nurses in the south-central area of the state. When approved the joint program called for a flexible curriculum, common admissions standards, one director responsible to both institutions, and a joint faculty.

The 1974 graduating class numbered 151, including 13 graduates of the nursing program, the first group to complete the associate of science degree in nursing. Tremendous community support was again evident as area legislators, doctors, hospital administrators, school counselors, and other area leaders joined in support of the program which allowed for an initial enrollment of 40 students.

Motlow began its fourth year of service to the community with 862 students, one more than the previous year. The new nursing program enrolled its first year quota of 25 students from a group of 75 who sought admission to the program. A new aerospace technology program was initiated as a model for other community colleges in the state. It was designed to prepare students for a career in areas including aerospace development, aerospace manufacturing, engineering aids, general aviation, airport management, and professional pilots. Also offered was a two-year transfer program for students who planned to work toward a bachelor of science degree in aerospace education. An army reserve officers training program was offered in conjunction with Middle Tennessee State University's ROTC program. It was designed to prepare students for advanced ROTC training and eventual second lieutenant commissioning at any four-year institution offering the program.

Another first in serving the educational needs of the community was realized as Motlow provided facilities for Middle Tennessee State University to offer undergraduate and graduate courses on the Motlow campus. Offered as "resident" courses, they allowed teachers and other students to continue work toward their degrees at MTSU without having to drive to Murfreesboro.

In sports, the high point of Motlow's young history came as the men's basketball team won the college's first state championship in a thrilling triple overtime victory over Columbia State Community College. Earlier the Motlow team had won its second consecutive Tennessee Junior College Athletic Association eastern division title qualifying it for the championship game. In the drive for the title, the Bucks notched their first 20-victory season as the college continued to build a competitive athletic program. Baseball was the other intercollegiate sport offered at Motlow, and its success was evident from the teams' winning 20 games and eastern division championships for two consecutive seasons. Eddy Daves in baseball and Jack Battle in basketball were named to All-American teams, becoming the first Motlow athletes to receive the honor.

A one-day program to inform women of educational, business, and volunteer opportunities was held in September. "New Direc-

Graduates prepare to receive diplomas. *Photograph courtesy Motlow State Community College.*

tions for Today's Women" was co-sponsored by Motlow College, Tennessee Valley Authority, and the University of Tennessee; it drew more than 600 women to the college to visit booths manned by representatives from approximately 50 industries, businesses, schools, volunteer and civic organizations. The program also included a four-week reentry phase designed to serve women interested in improving their self image, returning to work, going to work for the first time, or returning to school. South Central Tennessee Development District provided space on campus to house offices for an area economist. Offices of the Neighborhood Youth Corps and Emergency Employment Act were already in operation.

The fall quarter of 1973 marked the beginning of rapid growth in numbers of students. Enrollment exceeded 1000 for the first time; of the 1124 students registering, more than 300 were in evening classes. A study indicating that 43 percent of Motlow students were more than 25 years of age showed that more adults were returning to college to continue their educations. In line with growing

Classroom building. *Photograph courtesy Motlow State Community College.*

demands in this area, Motlow had, a few months earlier, appointed its first full-time director of continuing education and evening instruction. The large increase caused some logistical problems as many students found it difficult to find places to park; many parked among trees in wooded areas adjoining the lots. It also emphasized an impending need for more classrooms, offices, and additional space in the student center. Six new tennis courts were readied for classes, and approval was received for a $353,945 addition to the library, which would approximately double the size of the library and would include a multi-purpose lecture room, 35 listening carrels or individual study desks, and additional stack areas.

Motlow was one of several institutions cited by the U.S. Office of Education as a national model for statewide programming in the Tennessee consumer education program. The college also participated in the governor's summer youth program, which provided organized recreational programs for young people in the area. The children's drama class continued to produce successful programs for children's groups from schools and day care centers; more than

1000 children from surrounding counties attended a performance held in May of 1974. Also on campus during the year were several musical events, including a major symphony orchestra, a folk singer, and a rock group.

Students returning in the fall of 1974 for Motlow's sixth year found several changes in facilities awaiting them. Six new tennis courts and a 200-car addition to the student parking lot were complete. The library addition was proceeding on schedule with plans calling for it to be ready for use before the end of the year. Enrollment again increased with more than 1300 students signing up for courses, the highest number ever at Motlow. Many were taking non-credit courses as the college continued to expand its community service function.

The first women's basketball team at Motlow was organized, and games were scheduled with other two-year colleges within the state. Although their win-loss record was not good the first year, the Motlow team did an excellent job in the regional tournament and reached the semi-finals.

A team of reviewers from the Southern Association of Colleges and Schools made a three-day visit to Motlow in November for the purpose of recommending whether the college should be accredited by the association. Ten committees at the college had previously studied different areas of the college's operations and submitted a self-study report to the association. The college had been given a two-year accreditation earlier and, depending on the review team's report, could be accredited by the association for an additional 10.

In December of 1974, Governor-Elect Ray Blanton named Dr. Sam H. Ingram State Commissioner of Education. A search committee for a new president was appointed by the State Board of Regents; Dr. Don England, dean of instruction, was named acting president until the search committee could make a recommendation to the full board. At a special meeting of the Board of Regents held on February 5, 1975, Dr. Harry D. Wagner was selected to succeed Dr. Ingram. Dr. Wagner had been vice-president for student affairs at Middle Tennessee State University for four years and also had served as administrative assistant to the president and as dean of men at MTSU. He had served one year as president of Martin College in Pulaski prior to his tenure in Murfreesboro. Dr. Wagner began his duties at Motlow on March 1, 1975.

The first annual awards day to recognize outstanding academic, athletic, and service achievement at Motlow, was held in May, and 136 students received their degrees at commencement exercises in June. In August, Motlow served for the first time as host for the regular meeting of the State Board of Regents. During the same month Dr. Frank Glass of Murfreesboro was named dean of instruction replacing Dr. England.

Another record was set in the 1975-1976 term as 1391 students enrolled for classes. With a faculty now numbering 46 full-time and eight part-time professors, the college was offering seven associate degree programs and seven certificate programs. As the college continued to grow, requests were again submitted for additions to the student center and the classroom building to help relieve the overcrowding.

In December of 1975, the college received a 10-year reaccreditation from the Southern Association of Colleges and Schools at its annual meeting in Atlanta. As a result of a recommendation made the previous year by the association's visiting committee, a 10-member faculty council was organized.

During the winter quarter Motlow began offering classes at three off-campus locations—Shelbyville, Winchester, and Fayetteville— beginning their first major thrust into surrounding communities. An agreement was reached between Motlow and Middle Tennessee State University to offer courses leading to a bachelor of science degree in elementary education and to an associate degree in law enforcement, both on the Moore County campus. Students in the elementary education program were thus able to earn their associate degree from Motlow and their bachelor's degree from MTSU through courses available on the Motlow campus. In early 1976, air conditioning for the gymnasium was made possible by a gift to the college of $58,812.89 from Senator and Mrs. Motlow. Motlow State's women's basketball team, in only its second season of competition, placed second in the Region VII tournament and finished the season with a 19-9 record. Team member Karen Carter was named to the National Junior College All-American squad. Other sports teams at Motlow also were performing well. Bob Martin became the second men's basketball All-American in the college's history. Winning 27 games, the baseball team had its best season ever, bringing its number of victories to 114 games and three division championships in six years. A tennis team was formed, and 10 matches were scheduled. In April, the first annual Motlow arts and crafts show was held. More than 60 artists and craftsmen entered the two-day event.

A reorganization of academic units took place in July of 1976. Divisions of mathematics and science, social science and education, and humanities were merged into a single unit to be known as the liberal arts division. The career education division was kept intact.

Major changes in the college catalog were designed to assist high school students and guidance counselors, as well as currently enrolled students and faculty, in understanding course offerings. Under each university parallel major, 29 discrete emphases were identified, each listing courses to be completed in that emphasis. The redesign included five majors and nine emphases in career education. Initial successes in the multiple emphases concept led to the development of several new emphases under the university parallel major, including agriculture, preoptometry, preveterinary medicine, and social work. The prelaw, and dental/medical/pharmacy emphases were moved from the preprofessional major to the university parallel major; and separate emphases in predental, premedical, and prepharmacy were created to reflect changes in professional school admissions requirements.

In the career education division, emphases in real estate and banking and finance were implemented. An emphasis in insurance was developed to be implemented in the fall of 1977. Also approved, but not scheduled to begin officially until the fall of 1977, were an engineering major and an engineering technology major. The new program would offer a university parallel curriculum fully compatible with colleges of engineering in the State Board of Regents and the University of Tennessee systems. It would also include a two-year career curriculum for students who wished to enter engineering related jobs with area industries and governmental agencies. Included in the technology major were emphases in architectural engineering technology, industrial engineering technology, and general engineering technology.

The college was invited to set up an exhibit for the opening of Tullahoma's new indoor shopping mall. Named Motlow-in-the-Mall, this exhibit enabled the college to present its programs and services to a wide segment of the community through both static exhibits and live performances. Highlights included an art show, band concerts, and a blood pressure clinic.

Another record enrollment was realized during the fall quarter

Students conduct chemistry experiments. *Photograph courtesy Motlow State Community College.*

of 1976 as 1885 students registered for classes. The college had approximately 40 full-time and 30 part-time faculty members, the largest number in its history. A larger number of evening credit courses were offered both on and off campus. Off-campus credit classes were offered in Fayetteville, McMinnville, Manchester, Shelbyville, and Winchester, as well as on the campus of the University of Tennessee Space Institute. Non-credit offerings were refined and strengthened, and convenient mail-in registration procedures were instituted. The newest area of non-credit programming, the industrial and business improvement program, grew significantly during the year. More than 40 courses, workshops, and seminars were offered to a clientele of 1200 persons from Tennessee and surrounding states.

A revised honors program enabled Motlow graduates who had begun honors study during their first college quarter to enter university honors work upon transfer to a four-year institution. Increased emphasis was placed on student activities, and a counselor was designated student activities coordinator and advisor to the student government association. A new program, the Campus Forum, was initiated to highlight current topics of interest in the community. Forum topics during the year included capital punishment, abortion, child abuse, U.S. senatorial elections, and others. Also scheduled during the year were dances, a dinner theatre, mini-concert, and club day. Organizations such as the art club, Gamma Beta Phi, chorus, and Phi Rho Pi were active throughout the year. The college's first musical production, *The Apple Tree,* was a big success.

An appreciation dinner for Senator and Mrs. Motlow was held on February 17, 1977. Governor Blanton proclaimed the day "Reagor and Jeanie Motlow Day" in honor of the couple's many years of service to the community. Approximately 500 persons attended the event, including Governor Blanton, U.S. Senator Jim Sasser, Congressman Al Gore, Jr., Lieutenant Governor John Wilder, State Speaker of the House Ned McWherter, state cabinet officials, and many other members of the State General Assembly and friends from throughout the state. A "Reagor and Jeanie Motlow Student Loan Fund" was established and received contributions from persons throughout the area.

During the summer of 1977, the Motlow College Development Council became a viable and functional support organization. The council, made up of more than 100 trustees from the seven counties served by the college, provided support for all areas of college activities. Among the trustees were members of Motlow Boosters, Incorporated, an organization formed several years earlier to provide private financial support to the college athletic program. This function would now become a part of the council's expanded program. Approximately $50,000 was raised during the council's initial year, with approximately $30,000 in stock contributed by the Motlows and its dividends restricted for operational expenses of the council.

Motlow State was one of six institutions in the nation selected by the American Association of Community and Junior Colleges to institute a model program called the Community Education-Work Council. The council was to address problems of youth in transition between the worlds of education and work and to institute and promote means of overcoming the barriers of youth employment.

In July of 1977, the final phase of administrative reorganization was implemented with the naming of David Stults as dean of administrative services. The change consolidated the business office, computer center, and institutional research offices into one unit called Administrative Services.

In September of 1977, students again arrived in record numbers, and registration surpassed the 2000 mark for the first time. A total of 2119 students enrolled for credit and non-credit classes. The college again offered classes at six off-campus locations. More than 200 courses were offered in the evening during the academic year. A full-time assistant director of continuing education and evening instruction was employed to devote increased time to general interest programming and other public service functions.

During the year, a closed circuit television system was installed with a color production studio, a control room, editing equipment, and a distribution system to the classrooms. The industrial and business improvement program was elevated to division status, becoming the industrial and business institute. The institute developed many new programs to meet training needs of industries and businesses within the Motlow service area. More than 2000 people were served through 51 unique and individualized programs.

Throughout the year, a series of cultural events were brought to the campus, including a woodwind quintet concert, a brass ensemble concert, a voice recital, and a workshop and play featuring freelance theatre. Highlighting these activities was a special concert by the Louisville Symphony Orchestra, made possible through joint efforts of the local Kiwanis Clubs, the Motlow College Development Council, and the Tennessee Fine Arts Commission. Each activity was provided at no cost to students.

The Motlow College Development Council continued to provide needed support in many areas, including athletics, the new engineering program, a $500 outstanding faculty award, and other worthwhile projects. Student activities initiated in past years continued; they included a campus forum, which presented six different programs: dances for students, a film program, voter registration drives, mini-concerts, and two dinner theatres.

In March the college lost one of its most ardent supporters and friends when former state senator Reagor Motlow died at the age of 80. Senator Motlow was one of the earliest advocates of a community college for the area and, while in state government, supported education at all levels. Senator Motlow and other members of the Motlow family donated the land for the college. In addition, the senator and his wife gave more than $58,000 to the college to air-condition the gymnasium and made a contribution of stock worth almost $30,000 to the Motlow College Development Council.

Final approval came in March for expansion of Motlow's nursing program—one independent of the joint program begun in 1972 with Middle Tennessee State University. Under the new program, enrollment would increase to about 140 in three years, during which time students would be able to take courses before limited to a two-year span.

Sports activities at the college continued to be successful. The women's basketball team approached Region VII semi-finals with its first 20-victory season. The baseball team won its fourth division title. Two student athletes were named to All-American squads, Billy Holt in basketball and Mark Schueler in baseball. The tennis and men's basketball teams also showed improvement over previous years. In June Motlow was host to the Southeastern and National AAU Junior Olympics women's basketball tournament, which welcomed teams from throughout the nation.

In July, Miss Doris Evans became the dean of administrative services with responsibility for planning and supervision of financial and fiscal affairs, institutional management information systems, and appropriations requests.

Motlow State began its 10th year of service in September of 1978 with more than 2300 students registering for classes. This figure represented a 25-percent increase in credit enrollment and an 11-percent increase overall from the previous year. The history of the institution reflects the excellent support of its constituency in Motlow's seven-county service area and the capable leadership of the State Board of Regents, its governing body. The college views its first 10 years, 1969-1979, with pride and looks to the future with enthusiasm and optimism.

President Jack E. Campbell. *Photograph courtesy Walters State Community College.*

6

WALTERS STATE COMMUNITY COLLEGE
by Jack E. Campbell

Spreading over 134 acres of beautiful rolling land on the southeast boundary of Morristown, the main campus of Walters State Community College is the focus of an intellectual and cultural influence felt throughout upper East Tennessee. From Knoxville to Mountain City, the presence of Walters State has resulted in the involvement of increasing numbers of people from all walks of life in the educational process and in other enrichment activities designed to improve the overall quality of life in this region.

Most of the Walters State students take advantage of a comprehensive curriculum of programs and services at the modern and well-equipped educational complex which constitutes the college's main campus in Morristown. Also, as part of the college's widely acclaimed extension program, substantial numbers of other students attend classes in public schools, hospitals, municipal buildings, factory cafeterias, and additional rented facilities in several other communities.

Management of the college is based on the philosophy that each high school graduate or otherwise qualified person should have access to higher-education opportunities. The college is committed to providing this accessibility through an open-enrollment admissions policy and a comprehensive curriculum of programs and services—all based on an obligation to maintain delivery systems and satellite facilities so that programs and services are offered within reasonable commuting distances to the people in upper East Tennessee. Well-qualified faculty and staff undertake with pride the admission of a highly diversified body of students and meet the challenge of providing opportunities of the highest quality to satisfy students' needs.

In keeping with the college's primary mission, Walters State affords the student an opportunity to receive either an associate of science degree or associate of arts degree in a university parallel or in a career technology program. Also, the college provides a student the opportunity to achieve certification in a specialized career field or in a personal development activity.

Commitment to this primary mission has evolved since Walters State was established in 1970 and has enabled the college to enjoy phenomenal growth. Today nearly 4000 students fill the college's classrooms and labs. More than 3400 students are taking courses for credit, either in university parallel programs designed for transfer to four-year colleges and universities or in the 21 career technology programs designed to prepare students for immediate gainful employment. The remaining students are enrolled in the college's community service program taking non-credit courses for personal enrichment or career advancement.

The growth and development of Walters State reflect eight and one-half years of significant historical events representing dreams, plans, commitments, hard work, and progress. These historical events all stemmed from a genuine desire and diligent effort to build for the people a college based on a realization of the community college philosophy. The history of Walters State is actually a story of community service and community involvement—of people striving to improve and one that needs to be told and remembered.

The state's sixth regional, two-year college and the one farthest north and east, Walters State opened her doors in Morristown on September 23, 1970; the dream, however, began several years earlier. The community college program was initiated in 1963, when the Tennessee Board of Education developed plans for a statewide system that would bring the opportunity for higher education closer to the average Tennessean. A need for more widespread opportunities had been noted previously by the Pierce-Albright Report to the Tennessee Legislative Council in 1957. Because the goal of the General Assembly was to have a college within 30 or 40 miles of every citizen, the fact that more colleges were on the way was clear.

Morristown—the seat of Hamblen County and the geographical center of upper East Tennessee—seemed a logical choice for a two-year college to Jack Fishman, then executive director of the Morristown Area Chamber of Commerce. Hamblen, Jefferson, Grainger, Hancock, and Cocke counties, along with parts of Greene, Hawkins, and Claiborne counties, form an area called the Lakeway Region. The region ranges from the Blue Ridge Mountains through the Holston and French Broad river valleys (the Cherokee and Douglas lakes area) to join Union and Sevier counties in the foothills of the Smokies. Hamblen is a populous county with a variety of light industry and small family farms. The people are renowned for independence and determination, but for many of them education after high school was not easily accessible in 1965. Fishman, initiating the effort to locate a community college in Morristown, asked Della Jeffers, chairman of the chamber's education committee, for a study that would show how the Lakeway Region deserved and would benefit from a community college.

Former U. S. Senator Herbert S. Walters, a longtime benefactor of and public figure from the area, joined the cause, and in 1967, he accompanied Grayson Chandley, president of the Morristown Chamber, to petition the Tennessee Higher Education Commission for the college. Their arguments were persuasive, and the commission chose Hamblen County as the location for the sixth community college. Citizens of Morristown and Hamblen County demonstrated their support by donating 100 acres of land and $250,000 in funds. Mayor C. Frank Davis and Squire Roy Oakes championed the cause with the Hamblen County Court. During this gestation period, E. H. Kennedy of Newport and many others provided support outside the county.

The original campus site was personally selected by Commissioner J. Howard Warf of the Tennessee State Board of Education. An important factor in the choice was the site's proximity to the proposed Appalachian Regional Highway, which would connect Interstate 81 in Tennessee with Interstate 75 in Kentucky. As events unfolded, bids for the highway were received exactly one month before bids were opened for WSCC's first building. Groundbreaking for the original building, which was initially designed to house all facets of the college, was on September 22, 1969. The architectural firm chosen was Abernethy, Robinson, Abernethy of Johnson City; J. I. Cornett Construction Company of Elizabethton was the contractor. Government obligation bonds of $1,100,000 were matched by

Herbert S. Walters, former U. S. Senator and a friend of education.
Photograph courtesy Walters State Community College.

federal funds of $1,517,695. The additional $250,000, provided locally, completed the total capital necessary for construction of the
building.

On February 7, 1969, the State Board of Education named the
Morristown institution Walters State Community College in honor
of the former senator who had "achieved...distinction in public life
and in the services of his state and nation, and in his contributions to
education at all levels." Dr. James W. Clark had become the first president of Walters State by August 1, 1969. One of his first recommendations to the Board of Education was to find temporary space
for opening classes, a foresighted request as events developed.

The college welcomed its first students on September 23, 1970.
At that time, Dr. Clark and Dr. Darrell Simmons, who had been appointed dean of the college, along with 21 faculty and staff were
on hand. Characterized by youthfulness, enthusiasm, and lack of

experience, most of the faculty had never taught at a junior or community college. However, during August a faculty orientation on community college philosophy was conducted at Cleveland State Community College, and several of the Walters State faculty attended. What they learned there set a tone at WSCC that still prevails. Specifically, accessibility of educational opportunity, open-enrollment admissions, comprehensive curriculum, student-centered instruction, and multiple-teaching approaches continue to be important goals for the administration and faculty.

Inevitable delays in construction forced completion of the original building further into the future. The doors that opened to the first 414 students were those that the community made available to the college. According to Dr. James Ford, "The community shared its 'home' with the college." A new education building at the First Presbyterian Church of Morristown provided space for classes; faculty offices were situated in the church sanctuary's annex. A downtown building, rented from the chamber of commerce, and known simply as "The Green House," held administrative offices. A unique feature of this facility related to the counseling services offered. According to Dr. Ken Pearson, director of counseling, the requisite privacy was achieved simply by having the secretaries "take a walk" in the halls.

Technology classes were held in an unused building that belonged to the state; Bob Russell of the technology division lamented that, "After discovering why the building had been unused, the faculty requested that students bring umbrellas to class on rainy days." Kathryn Bass Flinn, learning resource center director, opened the library in the basement of the Morristown Public Library with one book—an unabridged dictionary that was a gift. A week after the opening of school, she made an unsuccessful bid to purchase the library of a parochial school, a failure which, happily, helped establish the nature of future library development. Today, the great majority of books have been bought new, and 90 percent have been selected by the faculty.

The community continued to demonstrate loyalty to the college during that first year. The program of the chamber of commerce's annual dinner in January of 1971 paid tribute to Walters State. This demonstrated involvement of many local businessmen in the college's career programs, particularly the manufacturing technology program. The businessmen, in the belief that their firms would benefit from the college's operation, gave advice and encouragement and offered tangible support in the form of scholarships. Local government officials provided invaluable aid in setting up the criminal justice technology program, founded with the assistance of the law enforcement education program. Criminal justice technology was well-established and eventually became one of the most productive programs at WSCC; equally significant, the program became one of the largest law enforcement programs in the state of Tennessee.

A committee of citizens, chaired by Howard Westhaver, met with various officials in early 1971 to stimulate progress on the building. Meanwhile, the First Baptist Church of Morristown provided space for students to congregate and to relax. Stemming from this cooperative relationship, the Baptist Student Union was initiated and became one of the most active groups on campus. Although two dances were held at the National Guard armory, there was not much organized student activity the first year. However, members of the student coordinating board were appointed and began writing a constitution.

The first group of students was young for a community college, Dean Simmons recalls. Most were from the immediate Hamblen County area and had been influenced to choose Walters State by their parents—the popular rationale being that the community college cost less and was closer to home. In ensuing years, as the technical program surged under the direction of Associate Dean James Coburn and as the evening and adult education programs expanded, the average age of the students rose to 27.

As previously mentioned, youth was a characteristic of the faculty as well. Actually, their resilience and enthusiasm were probably assets in establishing a new institution in those scattered, temporary quarters. Experience and maturity resulted naturally from the pursuit of their careers, and a unique sense of solidarity developed from the challenges of that first year. Of the 27 charter faculty members, 16 have remained with the college. Charter faculty and staff members who continue to be employed by Walters State in 1979 are Anne C. Armstrong, Kathryn Bass, William B. Biddle, Ronald J. Castle, Dr. James W. Ford, Jr., Linda B. Foutch, R. Lynn Gilmore, Glenora R. Hall, Sidney G. Hall, Evelyn J. Honaker, Dr. Kenneth V. Pearson, Samuel R. O'Dell, Gerald E. Risdahl, Robert T. Russell, Carolyn H.

Saylor, Lanny R. Saylor, Dr. Darrell D. Simmons, Brian V. Walter, and Curtis E. White.

During the first year, all basic academic courses were initiated except chemistry, physics, and biology. Significant is the fact that five career programs were started. In addition to law enforcement, programs initiated were secretarial science, manufacturing, library service, and architectural technology. Enrollments in these programs were reinforced by the fact that nine scholarships from local sources had been granted, and 65 students were able to receive financial aid from federal sources. A developmental studies curriculum provided English, mathematics, and reading for the student who was marginally prepared, while an advanced studies program was available to high school seniors. These were commendable programs for a first-year college. After a preliminary visit in April, the Southern Association of Colleges and Schools granted the college correspondent status, the first step in accreditation. Shortly thereafter, Greg Davis transferred from another institution to Walters State where he worked as a student helper in the admissions office. Having satisfied all the requirements, Greg became Walters State's first graduate during the institution's initial year of operation. Progress was truly in the making.

By the fall of 1971, WSCC enrollment had almost tripled. The faculty of the previous year had doubled to accommodate 1152 students, a total that was 50 percent greater than the projected highest enrollment of the institution. Ironically the college had outgrown its first building before it was occupied. Construction of an additional structure, a career technology building, was authorized during the year by the 87th General Assembly, but completion was still two years away. The first priority that fall was getting into the main building. On Labor Day a move into the first wing was accomplished, literally on the heels of the builder. Instructors who were teaching then recall that the final stages of construction were hindered during the fall quarter because laborers halted their work on nearby ladders as they grew absorbed in classroom lectures.

For the faculty, the second year was a period of designing programs with the instructors' own ideas and supplementing classrooms with equipment. The humanities department, for example, sought additions to its original equipment, a single tape recorder and a lone projector. The science faculty was anxious to incorporate laboratory

experience with the "chalk and talk" approach. The library embarked on another big book-buying year, aiming toward accreditation standards. Significant acquisitions of audio-visual materials and
other types of aids were made as the library strove to become a learning resource center, a goal that was fully realized with the completion
of a new facility in the fall of 1978.

Three new career programs—environmental health, child care,
and agri-business—were initiated during the year. Also, the services
of the career technology programs were made available to the community through workshops, conferences, and seminars held in conjunction with other agencies.

Students began their own efforts to give the college an identity
and to confirm their places within the college community. The first
elections for the student coordinating board were held, and Russell
Pruett was chosen president. The school colors—red, white, and
blue, to reflect the patriotic bent of the school's namesake—were
chosen in a second election after the first one was disputed. Seven
clubs—compass, karate, ski, Circle K, art, golf, and Theophilus—
were officially recognized during the year. In the spring the student
board sponsored the first collegewide event, a spring festival with
concerts, displays, and contests.

Even though the gymnasium was not completed until January,
physical education was offered in the fall at the Morristown Boys
Club and at local tennis and bowling facilities. Intramurals
flourished during the year with 11 flag football teams and 17 basketball teams. Soccer also was popular. The first athletic competition
with another college took place during the winter in the form of an
"extramural" basketball game with the best intramural players from
Walters State competing against the best intramural players from
Carson-Newman College.

The college became one of upper East Tennessee's two official
general education development (GED) testing sites in December
of 1971, and 113 people took the high school equivalency examination during the year. Also, the opening of the health clinic marked
the beginning of an important service. Over the years the clinic has
provided free testing and minor treatment, as well as health counseling for students. The scope of the clinic was broadened considerably
in 1977 when a health fair was introduced using the services of local
physicians and health agencies. Through the fair, school children,

their parents, and college students took advantage of educational services and glaucoma, blood pressure, and hemoglobin checks.

The seeds of an extensive community service program were planted with nine courses involving 174 students. One of these, karate, has remained particularly popular. The course is still taught by Dr. James Ford, a black-belt instructor and a charter faculty member in mathematics and science who later became dean of academic affairs.

In 1971-1972 the college was preparing for two important events. On May 21-24, the college received a Southern Association of Colleges and Schools visitation team, organized for the purpose of conducting a comprehensive evaluation of Walters State. The visiting committee prepared a detailed report of suggestions and recommendations and submitted the report to the admissions committee of SACS. At this point, Walters State had to wait until the following December to hear whether the report had been reviewed favorably by the committee and whether accreditation had been granted. On June 9 graduation of the charter class of 30 men and 26 women took place. After an address by Dr. E. C. Stimbert, state commissioner of education, Dr. Clark handed Walters State Community College's first diploma to Patricia Jean Baxley, a pre-education major from Morristown. With the completion of this vital step toward accreditation and with graduation of its first class, Walters State Community College's existence was recognized, but the institution was still in the process of growing to meet its potential.

In the third year, the original multi-purpose building was finished, equipment was in place, and science laboratories were a reality. The student body increased to 1358 with 43 percent of this number in career programs, a balance that remained consistent in ensuing years. In December, SACS announced that accreditation had been awarded Walters State. The comprehensive evaluation conducted by the SACS team the previous spring had been successful. The faculty and staff were proud.

The third year was a time for many distinguishing facets of the college to come into existence. Whereas development of a campus had been important the previous year, this year a significant step took place when off-campus courses were initiated. Dr. Lynn Gilmore, director of continuing education, led the charge. Courses were offered in September at Newport, Sneedville, Harrogate, and

Tazewell; and in January, law enforcement was taught at the University of Tennessee in Knoxville. Off-campus growth represented a major area in which Walters State demonstrated flexible service of a broad and diverse community by making the goal of "accessibility of educational opportunities" a reality.

In late August the community as well as the students welcomed the beginning of interscholastic sports when Bill Gardner was hired as basketball and baseball coach. On December 4 the Walters State fans cheered a first basketball victory over Ashville-Buncombe Technical School. The first baseball victory occurred on April 2, with a double-header win over Morristown College. A third aspect of the college's new athletic program was a golf team. Under the direction of Coach Wayne Quinton, this first golf team finished third in the Tennessee Junior College Athletic Association, an achievement which was to serve as a benchmark for years to follow.

In October, the early learning center opened in a mobile classroom on campus, providing a great service to the community and a unique laboratory experience for students in the child-care-technology program. The original group of child-care-technology students arranged the two-room facility to serve 12 three-to-five-year-olds. The facility was rearranged over the following years to fit the shifting needs of a group of children that had increased in number to 24. Each child-care student continued to get practical experience teaching in the early learning center.

During 1972-1973, activities on campus flourished. A faculty council, representing those faculty without administrative duties, was organized. The first lyceum program, which occurred on November 12, was fittingly entitled *Adam and Eve* and produced by the Alpha-Omega Players. A college-community symphonic band was established and gained the nickname "The Mighty Eight from Walters State." The debate team of Pam Shelby and Randy Clark won first place in novice competition at the Tennessee Intercollegiate Forensics Association, bringing the first trophy to the college. Melba Rose Greene was chosen the first Miss Walters State on November 18. The contest, sponsored by the Compass Club, was one of the most popular events on campus in 1972 and again in 1973 and 1975.

Over the years some student activities, like the Miss Walters State competition, were successful at intervals; and some, like production of the literary magazine *Gallery*, first published in the spring of 1974,

developed consistently. Student clubs, too, experienced a variety of
successes. In 1972-1973, 10 new clubs were recognized, making a
total of 16 on campus. Although the list of clubs in 1978-1979 included 18, only four—art, music, karate, and soccer—were the same
ones that had existed in 1972-1973.

The third year of Walters State's short history was quite promising insofar as activities and development were concerned and appeared to be the time when the faculty, staff, and students "settled
in." However, one sad event occurred. Herbert S. Walters died, and
this was a tremendous loss to the Walters State community.

In the fall of 1973, one of Walters State's most appreciated buildings opened, though a death knell for this particular building had
been sounded even before the college began. An old barn, left by the
previous occupants of the college site, was to have been razed years
before, but the manner in which the barn was used, first by the contractors and then by the college maintenance staff, made the facility
indispensable. By the spring of 1973, Robert Reed, head of maintenance and grounds, and art instructor Ron Castle reached a truce;
Reed would make part of the barn available to the art department if
the ceramists would remove their plaster of paris dust from the
classroom building. Kilns were installed and minimal construction
done. Subsequently, art activities in the barn grew to include paint-
ing, sculpture, and printmaking, as well as ceramics. Having long
outlived its expectancy, the beloved art barn was scheduled to meet
its demise when the fine arts building was complete; however, the art
barn's importance as a symbol and site of creativity on campus will
not soon be forgotten. The arts have always been valued at Walters
State, and the community has responded with leadership from supporters like Edith Davis. The first art auction and music department
concert featuring the WSCC chorale was held on December 6 and
showed a tangible result of that relationship; one thousand dollars
was raised for arts scholarships.

Another important community event of the year was an industrial fair held in January, when exhibits by 25 firms attracted more
than two thousand visitors. The event realized even greater success
the following year. Career programs in the areas of mental health
and computer science were initiated during the year and demonstrated how the college was continually striving to meet community
and student needs. However, response to an innovative mental

The art barn, beloved shelter for the arts. *Photograph courtesy Walters State Community College.*

health-technology program implemented during the winter quarter did not warrant continued existence, and, in the spring of 1976, the program was discontinued. Conversely, the program in computer science was successful. A computer was installed at WSCC during the fall quarter, adding efficiency to operations at the college and making possible the implementation of the computer-technology program. Improvements in the area of computers continued. A larger model was installed in 1976, giving the college on-line registration capabilities and greatly increasing the opportunities for hands-on experience for students. As the offerings in this department have grown, so has student response.

Because enrollment had continued to grow at unpredicted rates—1736 students for the fall quarter was a four hundred percent increase over the initial figure—campus construction was in the forefront. A scheduled groundbreaking on March 4 for the career technology building became an indoor "board-sawing" because of inclement weather. Nevertheless, the one million dollar building designed by Community Tectonics was underway. Also underway were plans for a combination student services and learning resource center project, but these plans were to see many changes, for funding for the project was delayed two years. By 1973-1974, Walters State had encountered and successfully overcome the many demands of a newly established college; the college was now headed into new dimensions of development.

A momentous change in the college took place prior to the beginning of 1974-1975. Dr. Clark resigned as president, and, on July 25, 1974, Dr. Jack E. Campbell was appointed his successor. Soon thereafter, Dr. Robert McElroy and Julian Jordan joined the administration as dean of students and business manager, respectively. On September 12, Walters State embarked on an intensive institutional self study, required by SACS as part of the process for reaffirmation of accreditation. This study—an 18-month evaluation of every phase of the college—involved representation by employees, students, and the community. The results provided a basis for initiating change and for guiding many facets of subsequent developments. Later the results were the basis for determining whether Walters State would be granted reaffirmation of accreditation. Another study took place during the same year as the result of a grant by the National Faculty for the Humanities. In a pilot program for two-year colleges, an examination of the humanities was conducted, resulting in substantial changes for the improvement of the instructional program.

One of the first challenges facing Dr. Campbell was the need to establish a nursing education program. A high priority with the local community since the initial planning days of Walters State, the proposed program was underwritten by pledges of $20,000 from local citizens as a measure of their commitment. Jack Fishman, publisher of the *Citizen-Tribune,* and Jean Keener, president of Morristown Federal Savings and Loan Association, headed the community effort. During the fall quarter, Emogene Jasper joined the faculty as director of allied health programs and began planning efforts to establish the nursing program. She made a careful study of community needs and initiated contacts with nursing organizations. After the study had been conducted, several conferences held, and approval from the State Board of Regents secured, THEC approved the nursing program to begin in September of 1975. Additional career programs implemented during the year were production-horticulture, tourism and recreation, accounting, management-technology, and radiologic-technology. Also approved for 1975 was a certificate program in fire-science.

The hiring of a veterans' coordinator in October of 1974 was one indication of a trend relative to enrollments that would occur at all institutions of higher education and particularly community colleges during 1975. The 650 veterans returning to classrooms at Walters State amounted to one-third of the enrollment, but they represented just one facet of the population that would come in increasing numbers to the campus in the face of economic and other pressures. Spring quarter enrollment actually reversed tradition by surpassing that of the winter quarter.

Bulging enrollments hit Walters State at a crucial time. The career technology building, begun two years earlier, was ready for occupancy in January of 1975, but funding for the proposed learning resource center and student services classroom project was not included in the year's budget. This delay in funding did, however, allow the faculty and staff to spend more time planning and developing project specifications. Community Tectonics, as a result of these updated specifications, returned to the drawing board to develop a plan that would provide more floor space for the same projected cost and solve some inherent problems in the original building as well. The new plan called for double-decking the existing learning resource center and student services area and moving the second floor classrooms and laboratories to a proposed academic building. In the final analysis, the new plan provided not only for more space in each area but also for more appropriately placed classrooms, separated from the noise of the gym and student activity areas.

Some campus improvements occurred with much imagination and very little funding. For example, the college allowed the Department of Transportation to move earth needed as fill dirt from the college property. In exchange, the college gained landscaping and desirable space for tennis courts, baseball fields, and a parking lot. Also, the maintenance staff constructed an observatory for the new Astrola 10-inch telescope and put together a lean-to greenhouse for the science department.

Special activities were important aspects of the college's development during this fifth year of operation. On May 7, 1975, the college's first honor society, Phi Theta Kappa, was established to recognize outstanding students. There were 80 initiates at the first meeting. Additionally, the first of three annual folklore festivals for craftsmen and artists from all over the region was held in March. Although the festival was later deleted from the college's program-

Chancellor Nicks and President Campbell break ground for academic building. *Photograph courtesy Walters State Community College.*

ming in order to support a duplicate activity which had been initiated by another community agency, the festival was one of the college's most popular events, drawing 7000 people in 1977.

In the area of community involvement, the reactivation of the Walters State Community Advisory Council and the initiation of a Walters State Foundation in March of 1975 were important steps. The size of the existing, but inactive, council was doubled; each member was asked also to become a trustee of the WSCC Foundation, which was designed to provide the college with a citizens' body for fund-raising, promotion, and development. This move resulted in a body of 50 supporters' being named the Walters State Community Advisory Council and Foundation. The original officers were Howard Westhaver, president; Bud Abbott, vice-president; Paul Capps, secretary; and Bob Pratt, treasurer. Lon Price later replaced Abbott, while the others continued to serve. The Senators Club, with William Denton serving as chairman, was the first subgroup of the Walters State Foundation. Pledging their support, financial and otherwise, the members of the Senators Club were instrumental in making the faltering Walters State men's basketball program one of the most respected in the state and region. The following two years, under the direction of Coach A. W. Davis, the college's basketball team, known as the Senators, finished second in the state in 1975-1976 and won the state championship in 1976-1977. Subsequently, under Coach Bill Carlyle the team finished second in the state in 1977-1978 and third in the state in 1978-1979.

An unusual community-college relationship developed during the spring of 1975 as Hamblen County residents made it known that they would not allow completion of a regional prison being built near the campus. Construction halted, and there was much interest in seeing the college acquire the site for future development. In August, after a proposal had been developed by Dr. Campbell and his staff who were working with the staff of the State Board of Regents following a request from state officials, the state officials made a proposal to town and county officials for converting the prison to use by WSCC. The county followed through in January of 1976 by approving a bond issue for purchasing 34 acres of land that would connect the campus with the prison site. The acreage was deeded to the college in the fall of 1977, but no further steps were taken by the state toward developing the proposed prison facility as a component of Walters State.

At the end of the 1974-1975 year, the number of students comprising Walters State's fourth graduating class totaled 170. For the first time the honor students and Phi Theta Kappas were given special recognition in the graduation ceremony. Also, in a time of public concern and expression over government, it was significant that Senator Howard Baker, who had co-chaired the Watergate investigation, delivered the commencement address.

The fifth year of operation at Walters State was a year of new dimensions. Changes in personnel, organization, and overall campus appearance occurred. Studies were conducted and new pro-

Commuting graduate heads for commencement. *Photograph courtesy Walters State Community College.*

grams were developed. Community relations were reaffirmed. Plans for the future were unfolded, but not without some apprehension that external forces might affect the college's overall movement.

By the fall of 1975, a sluggish economy was making a noticeable impact on higher education. While sending students back to college at an unprecedented rate, the economy was also having an unfortunate effect on funding for colleges and universities in Tennessee. These institutions of higher education found themselves searching for ways to accommodate record-breaking enrollments with minimal increases in funding. For Walters State, the result was the development of a comprehensive management and evaluation system designed to provide for the needs of students and to stimulate continuing development of programs and services. At the same time, the system was designed to ensure greater efficiency and quality control in all aspects of the college's operation and a high degree of accountability to the general public. In other words, the college began a year of "belt tightening."

With the veteran students having the greatest impact, Walters State's enrollment soared to 2877, a figure 58 percent higher than that of the fall of 1974. Off-campus classes were taught at 14 sites throughout upper East Tennessee, necessitating a greater allocation of manpower to continuing education to ensure appropriate structure and effective supervision of instruction. Walters State coped with the unexpected enrollment increase and lean budgeting by making extensive use of available community talent as adjunct faculty, both on campus and in the widely dispersed off-campus sites. In addition, full-time faculty taught overloads more extensively than ever before.

The financial squeeze sparked a dramatic growth in programs which provided financial assistance. The Basic Educational Opportunity Grant, which assisted 19 students at Walters State when it became available in 1973, had 283 participants in 1975. With a record participation of 359, the Law Enforcement Education Program (LEEP) was one of the most active in the state among community colleges and four-year institutions.

At a time when spending was being closely scrutinized, the administration introduced a management and evaluation system as a means to improve the overall quality of the institution and to be responsive to the people's cry for greater "accountability" in the use of public funds. The system was initiated at the administrative level in 1975 and later extended to every area of the college. Each unit within the college developed precise objectives at the beginning of the year and subjected them to an evaluation at the end. This management practice was in keeping with the administration's commitment to participatory governance by students, faculty, staff, and the general public in decision making and curriculum planning. While promoting accountability, yet being innovative and open for dialogue, constructive criticism, and feedback, the management system was an ideal for which the college continually endeavored.

Efforts were made during the year to improve communication in areas of college life in order to increase awareness of the participatory governance philosophy. A college committee handbook, for example, pointed out the reorganization of committees that had taken place the previous year. A weekly news bulletin and quarterly bulletin for continuing education were initiated. The faculty mail system and information center also were made more effective.

Two management practices implemented during 1975-1976 related specifically to the areas of campus development and faculty salaries. First, a comprehensive 10-year plan was developed for campus construction, and in the spring of 1976 the first step of the plan was implemented when the General Assembly authorized $2.2 million for the learning resource center and student services classroom project. Second, guidelines were developed that allowed a faculty salaries to be brought up to the level of other area institutions and provided for equity and merit among the Walters State faculty. Exhibiting keen insight, the General Assembly and the Board of Regents permitted flexibility in their salary requirements for community colleges, thus allowing needed salary increases for the following year.

Careful management did not preclude progress on campus in the academic and student activity areas during this sixth year of operation. The nursing and fire-science programs, for example, enrolled their first students, and a greenhouse was completed for the developing production-horticulture program. An energetic drama program, which was well-received by the students, faculty, and community, also was initiated. According to Director Terry Holcomb, "Theatre is fun." To prove his point, Holcomb chose for his first production *Love Rides the Rails, or Will the Mail Train Run Tonight?*—a combination of music, comedy, and melodrama set in the railroad boom of the 1890s. This successful endeavor was the beginning of a new era in drama, which eventually resulted in the providing of quality instructional experiences and high grade entertainment for Walters State students, faculty, and interested community representatives. The student newspaper, *Filibuster,* also was revitalized by the addition of a faculty supervisor who had been a professional journalist and photographer and who demonstrated high enthusiasm for student involvement, believing that the newspaper was an invaluable instructional tool. Other instructional activities included the implementation of 26 courses during the year, one of which was an ROTC program in cooperation with Carson-Newman College. A biology greenhouse and head house also were put into operation, and plans were unfolded for computer-assisted instruction, television-radio broadcasting courses, and an audio-video production studio.

In athletics, women's basketball made a debut as the result of a promise made by Dr. Campbell to three students the previous year. A modest amount of money was squeezed out of the existing athletic budget for financing the team; a coach was employed; and the team recorded a respectable 9-9 season. A tennis coach was hired to add support to a co-ed tennis team and to fully utilize the tennis courts, completed the year before. Student activities continued to thrive during 1975-1976; on May 26, at Walters State's first honors day ceremony, students received formal recognition for outstanding achievement in extracurricular activities.

By February the self study, initiated 18 months earlier, had been completed and the results published. The college awaited a visit from the Southern Association evaluation team that would review the self-study document, investigate the actual operation of the college, and subsequently determine whether the college was, in fact, doing what was stated in its document; it would also be evaluated in terms of the standards of the association. The committee arrived in March, conducted the comprehensive mission, and later submitted a highly favorable report. At this point the college felt reassured but had to wait until the following December to receive a final decision regarding reaffirmation of accreditation. However, the year of record enrollment and low level funding had been dealt with successfully, and Walters State was in stride.

The growth in all phases of operation, as well as growing requirements from external agencies, prompted the establishment of a new administrative position, that of the dean of administrative services. This top level position, along with those of dean of student services, dean of instruction, and business manager, was placed directly under the president on the organizational chart and was designed to streamline various educational services within the college and to help meet the demands from outside. Dr. James Ford, who had successfully directed the institutional self study, was named for this position. Approximately one year later, on August 1, 1977, Dr.

Ford again changed positions when he was appointed dean of instruction upon the resignation of Dr. Darrell Simmons. Dr. Simmons, who had worked in education 28 years, resigned, effective July 1, 1977, to return to the classroom as a professor of technology. However, because of Dr. Simmons' commitment to Walters State and his vast experience and expertise, in addition to his teaching responsibilities, he was asked to continue to assist in certain phases of administration as special assistant to the president.

In December of 1976, the event toward which the entire college community had dedicated untold time, effort, and commitment took place. The favorable report of the SACS evaluation team was accepted, and Walters State was granted reaffirmation of accreditation. The years of preparation and months of study had been rewarded!

On March 11, 1977, another significant event took place. The long-awaited learning resource center and student services classroom project was launched with a groundbreaking for the classroom building. Fruits of past efforts also were evident in other areas. Community service activities had grown, along with the other divisions of the college, to the extent that a full-time director, Janice Houston, was employed. With her enthusiasm and leadership providing the impetus, the community service program attracted 2764 participants in 66 conferences and 851 students in non-credit courses. Additionally, non-credit courses were offered for the first time at off-campus sites.

Each academic division of the college had realized a substantial increase in enrollment the previous year and had accommodated this increase with adjunct faculty. An immediate objective for this fall quarter of 1976 was to reduce the ratio of full-time faculty to adjunct faculty, for the number of adjunct faculty had grown to 91 while the number of full-time faculty remained 55. To accomplish this objective, which supported the college's desire to ensure quality instruction, 19 new full-time faculty members were employed in the academic divisions. Undergirding the employment of the new faculty members was a well-designed affirmative action program; it ensured fair employment practices and maintenance of desegregation efforts. By utilizing the affirmative action procedures, Walters State officials employed a sufficient number of black faculty members in order to exceed the college's 1980 desegregation goals.

Another significant occurrence in the academic area during this 1976-1977 year was the amount of attention given to articulation. The general education requirements of the associate degree came under scrutiny by local and state officials in an effort better to articulate the university parallel requirements in community colleges with requirements at four-year colleges and universities. Related to this effort, Bill Hodges, a counselor at Walters State, conducted his own study as part of a dissertation and produced data to show that graduates from Walters State did just as well after transferring to four-year schools as did the students who started at these four-year schools.

The offerings in humanities, under the direction of Dr. William Biddle, continued to develop during 1976-1977. To stimulate further interest and to exhibit what was being done, a week-long humanities festival involving students, faculty, and the general public was planned and conducted in the spring. Drama, arts, music, journalism, and literary works were featured. Later, in 1978, this festival grew into a Morristown-Hamblen County observance.

The college's nursing program added an innovative feature characterized as the "career mobility option." Begun in the fall quarter, it allowed a licensed practical nurse to take a series of National League of Nursing proficiency examinations; if scores on the exams met a required standard, the nurse was allowed to enter the Walters State registered nursing program at the second-year level, thus increasing the number of sophomores and resulting in the program's having a spring graduating class of 59—three more than the entire charter class of 1972.

In athletics, the college's tennis team, under the direction of Coach Judy Morgan, was not to be outdone by the men's basketball team, which had just won the state championship. For the first time, Coach Morgan was able to award scholarships to her players, and her team placed a highly regarded second in both the state and regional tournaments. Subsequently, the tennis team competed in the National Junior College Athletic Association's tournament; no other Walters State athletic team has had that distinction.

In addition to athletics, new directions in other student activities were realized. A yearbook was published, and a joint project was coordinated by the *Filibuster* staff and the student government association to elect the year's outstanding faculty member. The *Filibus-*

ter announced in its June edition of 1977 that, "as of May 11, 1977, Dr. Larry Fleming became the first recipient of the Outstanding Faculty Award." The next year, 1977-1978, the recipient of this distinguished award was Terry Holcomb. A "varsity sport of the minds," officially known as the college scholars bowl, was organized as an interscholastic activity, and the Walters State team, under the direction of Dr. Larry Fleming and Dr. Sam O'Dell, competed for the first time at Berry College in Georgia. Stemming from the Walters State team's experience, a high school scholars bowl was conducted the next year with four area high schools competing. The activity grew each year, and in 1979 Dr. Bill King and Dr. Sam O'Dell took the Walters State team to Berry College and finished a respectable third among 12 teams representing colleges throughout the Southeast.

A drug and alcohol abuse study in Hamblen County was completed and published in the spring of 1977. Sociology students had begun the study the previous year by surveying 1000 homes in the county, as well as schools and public institutions. With additional studies, the college continued efforts to be an educational instrument for the whole community. One such project, made possible by a federal grant, was a study in 1978 of metropolitan government for Hamblen County and Morristown. The same year a survey of vocational interest among high school students was conducted in conjunction with the Explorer Scouts. These extended services to the community were integral parts of the college's programming; while providing these services, the faculty and staff remained cognizant of a need to maintain the highest degree of quality in everything that bore the Walters State label.

In March of 1978 the *Filibuster* headlined "Beginner Chemistry to Start in Spring." According to Chemistry Professor Carl T. Bahner, the development of this course stemmed from a desire of the faculty to provide a course for students with a limited background in chemistry or for those who had not been introduced to chemistry at all. Dr. Bahner, who became Walters State's first retiree in June of 1978, indicated that he wanted a course relevant to the needs of students at the marginal level in order to stimulate interest and ensure quality in the upper-level courses. Dr. Bahner's actions exemplified the attitude of most faculty and staff for the year 1977-1978, for it was then that the college accepted the challenge of certifying and documenting the maintenance of quality in all programs and services. This timely undertaking began when programs and services were being extended to increasing numbers of constituencies throughout upper East Tennessee.

The college's management system was brought into focus again because of two occurrences—the college's endeavor to document existing quality in the instructional program and the State Board of Regents' early efforts to develop a comprehensive five-year plan. The outline for the Regents' plan complemented what had already been done at Walters State. One initial and quite significant aspect of the plan was the development of "The Walters State Role and Scope Statement," which contained a comprehensive listing of five-year goals.

A major goal developed by the Walters State faculty and staff was to "establish means to ensure that an associate degree from Walters State is meaningful in that the degree represents an achievement of certain basic skills and an attainment of specified competency levels." A considerable amount of time was spent in determining how this goal could best be achieved and in establishing appropriate mechanisms to reflect activities directed toward this end. Courses on and off campus were reviewed, with special attention being given to monitoring of off-campus classes through formal feedback mechanisms. The faculty and staff evaluation system was reviewed and modified, and a comprehensive orientation program was devised for adjunct faculty. Division chairmen began to exert more time and energy toward evening on- and off-campus programs. Faculty loads and low-producing programs were scrutinized not only at the local level, but at the Regents' level as well. In the final analysis, a committee was appointed to conduct a comprehensive study of the entire curriculum, course by course, to ascertain what a degree from Walters State signified and what changes were necessary, if any, to ensure that it was meaningful.

The far-flung community was receiving increased attention as off-campus enrollments continued to grow. As a cooperative effort between the college and the Tennessee Valley Authority, preparation courses for the high school equivalency examination were offered at a number of sites. The total of GED graduates in the involved area, which included Hamblen, Hawkins, Grainger, Greene, Hancock, and Sullivan counties, went from approximately 500 to almost 900 during the first year of the program.

Evening falls and classes begin again. *Photograph courtesy Walters State Community College.*

Course offerings that gave students a substantial portion of their junior college education were provided at off-campus sites in Rogersville, Knoxville, Sevierville-Gatlinburg, Newport, Tazewell, and Greeneville. Response was so positive in Greeneville that in 1978 the college rented a facility and attracted 365 students the first quarter. Several additional courses were specifically planned and taught for new industries being established in the area; courses in German for local workers who were to be trained in Germany and in English for German supervisors and their families were offered for MAHLE, Incorporated, a Germany-based industry that was establishing a factory in Morristown. Through these efforts the college was true to its commitment to offer programs and services based on needs and to offer them within reasonable commuting distances for the people in upper East Tennessee.

On campus, a new career program, medical technology, broadened the scope of the college in the health field. An interesting aspect of this program was that students entering the program were certified lab technicians who had been given one year's credit for their previous training and experience. These students enrolled primarily in general education classes at Walters State.

The Walters State Foundation continued actively to support the college. Two substantially endowed scholarships, in memory of Selina Gill and Ellen Nabors, were established. Roland Dicks was named chairman of the Selina Gill Scholarship Fund, and Clay Walker headed a committee to manage the Ellen Nabors Scholarship

Fund, which was established by Dr. Luke Nabors in memory of his wife.

As community assistance was received, the college, in turn, took pride throughout the years in responding to the community's needs by opening campus facilities to the public. During 1977-1978, Walters State was host for a number of important functions, locally and statewide. The Community-Junior College Conference, sponsored by the University of Tennessee, brought 200 people from across the state. When the Tennessee Higher Education Commission met on campus for the first time, a resolution was passed honoring the contributions of John M. Jones of Greeneville, who was retiring from THEC. The college was honored that THEC chose to recognize this distinguished East Tennessean on the Walters State campus. Locally, the college co-sponsored (with the Morristown Lions Club) a lecture by Paul Harvey and served as host for the chamber of commerce annual dinner, an event which was attended by 600 highly appreciative community members.

Organizational changes within the college during 1977-1978 resulted in Dr. Neal Fentress' being named dean of administrative services; that position had been vacated when Dr. Ford became dean of instruction. A new office was established which provided for the consolidation of community relations, alumni affairs, public information, and recruitment; at the same time it added credibility to the college's effort to recognize a new standard of the SACS relating to institutional advancement. The new office was named institutional advancement, and Victor Duggins was named director. From an organizational standpoint, the president desired to receive greater input from students and faculty; therefore, he established the president's faculty advisory council and the president's student advisory council with which he personally met throughout the year. As a public relations effort, the Senators' Pages, a small group of selected students, were organized to assist the president at official functions and to be effective spokesmen for the college in the community.

A showcase in the area of community involvement was the music department, where two significant projects were undertaken during the year. First, the college incorporated the Kindermusik program, designed by a professional musician in Morristown, to give children of the Lakeway Region the ability to appreciate and enjoy music and to develop skills for pursuing music professionally. The other exciting development involved the community chorale, directed by Will Kesling. Their spring concert, featuring 42 citizen-singers accompanied by volunteers from the Knoxville Symphony, was one of the most ambitious choral programs presented in Morristown. In support of the music program and other aspects of the campus operation, the college received funding in the spring of 1978 for a $3.1 million Campus Development, Phase II project which incorporated a fine arts building, maintenance building, and a central energy plant. Projected for completion in the spring of 1980, the building expansion was designed to satisfy the critical needs of the present and to provide opportunities for the future.

When in December of 1978 the State Board of Regents met at Walters State for a second time, the campus design called for in the master plan of 1975 was closer to reality. Construction on the fine arts and the maintenance buildings was about to begin. The classroom building was ready for the opening of the winter quarter, and the additions to the student service and learning resource center areas were almost complete. The new additions were designed to provide Walters State students with facilities which were desperately needed and to bring to full realization the learning resource center—a concept Kathryn Bass Flinn had envisioned when the facility consisted of only one room in the basement of the city library. Upon completion of these additions to the campus, the college would reach a state of development that could not have been foreseen eight and one-half years earlier when the Lakeway citizens first opened their hearts and homes to Walters State Community College. During this period Walters State has proudly joined with other state community colleges in vastly expanding the scope of higher education in Tennessee.

The story of these years does not evolve from the mere construction of buildings, development of curricula, or assemblage of faculty and students. The college's growth in appropriations, enrollments, and employees has been derived from the vision, dedication, and hard work of East Tennesseans representing every walk of life. Through an organic process, Walters State Community College was conceived and has been nurtured by the community the college was called to serve. Inspired by the goodness and generosity of a great people, sustained by their energy, and challenged by their independent spirit, the college has embarked upon a course of service which promises a worthy future firmly established on the secure foundation of a distinguished past.

7

VOLUNTEER STATE COMMUNITY COLLEGE
by Hal R. Ramer

*T*he love of learning and the rich tradition of higher education in the Sumner County region have been ably chronicled by Walter T. Durham, Gallatin scholar and businessman, in his book *A College for this Community,* which surveys the history of the local colleges antecedent to Volunteer State Community College. The cultural heritage of this area of Tennessee is substantial. In a real sense, Vol State is the legacy of Samuel Black and others, and of Wirt College, Howard Female College, Neophogen College, Tullatuskee Normal College, Isaac Franklin Institute, Pythian College, and other schools that rose and fell only to rise again as Vol State. In Durham's words, Vol State " . . . fulfilled the heretofore frustrated dreams of local partisans of education—dreams that can be dated back to the early 19th century . . . ."

In contemporary times, developing local plans and support for a unified proposal to the state toward the location of a new community college in Sumner County involved the work of many citizens and local officials. This effort culminated in the preparation of a brochure, *Gallatin–The Most Promising Location in North Central Tennessee for a New Community Junior College,* which was formally presented by Robert L. Wendling, spokesman for the Sumner County delegation in attendance, to the Tennessee Higher Education Commission at its Nashville meeting at the Capitol Park Inn on September 11, 1967. This local initiative anticipated future General Assembly action to authorize and appropriate funds for additional community colleges in Tennessee.

Following such action by the State Legislature, the Tennessee Higher Education Commission, at its meeting on June 2, 1969, adopted a resolution authorizing the State Board of Education to establish a community college in Sumner County at a site to be chosen by State Education Commissioner J. Howard Warf and the authorizing board. Subsequently, Commissioner Warf and his staff members, T. Wesley Pickel and H. R. Ramer, visited the area to inspect four prospective sites provided by the county. Hosts for the visit were county and city officials and civic leaders of the county. Commissioner Warf notified County Judge I. C. McMahan by letter on July 29, 1969, that a 100-acre tract on Nashville Pike (known locally as the Frost property) had been chosen for the new campus. The county paid Louis Green, Sr., owner of the land, $200,000 and deeded the tract to the state for the college on December 4, 1969. In accordance with state requirements, the county also provided $250,000 to the state toward initial construction costs. The city of Gallatin agreed to extend all utilities to the site, and both city and county agreed in perpetuity to protect land zoning of the area in conditions that would enhance the college environments, as well as to provide the usual police and fire protection services.

Included on the agenda of the State Board of Education meeting in regular quarterly session at Nashville on May 8, 1970, was designation of executive heads for the yet-to-be created state community colleges in Shelby, Roane, and Sumner counties. Chairman J. H. Warf stated that, although the board had authorized him to appoint founding presidents for the new colleges, he preferred to present his recommendation for each position and request the board's action thereon, having considered and screened numerous candidates before arriving at his final recommendation.

Warf presented the name of Hal Reed Ramer as founding president of the institution to become Volunteer State Community College. Ramer, a native of Kenton, Tennessee, and a graduate of Peabody College and the University of Tennessee, had received his Ph.D. from Ohio State University where he had also served in the positions of assistant to the president, assistant dean of men, and director of the international center. For the preceding seven years, he had been assistant state commissioner for higher education, associated with Commissioner Warf in providing staff administrative services for the board in the governance of the six regional univer-

President Hal Reed Ramer. *Photograph courtesy Volunteer State Community College.*

Left to right: John R. Long, President Ramer, William H. Coley, John H. M. Smith, Commissioner Warf (at lectern), I. C. McMahan, Cordell McDonald, Melvin Briley, and Nolen E. Bradley, Jr., at ground-breaking ceremony, November 5, 1970. *Photograph courtesy Volunteer State Community College.*

sities and in the establishment of the new system of state community colleges. Board member Edward L. Jennings moved approval of Ramer to become the founding president effective July 1, 1970. The motion was seconded by James H. Jones, Jr., and the appointment was approved unanimously.

Selecting a suitable official name for a new college is important. The name chosen should be as broadly acceptable as possible and lend prestige and visibility to the institution. The president of the newly authorized college considered several names to propose to board chairman Warf. Inasmuch as the capital city of the Volunteer State comprised a major part of the college's service area, Ramer recommended "Volunteer State Community College" to Warf, who discussed the proposal with Jennings. At the called board session on July 2, 1970, Jennings presented a resolution to name the institution "Volunteer State Community College." The motion was seconded by J. Frank Taylor of Huntingdon and was unanimously adopted by the board.

At 10:30 a.m. on the cold, damp, and blustery day of November 5, 1970, the campus groundbreaking ceremonies, complete with silver shovels, were held under the direction of ceremonial chairman E. G. Mattox to officially launch the construction of the new college.

The ceremonies were followed by luncheon at Bluegrass Country Club. Presiding at the program, William H. Coley, president of the Gallatin Chamber of Commerce, welcomed the large assemblage and forecast "years of much academic, economic, and social improvement" that the college would bring to the area.

After the invocation by the Reverend Charles Moffatt, presentations were made by Barry Cecil and Robert L. Wendling, both past presidents of the chamber, and by Judge McMahan, Commissioner Warf, Tennessee Higher Education Commission Chairman John R. Long, and President Ramer. Governor Buford Ellington could not be present for the event but sent a telegram expressing his personal good wishes and characterized the advent of Volunteer State College as "a major step forward" in Tennessee's effort to bring public higher education within commuting range of every citizen.

In tracing from 1965 the succession of local initiatives to acquire a state college (including the speech in July of that year by Commissioner Warf before a joint meeting of local service clubs), Wendling and Judge McMahan cited the chamber of commerce, county court, city council, area business and industry, and the efforts of civic leaders and elected officials in the success of this enterprise. Especially acclaimed for their persistent leadership were James W. Hawkins, Barry Cecil, E. G. Mattox, Fred Kelly, John Phillips, John Boyers, Judge Stokley Dismukes, Ottis Kemp, Cordell McDonald, Dan Calgy, Walter Durham, Felix Fly, Randy Wood, Mary Suddarth, State Representatives Melvin Briley and John Steinhauer, and State Senator William Baird. Cited for special assistance and final authorization at the state level were Governor Ellington, Commissioner Warf, Chairman Long, THEC executive John K. Folger, and members of the General Assembly of 1969, the State Board of Education, and the Tennessee Higher Education Commission.

Among other Sumner Countians especially prominent in the leadership at various stages over the months and years in the successful effort to acquire the college were Billy Dick Brown, William P. Wade, Sarah Berry, Ruth Russell, Noble Caudill, J. O. Templeton, L. H. Newman, A. Byron Charlton, Jr., Nathan Harsh, William Puryear, Clyde Riggs, Thomas Boyers, III, George Hamilton, Edward McDonald, Thomas Carter, Dan Herron, John Malone, Oscar Martin, Reverend Ben Alexander, J. C. McMurtry, J. H. Cage, John Garrott, William David Doyle, William Black, Tom Bruce, Robert

Kulakowski, Dorma D. Smith, Mrs. Johnny Dake, Howard Hitch-cock, Andrew Swaney, Harold Whitaker, Charles Tomkins, Jr., Robert Ramsey, Louis A. Green, Sr., Jack Roth, Robert Bennett, El-wood O'Neal, John Thomas, Charles Parks, Jack Settle, Charles Payne, James Draper, Harry Smith, Jimmy England, H. H. Burrum, Fred White, Roy Shoulders, O. E. Ausbrooks, Gene Brown, Mrs. James Creasey, Russ Melvin, Charles Brewer, Lee Raines, and Dan Lewis.

Goals and objectives for the college were formulated by its ad-ministrative staff as the college began in 1971, with an intent of pro-viding comprehensive educational opportunities day, evening, and year-round to Tennesseans and others inside a 40-mile commuting radius of Gallatin and within the economic limits of those desiring such opportunities. Specific objectives provided for the following: an academic program preparing students to transfer two years of college work to four-year colleges and universities; programs of occupational-technical and preprofessional work preparing stu-dents to enter industry, business, and the service professions; a pro-gram of adult and continuing education for students primarily earn-ing a living or making a home; student counseling and guidance services in accordance with personal, occupational, and academic needs; work with high schools, area vocational-technical schools, technical institutes, adult education programs, other colleges and universities, and businesses and industries within commuting range; and community service to create a cultural atmosphere and to make the facilities of the college available to the community.

The six original declarations of purpose were not altered until mid-year of 1977 when the college's first self study was completed for reaffirmation of accreditation by the Southern Association of Colleges and Schools. At that time, the campus committee on pur-pose recommended that a seventh statement of intent be added which broadened the college's commitments:

> To provide low-cost, quality education on an "open-door" admis-sions basis by providing high quality faculty and facilities, to provide an educational experience based on individual student needs and to implement programs designed to elevate academi-cally deficient students.

The requests for "role and scope" statements from external sources resulted in the formation of an ad hoc committee on role and

Charter personnel at Volunteer State. *Photograph courtesy Volunteer State Community College.*

scope in the fall of 1977. Their project, like that of the self study, provided additional opportunity for involvement of campus personnel in the development of statements relative to role and scope. Furthermore, it was through projects such as these that Volunteer State's primary managers enhanced their abilities to integrate goals and objectives with long-range planning efforts. Such a blending of effort was evidenced in 1979 in the college's five-year comprehensive plan, with implementation scheduled for September of 1979. The success of implementation will be another measure of the appropriateness of the college's goals and objectives. This plan, which includes the college's statement of role and sctpe, will serve as the blueprint for institutional development from 1979-1984. It is with faithfulness to the seven aforementioned objectives that Volunteer State Community College has continued its growth and development.

To begin the work of planning the new college—selecting its administrative staff and faculty, developing curriculum and facilities—and to enlist students and community support, the president opened temporary offices in September of 1970 in the Cordell Hull Building at Nashville. Especially helpful to the president at this incipient stage of Vol State were Nolen E. Bradley, Wade Powers, Jess Mallory, James Tuttle, Walter Thigpen, and Peggy McMurtry, all initial college staff members, and later Bill Hillard, Scott Fry, Don Goss, Charles Lee, Wayne Sullivan, John Bell, Franklin Conley, Sue

Greenfield, and John Samples, also charter staff members of the college. Commissioner Howard Warf, T. Wesley Pickel, Violet Parrish, John H. M. Smith, Ronald Brinkley, H. Lynn Banks, George Roberts, and Ben Groce, all of the State Department of Education staff, gave notable assistance from the state level. In May of 1971, additional temporary offices were opened at the Cordell Hull Hotel in Gallatin. The college began instruction in October of 1971 with classes taught for the first quarter in Gallatin in the hotel, the First United Methodist Church, the Gallatin Church of Christ, the First Presbyterian Church, the First Baptist Church, the National Guard Armory, and the Gallatin Junior High School.

Beginning students that opening quarter totaled 581, resulting in a full-time equivalency of 411. The first two students enrolled were John Newman and Joni Steinhauer, both of Hendersonville. Only 23 of those included in the total enrollment were students taking non-credit courses, with the remainder being students enrolled in credit courses. The majority of the students in this first class were residents of Sumner County. Students were enrolled from 11 other counties, with Davidson County having the second largest number of students. This group of students was almost evenly divided between those classified as full-time and those classified as part-time students. The full-time male student body more than doubled the number of full-time female students, while there were significantly more females among those students attending part time. Approximately 10 percent of this first class was composed of black students, and the average age for the student body was 23.

The second year of operation reflected a dramatic increase in enrollment with the total enrollment reaching 1408 with a full-time equivalency of 1023. The total college enrollment continued to increase about 13 percent for several years and then, in 1975, a 45-percent increase occurred. In the fall of 1975, the total enrollment increased to 2620 with a full-time equivalency of 1682. Interestingly, the student body continued to be evenly divided between males and females. However, the enrollment of 1975 started a trend of more part-time students than full-time students, and this tendency has continued to increase this ratio each year since that time. The average age of the student body increased in 1975 to 28, with the under-21-age category being the largest group and with the over-35-age category being the second largest.

TABLE I
VOLUNTEER STATE COMMUNITY COLLEGE
CHARTER PERSONNEL—July 1, 1970 to June 30, 1973
HAL R. RAMER, President
(1970)

ADMINISTRATION

Bradley, Nolen E. (1970)
Fry, James Scott (1971)
Hillard, William M. (1971)
Lee, Charles E. (1971)
Mallory, Jesse D. (1971)

Powers, R. Wade (1971)
Thigpen, Walter K. (1971)
Tuttle, James L. (1971)
Watts, Wallace B. (1971)
Woods, James R. (1972)

FACULTY

Armstrong, Robert O. (1971)
Bell, John Roney (1971)
Bills, Doris A. (1971)
Boyer, Donald H. (1972)
Bozarth, Rona Suzanne (1972)
Bradley, Eloise M. (1971)
Brinkley, Velma S. (1972)
Carson, Glenn Moore (1971)
Coleman, Richard D. (1972)
Conley, Bonnie W. (1971)
Conley, Franklin D. (1971)
Cozy, Helen B. (1971)
Freedle, Joe T. (1971)
Fry, Janice W. (1971)
Gill, Nancy L. (1972)
Gonsoulin, Gene J. (1971)
Goss, Donald R. (1971)
Greenfield, Virginia M. (1971)
Harville, James R. (1972)
Hawkins, Betty L. (1971)
Henson, Allen M. (1971)
Herrmann, Jeanette C. (1972)
Herrmann, Richard E. (1971)
Higdon, William D. (1971)
Jewell, Charles D. (1971)
Jones, Patricia M. (1971)
Kelley, Jane (1971)

Kirby, James Thomas (1972)
Lawler, Charles A. (1972)
Lebkuecher, Patricia B. (1972)
McGee, Drenda R. (1972)
Miller, Paul Thomas (1971)
Moore, James C. (1972)
Moore, John Richard (1971)
Moore, William Frederick (1971)
Moser, H. Ronald (1972)
Murphy, Joseph M. (1971)
Murray, Beulah B. (1972)
Nicar, Daphne M. (1972)
Peay, Moiselle (1971)
Phifer, John Winston (1972)
Simmons, Frank W. (1972)
Snider, Jimmie L. (1972)
Stephens, Louise M. (1971)
Stewart, Mary E. (1971)
Sullivan, G. Wayne (1971)
Sutcliffe, Rita J. (1972)
Thigpen, Virginia A. (1972)
Tucker, John Mark (1972)
Voorhies, Marguerite (1971)
Ward, James K., Jr. (1972)
Watlington, Joseph C. (1972)
Weaver, Joan C. (1971)

SUPPORT STAFF

Adams, Cretdell (1972)
Anderson, Helen L. (1971)
Borden, Marie (1972)
Borden, Ralph (1973)
Burgett, Herman (1973)
Bradley, Howard T. (1972)
Butler, Austin (1972)
Crouse, Devonnia G. (1971)
Draper, Beth (1972)
Duncan, Rosie L. (1971)
Eddy, Karen (1972)
Eden, Thomas C. (1972)
Farris, Barbara M. (Hager) (1972)
Fleming, Woodrow W. (1972)
Fly, Lynn (1972)
Flynn, Lynn (1972)
Frakes, Sam B. (1972)
Frakes, Veda (1972)
Fykes, Virginia (1971)
Gagnon, Catherine (Greer) (1971)
Gibson, Betty (1972)
Goad, Patricia (Austin) (1971)
Hall, Donah F. (1971)
Harper, John E. (1972)
Higdon, Susan (1972)
Hodges, James B. (1972)
Holland, Susie L. (1971)
Jewell, Joyce (1972)
Jones, Robert A. (1972)
Jones, Robert J. (1972)
Keith, Frances K. (1971)
Kelsey, JoLaine (Bloodworth) (1972)

Lewis, Regina (1972)
Malone, Hubert (1972)
Maynard, Evelyn R. (1971)
McMurray, James (1972)
McMurray, Roy (1973)
McMurtry, Peggy L. (1970)
Metcalf, Larry (1972)
Miller, Nell L. (1971)
Oates, JoAnne (1971)
Odom, Joe Thomas (1972)
Pearson, Sheila E. (1971)
Pedigo, Rebecca S. (1971)
Pippin, Danny (1972)
Pippin, David (1972)
Pollock, John W. (1972)
Primm, Edgar W. (1972)
Redmon, Sharon L. (1972)
Roark, Janice (Duke) (1971)
Russell, J. B. (1972)
Russell, Sherry (Helms) (1972)
Samples, John (1971)
Seaton, Chester (1973)
Seaver, Elizabeth R. (1971)
Segroves, Bill (1972)
Smith, Gloria (1972)
Strong, Betty (1972)
Taylor, Gail (Grab) (1971)
Templeton, Joyce A. (1971)
Williams, Ralph (1972)
Wix, Gail (1972)
Wooten, Jane P. (1971)

The total enrollment of the college has continued to increase each year to an enrollment of 3625 students in the fall of 1978. Because of the growing number of part-time students enrolling, the full-time equivalency of the college has slightly declined each year after 1975 until in the fall of 1978 this number was 1577. The segment of the enrollment which increased more rapidly was female students classified as part-time. In the fall of 1978, about 62 percent of the student body was female. During the years from 1975 to 1978, a significant growth was experienced in the enrollment in non-credit courses designed for personal enrichment. Since its beginning, more than 28,300 individual persons have taken some type of course or seminar offered by the college through June of 1979. Vol State has served the older student from the outset. The mean age of students in 1971 was 23 years, whereas in 1979 that mean age of the student body had risen to 28.9 years. Some 32.1 percent of the 1979 students were under age 26, and 23.8 percent were over age 35.

In 1975, the college started developing strategies to deliver instruction and services at locations away from campus. Several different sites were utilized in an effort to provide educational opportunities in the areas in which people live or work. A consortium was formed in 1976 that included Volunteer State, Tennessee State University, and McGavock High School for the delivery of college courses at McGavock High School in Donelson. Plans are underway to open other cooperative educational centers. In the meantime, classes have been offered at Lafayette, Westmoreland, Springfield, Hartsville, and at other off-campus teaching sites. Similarly, off-campus offerings of evening courses of universities on the Vol State campus were facilitated by VSCC whose consortium, with Board of Regents' approval, established a university center at Vol State. Directed by Ed Cullum and a steering committee, the center provided for coordinated upper-division undergraduate and graduate instruction by Tennessee State University, Middle Tennessee State University, LIT Nashville, and by Tennessee Tech.

As the enrollment of the college has grown so has there been a growth in the number of courses offered and in the variety of curriculum options. When the college opened, university parallel degree programs were offered to permit students to pursue a degree to transfer to most university majors. The curriculum also included career degree and certificate programs to prepare students for employment after graduation. The initial career offerings included four associate degrees and six certificates.

Some adjustments have been made in the university parallel programs to more adequately meet the needs of students who plan to transfer. Community needs have been assessed at various times during the college's existence (under the guidance in recent years of Jim Moore) to ascertain the need for additional career degree and certificate programs. These programs are developed after an advisory committee has been formed and recommendations received indicating such career programs would aid the community. The college in 1979 offered career associate degrees in medical laboratory technician, medical records technology, physical therapy assistant, conservation and environmental technology, general business administration, human services, office occupations, and surveying engineering technology. Career certificate programs now being offered are basic management, broadcasting, data processing, dental assistant, food service administration, human services, marketing and distribution, office occupations, real estate, respiratory therapy, and teacher and child aide technology.

Led by Carol Horn, a business and industrial institute was formed in 1978 to serve the needs and interests of those segments of the economy by assisting with employee development. Programs were designed for the training of high potential, newly appointed, and experienced personnel. Instruction includes short courses, workshops, seminars, and special training sessions. The training provided can be in-plant, on-campus, or at a neutral location. All instructors utilized are professional practitioners with years of personal experience in the areas of expertise. Continuing education units and certificates of completion are awarded for successful performance in training. In 1978-1979, 20 seminars and courses were conducted which provided training for 574 employees of more than 30 companies.

From a modest start, Vol State's program of community services has experienced steady development through the years. Additional enrollment of some 750 persons in more than 70 non-credit CEU courses occurred in the fall of 1978 under the immediate supervision of Hilary Marabeti. Responsiveness to community interests and needs has been the hallmark of program design and delivery as the college worked with myriad citizen groups whose clientele ranged from senior citizens to pre-college. Similarly, attention has been given to those adults whose formal educations were interrupted for diverse personal reasons. The college began its approved general educational development testing service in January of 1972, and in January of 1975, upon demonstrated need, instituted non-degree-credit courses in GED pre-test preparation. Through June of 1979, some 2395 persons received their high school equivalency diplomas from the State Department of Education as a result of the college's GED instruction and testing service. Incalculable assistance was thereby rendered to these adults in their continuing education, personal enrichment, and self-esteem, and in the opportunities for upward mobility in careers.

In 1971, the American Library Association *Standards for Junior College Libraries* and "Standard Six" of the *Standards* of the Southern Association of Colleges and Schools provided goals and guidelines for developing a library. Furnishings were specified, bid, and ordered, and books listed in *Choice Magazine's* "Opening Day Collection" were ordered. An early decision to have a card catalog record of all books, periodicals, and audio-visual materials available to the general public—regardless of the department ordering or the funding account used—was important and cost-effective. By 1972, the decision was made jointly by the library and the library committee to buy backruns of periodicals in microfilm format rather than to bind space-consuming paper copies which had the additional disadvantage of being prone to mutilation.

By 1973, audio-visual demands were sufficient to require increased emphases. The library was rethought as an integrated print and audio-visual information complex, and, subsequently, the College of Dupage, William Rainey Harper Community College, and the A.L.A.-American Association of Colleges and Junior Colleges-Association for Educational Communications and Technology's joint *Guidelines for Two-Year College Learning Resources Centers* provided the philosophical and practical bases for the emergence of the college's library-learning resources center. Print and non-print procedures in acquisitions, cataloging, circulation, and in acquisitions, cataloging, circulation, and reference were merged, and a darkroom, small video studio, and sound booth were incorporated within the enlarged L-LRC. The public area increased from 7240 square feet in 1971 to 13,500 square feet in 1978. Off-campus cooperation involved sharing of resources with proximate county libraries, with the teaching of library courses at McGavock High School, and at Donelson and Springfield public libraries, and with management and operation of the McGavock High School library for evening students.

The L-LRC collection at the beginning of the 1978-1979 year had 30,000 books, 1632 reels of microfilm, 250 periodicals, and 1273 units of audio-visual materials. An electronic book detection system enhanced security of materials. SOLINET connected the L-LRC with almost all major libraries through the eastern part of the U. S. (with VSCC loaning books to libraries such as Emory University, Joint University Libraries, University of the South, Eastern Michigan University, Tennessee Technological University, and Emory and Henry). On-line cataloging data provided the campus computer with a complete listing of L-LRC materials which, in print-out form, were provided every academic division on campus and to all L-LRC areas. The quality of these services by L-LRC personnel brought a "commendation" from the third visitation committee of the Southern Association of Colleges and Schools to Director Walter Thigpen and his staff.

Volunteer State Community College began its work toward accreditation shortly after the college became operational. A candidacy committee of the Southern Association of Colleges and Schools visited the college during April 11-14, 1972, and issued a comprehensive report that proved to be quite valuable to the administration, faculty, and staff as the work continued toward seeking accreditation. The report of the committee provided candidacy status by SACS and information that would assist the college in its development so that the numerous accreditation requirements could be fulfilled for initial accreditation. This report also served as the benchmark for the SACS evaluation committee which visited the college during May 22-25, 1973, to measure the college for initial accreditation. As a result of this visit, VSCC was awarded full and retroactive accreditation by SACS at its December of 1973 annual meeting.

In September of 1976, the college began an 18-month institutional self-study process, extensively analyzing every aspect of the institution. Virtually every employee provided input through various committees organized to meet the SACS standards. The self-study steering committee guided the progress of this campus analysis; it merits recognition for what culminated in a most comprehensive and useful institutional examination. Steering committee members and the areas they represented were Director Patricia Lebkuecher; Wayne Sullivan, divisional chairman; Hilary Marabeti, faculty; Rod Thorland, faculty assembly; Jane Wooten, support staff; Joan Oathout, at-large; Ron Edwards, student services; and R. Wade Powers, administration. Functional subcommittees of the parent committee were chaired by Bob Sibert, purpose; Linda Doran, organization and administration; Richard Herrmann, educational program; Richard Coleman, financial resources; Rosemary Craighead, faculty; Shirley Reeves, library learning resources; Jane Kelley, student development services; Edgar Lowe, physical plant; Howard George, special activities; Robert Ruff, plans and projections; and Virginia Thigpen, editor. During March 7-10, 1978, a SACS committee visited the college to evaluate the self study and to prepare a report to SACS for the purpose of determining eligibility for reaffirmation of accreditation. On December 19, 1978, the SACS commission on colleges notified VSCC that it had successfully completed the institutional self-study process and that accreditation was reaffirmed at the SACS annual meeting in December of 1978.

In the fall of 1972, an ad hoc committee of faculty and administrators was appointed by the president of the college to explore the possibility of establishing a college assembly. After several meetings, during which the purposes, constituency, and representation were discussed, it was decided that the scope of the organization would be limited to representatives of the teaching faculty. During the ad hoc committee meeting on January 18, 1973, the first spokesman of this representative body, P. Thomas Miller, was elected from committee membership and designated speaker of the faculty assembly. The president of the college expressed his interest in the assembly, reflected on the possibilities of such a body, and pledged his support of its activities.

After election of the first speaker, the faculty assembly spent the remainder of its first year, 1972-1973, in drafting and ratifying its constitution and bylaws. Upon ratification by the faculty, the constitution was presented and defended by the speaker before the administrative committee of the college. It was unanimously approved. Understood from the outset was that this body should serve in an advisory capacity to the administration on matters of concern to the faculty. The purposes as stated in the preamble were

> ... to promote faculty participation in academic decision-making according to sound principles of higher education, to provide an orderly process for improving communication and mutual understanding between the administrative officers and the faculty of the college, to foster mutual trust and respect, and to facilitate the expression of the collective opinion of the college faculty.

Original members of the ad hoc committee and of the assembly during the first year when the constitution was being written and ratified were Franklin Conley, counseling; Janice W. Fry, humanities; Gene J. Gonsoulin, career education; Patricia L. Jones, social science and education; Patricia B. Lebkuecher, social science and education; Charles E. Lee, adult and continuing education; P. Thomas Miller, mathematics and science; Louise M. Stephens, career education; Virginia H. Thigpen, humanities; Walter K. Thigpen, library services; and Joseph C. Watlington, mathematics and science. These same members served as the first elected representatives of the initial faculty assembly (1973-1974). P. Thomas Miller was elected as the first speaker. Subsequent speakers were Patricia B. Lebkuecher (1974-1975), Richard E. Herrmann (1975-1976), Hilary B. Marabeti (1976-1977), Robert M. Ruff (1977-1978), Larry J. Adams (1978-1979), and Lynda Taylor Thorland (1979-1980).

Major accomplishments of the first faculty assembly under the new constitution were to establish and/or improve lines of communication between faculty and administration; to design a comprehensive educational advisement system for the college; to design an administrator evaluation instrument and to initiate the process of regular evaluation of administrators; to design, conduct, and analyze data; and to publicize the results of a study of faculty morale. Among accomplishments of succeeding faculty assemblies have been the following: to present recommendations for formulation of Volunteer State and State Board of Regents guidelines for faculty promotion at community colleges; to recommend a new payment policy on ACE non-credit courses taught by full-time VSCC faculty based on a new method of computing teaching load equivalents (TLE) and a higher rate of pay for each TLE; to recommend a new "hazardous weather" policy; to form an ad hoc college welfare committee to study problems concerning insurance programs, credit unions, tax-sheltered annuities, etc.; to recommend changes in the committee system of the college based on a thorough study of the standing committee system; to recommend specific improvements in the college calendar; to review and submit extensive recommendations to the Board of Regents through the president of the college on the original draft of the newly formulated tenure policy for college faculty; to take a lead role in forming a statewide faculty organization among SBR colleges; to initiate formal communications with the Tennessee General Assembly concerning faculty salaries in community colleges by sending a VSCC delegation to make a presentation before the House Finance, Ways, and Means Committee; and to consider draft documents and make extensive recommendations to the administration and to the Board of Regents concerning the overload compensation policy. Accomplishments of the faculty assemblies of VSCC since 1973 have indeed made an impact on the morale of the faculty, the attentiveness of the administration to faculty needs, and the recognition by the administration of the college, the Board of Regents, and state legislators. Faculty members can and do provide a great deal of expertise in molding the educational system.

From the austere beginning, the college moved during the winter of 1972 to permanent facilities on its 100-acre site on U. S. Highway 31-E between Gallatin and Hendersonville. Table II summarizes the facilities development and occupancy at Vol State through the years. The college in 1979 had 975 parking spaces. Completion of the new campus center addition project would provide approximately 1100 parking spaces. Six tennis courts and the present baseball field were constructed in 1974. As of June 30, 1978, the college accounting records indicated a book value for the seven buildings of $5,186,080. A conservative estimate of the replacement cost would be in excess of $15 million at 1979 construction levels. In addition to the buildings, the other improvements, such as parking lots, tennis courts, baseball field, along with library books and movable equipment, were capitalized at a cost of $1,711,372 as of June 30, 1978. It was estimated that the replacement cost of these improvements would exceed four million dollars at 1979 prices. By the summer of 1979 a major expansion of the campus center and the

TABLE II
VOLUNTEER STATE COMMUNITY COLLEGE
FACILITIES DEVELOPMENT
1972-1979

BUILDING NAME	PRIMARY FUNCTIONS	GROSS SQUARE FEET	OCCUPANCY DATE	COST	ARCHITECT	CONTRACTOR
Administration Building	Provide administrative and faculty offices, library/LRC, and classrooms	49,350	1/72	$1,085,889	Schlott, Norman, and Cain	Hardaway Constn. Co.
Campus Center Building	Provide bookstore, cafeteria, student services offices	30,264	2/72	$ 505,742	Schlott, Norman, and Cain	Hardaway Constn. Co.
T. Wesley Pickel Fieldhouse	Provide gymnasium, classrooms, offices for physical education, music, allied health	51,801	2/72	$ 998,236	Schlott, Norman, and Cain	Hardaway Constn. Co.
J. Howard Warf Science Building	Provide offices, computer center, laboratories, classrooms for math and science	28,337	3/72	$ 711,599	Schlott, Norman, and Cain	Hardaway Constn. Co.
New Classroom Building	Provide offices and classrooms for social science and education, auditorium	25,875	6/75	$ 775,342	Schlott, Norman, and Cain	Roberts Constn. Co.
Art Building	Provide art offices, laboratories, classrooms, maintenance	8,500	8/75	$ 132,270	Johnson and Collier	Woodmore Constn. Co.
Ray Blanton Career-Technology Building	Provide offices, classrooms and laboratories for business, medical records, CET, SET	22,000	6/78	$1,470,000	Johnson and Collier	Woodmore Constn. Co.
Greenhouse	Provide greenhouse nursery for CET	600	6/78	Incld. above	Johnson and Collier	Woodmore Constn. Co.
Field Station	Provide scientific labs for air, water testing, astronomy, etc.	1,500	1979	Approx. $ 92,000	Johnson and Collier	CTC Constn. Co. and Hardaway Constn. Co.
Campus Center Addition and Coal-Fired Heating Plant	Expand existing functions and add student activity spaces, classrooms, and testing center. Convert from natural gas to coal as primary fuel for heat.	31,550	1981	Approx. $3,255,000	Hart, Freeland and Roberts; Johnson and Collier	Ray Bell Constn. Co.

addition of a coal-fired heating plant were underway. Capital outlay funds of $3,255,000 were approved for this new project by the 1978 legislative session. A campus facilities master plan was developed in April of 1977 with Burkhalter-Hickerson Associates, Incorporated, to provide a guide for future campus growth.

A stated goal of Vol State is to provide community service, create a cultural atmosphere, and make college facilities available to the community for better citizenship and profitable use of leisure time. To accomplish this aim, procedures have been outlined by the college. The campus center was utilized in 1978 by more community groups, organizations, and families than any other college facility. In addition to affiliated organizations using the campus center, 66 outside groups scheduled and used the facility. The auditorium was used by 21, the Pickel Fieldhouse by 14, and the classrooms by 13 such groups. When other campus facilities are included, it is not uncommon for as many as 120 non-affiliated organizations to avail themselves of this college service to the community over the course of a year, leaving little doubt that taxpayers harvest a good return on their investment.

A brief summary of Vol State's financial growth shows that in the first year of operation, 1971-1972, the college programmed a total education and general budget of $807,800 of which $585,000 was from direct state appropriation. In the 1978-1979 budget, the education and general expenditures were allocated at $3,507,244 of which $2,665,600 was from direct state appropriation. The average faculty salary for the 1971-1972 academic year was $8,406 compared to a 1978-1979 academic year average of $15,717. For the 1978-1979 fiscal year, approximately 334 students received from all sources a total of $234,276 in student financial assistance to pursue their education.

In an innovative effort to conserve energy resources, the college implemented an experimental four-day week during January through March of 1978. Adjusting operating timetables to meet standards, classes and lengthened office hours were scheduled Monday through Thursday, with facilities closed on Friday, Saturday, and Sunday. The energy savings during this experimental schedule were significant when compared to the same time period of the previous year. The college reduced electric consumption by 29 percent and natural gas consumption by 17 percent. Cost of transportation for students and staff was not measured, but a significant reduction was also apparent. Favorable reaction from the college community and a commendation from the state energy office resulted, together with numerous inquiries from other institutions.

The college joined the "computer age" as it installed its first electronic data processing equipment on April 14, 1972. The original computer configuration and staff remained unchanged until April 1, 1974, when James Winters became the director of data processing. It was shortly determined that the original computer configuration was inadequate, and requests were made to upgrade the system to more fully meet the needs of the institution. After lengthy conversations among Vol State, the vender, and the State Board of Regents, extensive modifications were made to the system during December of 1974 and October of 1975, which resulted in an upgraded configuration.

During 1976-1977, the last major modification was made; it consisted of a communications hookup between the computer at Middle Tennessee State University and Vol State equipment. In July of 1977 the computer center greatly expanded its capacities with the installation of a terminal-oriented computer system, and in June of 1979 an additional 12 computer terminals had been added, bringing the total number of terminals to 27. The computer center provides services to students through the instructional program, to the faculty and college administrative units, and to several nonprofit agencies in the community on a contractual basis.

The personnel office was established on April 1, 1977, with the following responsibilities assigned to its director, Joan Weaver, and staff: assistance in development and administration of personnel program and employee benefits; assistance in formulation of personnel policies and procedures; maintenance of personnel records and generation of reports and statistical information; recruitment of personnel and maintenance of appropriate applicant pools; and assistance in monitoring affirmative action policies and procedures. Placement in employment of students and alumni was carried forth as a portion of the director's role.

Striving to expand services to employees and the college, the personnel office duties have continued to increase. By July of 1977, the personnel office had established a centralized employee and applicant file system. A terminal was also installed in the personnel office facilities, and the computerization of personnel information was begun. In September of 1977, the responsibility for employee benefits determination was transferred to this office.

In January of 1978, the personnel office prepared the employee payroll for the first time. This was a concerted effort in cooperation with the staffs of the business office and computer center. Payroll checks were first written by the computer center in April of 1978 and validated by the business office. The personnel office has served on two pilot projects for the State Board of Regents, namely, the computerized personnel update system and the staff classification study. In January of 1979, a staff classification system was implemented by the college.

Utilizing findings and recommendations contained in the 1977-1978 institutional self study along with evaluations made by the president, the college was reorganized on July 1, 1978, to incorporate a management-by-objectives process and in order better to align functional responsibilities with accountability factors. Although the original organization served well to that point, the revised structure grouped kindred operations and academic disciplines and provided for more effective use of human, financial, and physical resources. The approval and assistance of Chancellor Roy S. Nicks, and of the faculty, students, staff, and college committees contributed immeasurably in the smooth transition to a new mode of administration.

A wide variety of college musical and dramatic events and of student and faculty recitals have been produced before appreciative audiences through the years, providing rich experience in the multi-faceted aspects of the performing arts and requiring the cooperative efforts of talented personnel in the disciplines of drama, music, set design, costuming, sound, lighting, advertising promotion and business, hospitality, and other forms of stagecraft. Among these, 14 drama productions have been held at the college over the past eight years, culminating in the outstanding performance of "Klokeye," an original fantasy play written by Professor Dan Jewell and whose music and lyrics were composed by Charlie Chappelear, a VSCC student.

Music ensembles established over the years and available for participation by all students are the Camerata Singers, the concert band, the chamber music ensemble, and the Volunteer Concert Choir.

TABLE III
VOLUNTEER STATE COMMUNITY COLLEGE
PERSONNEL—July 1, 1978 to June 30, 1979
HAL R. RAMER, President
(1970)

ADMINISTRATION

Gray, Thomas E. (1974)
Moore, James C. (1972)
Powers, R. Wade (1971)

Thigpen, Walter K. (1971)
Tuttle, James L. (1971)
Woods, James R. (1972)

FACULTY

Adams, Larry J. (1976)
Amonette, Alice (1974)
Barstis, Lynn (1976)
Bell, John R. (1971)
Bible, Ondis N. (1977)
Blecha, Janet (1975)
Boehmer, David (1974)
Brown, Helen D. (1976)
Bush, Perry K. (1978)
Carman, W. Craig (1976)
Coleman, Richard D. (1972)
Coleman, Ronald R. (1976)
Conley, Franklin D. (1971)
Constantin, George N. (1976)
Curp, Sara E. (1974)
Doran, Linda K. (1973)
Edwards, Ronald R. (1973)
Farish, John P. (1976)
Forrester, Robert A. (1973)
Fry, Janice W. (1971)
George, Howard (1974)
Goss, Donald R. (1971)
Hackney, Ronald W. (1973)
Hardy, Faye R. (1973)
Harville, James R. (1972)
Hawkins, Betty L. (1971)
Herrmann, Jeanette C. (1972)
Herrmann, Richard E. (1971)
Hester, Brenda E. (1976)
Highers, Michael R. (1974)
Hillard, William M. (1971)
Horn, Carol D. (1975)
Jackson, Howard J. (1977)
Janaway, Paulette (1978)
Jewell, Charles D. (1971)
Kelley, Jane (1971)
Kirby, James T. (1972)
Knobeloch, Lois A. (1977)
LaBounty, Lynn A. (1976)
Laude, Walter R. (1973)
Lawler, Charles A. (1972)
Lebkuecher, Patricia B. (1972)
Lee, Charles E. (1971)

Lowe, James E. (1971)
Marabeti, Hilary B. (1973)
Martin, Kathryn J. (1976)
McClellan, Paul L. (1975)
McDonald, Michael R. (1978)
Miller, Paul T. (1971)
Mingledorff, Glenna L. (1976)
Moore, J. Richard (1971)
Moser, H. Ronald (1972)
Murphy, Joseph M. (1971)
Murray, Beulah B. (1972)
Nance, Jesse J., Jr. (1978)
Nelson, Betty F. (1977)
Nelson, Janice S. (1974)
Nicar, Daphne M. (1972)
Oathout, Joan B. (1975)
Reagan, Larry Gay (1975)
Reeves, Shirley B. (1974)
Rivers, Victoria L. (1974)
Rouch, Richard D. (1976)
Ruff, Robert M. (1973)
Sale, June T. (1977)
Schibig, L. Joseph (1973)
Sharp, Julie E. (1977)
Sherrill, Vanita L. (1973)
Sibert, Robert S. (1973)
Smedley, Bruce R. (1973)
Smith, James L. (1974)
Snider, Jammie L. (1972)
Stephens, Louise M. (1971)
Stine, Karen E. (1976)
Sullivan, G. Wayne (1971)
Thigpen, Virginia A. (1972)
Thorland, Lynda T. (1976)
Thorland, Rodney H. (1973)
Tison, Gaye W. (1978)
Voorhies, S. Marguerite (1971)
Ward, James K., Jr. (1972)
Watlington, Joseph C. (1972)
Weaver, Joan C. (1971)
Webb, Gary S. (1977)
Whitsell, Roland D. (1978)
Wright, Neil H. III (1975)

SUPPORT STAFF

Adams, Cretdell (1972)
Adams, Denise (1973)
Adams, George A. (1979)
Adams, Herschel (1978)
Apple, Debbie (1979)
Barnes, Charles (1979)
Bayman, Vessie O. (1975)
Beasley, Bonnita K. (1976)
Borden, Marie E. (1972)
Bridges, Peggy J. (1978)
Brown, Betty S. (1974)
Burgett, Herman (1973)
Carter, Lillian H. (1978)
Casteel, Larry W. (1973)
Cliburn, Sherry L. (1978)
Cothron, Billy (1975)
Cravens, Mary L. (1973)
Daughtry, Darlene (1974)
Deathridge, Ann B. (1974)
Donoho, Elaine M. (1974)
Dorris, Inez O. (1975)
Eden, Thomas C. (1972)
England, Paula R. (1978)
Farris, Barbara (1972)
Featherston, Nancy D. (1978)
Fleming, Marge J. (1974)
Fleming, Woodrow W. (1972)
Fly, Lynn B. (1972)
Flynn, Lynn H. (1972)
Flynt, Beth M. (1979)
Fox, Joe T. (1973)
Frost, Louise H. (1978)
Gibson, Betty J. (1972)
Gossett, Holly E. (1978)
Hackett, Jewell E. (1973)
Hamilton, Felice F. (1973)
Hammer, Natalie A. (1974)
Hodges, Robert B. (1974)
Hodges, James B. (1972)
Hodges, William G. (1974)
Hof, Patricia E. (1976)
Honeycutt, Teresa J. (1979)
Hosier, Susan C. (1973)
Jewell, Joyce (1972)
Jones, Joan C. (1978)
Johnson, Debbie G. (1977)
Kane, Dora A. (1979)

Kirklin, Suzanne C. (1973)
Lyles, Eldon (1977)
Marlin, Orsie (1977)
Maynard, Evelyn R. (1971)
McCormick, Henry K. (1978)
McCormick, Rosemary T. (1978)
McMurray, James (1972)
Miller, Neil L. (1971)
Milliner, James (1974)
Moseley, Alfred (1979)
Murrell, Trina H. (1978)
Oates, JoAnne B. (1971)
Odom, J. Thomas (1972)
O'Neal, Judy L. (1977)
Ohman, Peggy (1978)
Page, Brenda M. (1979)
Pedigo, Rebecca S. (1971)
Pollock, John W. (1972)
Porter, Donna B. (1975)
Ransdell, Nan T. (1977)
Roark, Janice K. (1974)
Roberts, J. B. (1978)
Robnett, Jean E. (1975)
Seaton, Chester (1973)
Shaub, Charles (1978)
Simpson, Mary M. (1976)
Sinks, Nancy F. (1977)
Sloan, Sherry F. (1977)
Smith, John T. (1974)
Spivey, Cynthia K. (1974)
Stiles, Ray (1978)
Stinnett, Mildred (1973)
Swoopes, Debra Y. (1977)
Templeton, Joyce A. (1971)
Tinsley, Elizabeth S. (1978)
Titus, Greg (1978)
Trout, Janice E. (1975)
Trout, Robert G. (1974)
Ventress, Alvin W. (1975)
Williams, Ralph (1972)
Wilson, Vicki F. (1977)
Winters, James L. (1974)
Wix, Gail F. (1972)
Wooten, Jane P. (1971)
Worsham, Phillip W. (1976)
Wright, Floy B. (1973)
Wright, Peggy (1979)

These groups have regularly performed with acclaim on campus and before varied community audiences since the founding of the college.

Sensing the need for an annual publication expository of original art and literary works of students, faculty, and staff, the division of humanities established in 1973 a magazine, *Number One,* which takes its title from the community of the same name adjacent to the campus. Through 1979, seven volumes have been issued, drawing considerable visibility and affirmative reviews, and serving well as an exemplar of creative forms of printed expression.

In 1976, under the leadership of Sammy Parker, instructor of communications, and Donald R. Goss, chairman of the division of humanities, the college made application to the Federal Communication Commission for a license to operate an educational FM radio station on the campus. On February 9, 1978, the college was issued a construction permit for a 400-watt station to operate on a frequency of 88.3 megahertz. The college selected as a call sign for the station the letters WVCP which signify "We are the Volunteer State Community College Pioneers."

Through the generosity of several local commercial broadcasters, who donated equipment and advice, and with the aid of consulting engineers, Scott Baxter, Rudgyard Forrester, and Tom Park, the station began operating on January 7, 1979. An open house was held on that day celebrating the inaugural broadcast and featured statements by State Senator T. Tommy Cutrer, State Representatives John Steinhauer and Jack Burnett, U. S. Senator Jim Sasser, Congressman Albert Gore, Jr., Wray Buchanan of the State Board of Regents staff, Student Government Association President Guy Jones, Mike McDonald of the faculty, and President Ramer, with Reverend Alfred Bennett offering the invocation. Ruth Ann Leach of TV Channel 5 represented the commercial broadcast media.

The first student organization formed at Vol State was the student government association, initiated by the college because of its democratic and creative implications. Each student upon enrollment is a member and is encouraged to participate. Student government was seen as the representative agency for student involvement in the decision-making process at the college. The charter class in the fall of 1971 elected officers and representatives, and a working group began to draft a constitution. In the fall of 1972, it was presented to the entire student body for approval and was subsequently ratified. A revision was ratified in the spring of 1978. The student government association, referred to as SGA, was organized into three branches: the executive, the legislative, and the administrative.

Purposes for the association were identified by the students: "to promote the welfare of each student attending this institution; to train ourselves in the general principles of democratic government; to provide official channels through which student opinions may be expressed; to promote academic freedom and responsibility; to promote students' rights and responsibilities; to promote full cooperation between students, faculty, and administration; to foster awareness of the students' position on campus and in the community; to coordinate all student body activity; and to prepare ourselves to assume the privileges and responsibilities in the State of Tennessee and the United States of America."

The following persons have served as president of the student government association: Edward Mayberry (1971-1972); John Newman (January-June, 1973); Kenneth Hanson (1973-1974); Shan Payne Rhea (interim); Denney Coarsey (1974-1975); Joe Loftin (1975-1976); Teresa R. Ware (interim); Anthony Pratt (1976-1977); Timothy Bass (1977-1978); Timothy Holder (interim); Del Lloyd (1978-January, 1979); and Guy R. Jones (1979-1980).

Following the establishment of the student government association, other student clubs and organizations were formed through the years. Some were a result of student initiation, while others were a result of faculty or community interest. Active and contributing student organizations through 1979 are Gamma Beta Phi Honor Society, Baptist Student Union, Black Student Association, *The Settler* staff, Fellowship of Christian Athletes, Delta Psi Omega, HER Group, Returning Women, Environmental Action Organization, Single Parents Group, and the Student Teacher Education Association.

In 1976, the college initiated homecoming ceremonies to take place annually at a winter basketball game. Elected by the student body, homecoming queens have been Kay Murray (1976), Melissa Aston (1977), Patrice Sanders (1978), and Linda Hendricks (1979).

The Settler, the campus newspaper, serves as a laboratory for student journalists and as a medium of expression and information for the student body and campus community. The content of the paper includes current news, editorial views, sports, special features, ads, cartoons, faculty and administrative comments, and activities at Vol State. The following students have served as editor: Joni Steinhauer and Barry Witcher (1971-1972, co-editors); Phillip Worsham (1972-1973); Lynn Casey Marshall (1973-1974); Herbert Parker (1974-1975); Kay Murray (1975-1976); Sam Weakley (1976-1977); Terry Shart (1977-1978); and Floretta McDole (1978-1979). In 1978-1979, *The Settler* was awarded third place in national competition by the Columbia Scholastic Press Association at Columbia University, New York, in its 55th annual contest. Publication is supervised by the committee on student activities.

Pioneer Trails was established as the college yearbook in 1971. The purpose was to record the year's activities in a publication for students. Student editors of *Pioneer Trails* were, 1971-1972, Phillip Worsham and Rhonda Gilbert; 1973-1974, Patti Stanton; 1974-1975, Linda Connolly; and 1975-1976, Annette Ragland. Editors Stanton, Connolly, and Ragland were assisted in composition and format by Barbara Hager of the college staff. In 1972-1973, *Pioneer Trails* was published and edited by William M. Hillard, dean of students, and Dan Jewell, professor of English. In 1976-1977, the publication ceased due to a lack of student staff.

The year 1978-1979 saw a revival of student concern for a publication to chronicle the year's activities and student life. The student government association initiated a replacement publication called *Campus Scene*. Under the capable leadership of Co-editors Mike McReynolds and Penny Gentry, a magazine format with soft cover accurately captured and reflected the Vol State atmosphere and its students, faculty, administration, and staff.

In the first year of operation, 1971-1972, the college sponsored an intercollegiate men's basketball team under Coach Glenn Carson. All home games, except the final game, were played at Hendersonville High School and Union Elementary School in Gallatin. The final game of the season was played in February of 1972, in the T. Wesley Pickel Fieldhouse on campus, when dedication services for this permanent facility were conducted.

The following year, 1972-1973, intercollegiate baseball under Coach Tom Kirby and intercollegiate golf were added, and VSCC became a member of the National Junior College Athletic Association and the Tennessee Junior College Athletic Association. Richard

Moore was named head basketball coach and was selected as Co-Coach-of-the-Year for the TJCAA Western Division. Larry Knight of the men's basketball team was voted as the Co-Most-Valuable-Player for the Western Division of the TJCAA. The women's basketball team under Coach Patsy Jones was the first junior college team in the area and therefore played primarily junior varsity teams from four-year institutions.

The year of 1973-1974 marked the first use of the newly constructed baseball field and the first year of intercollegiate tennis. Larry Knight of the men's basketball team was selected to the all-division and all-conference teams. Dickie Moran of the golf team placed 28th in the nation at the NJCAA play-off in Fort Myers, Florida, and Bob Hardin of the baseball team was selected to the all-conference team.

The women's basketball team highlighted the 1974-1975 intercollegiate athletic scene. This team under Coach Patsy Jones won the Region VII championship, finished in the top four teams at the first national tournament for women's junior college basketball held at Overland Park, Kansas, and was ranked seventh in the nation in post-season polls. Kim Grizzle and Sandra Smallwood were named to the junior college All-American team. Ed Haddox of the men's basketball team was selected all-conference honorable mention, Bob Hardin of the baseball team was selected all-conference, and Steve Connor of the baseball team was selected as the number two draft choice of the San Diego Padres. Golf was discontinued as an intercollegiate sport. Tennis was under first-year Coach Alice Amonette.

The men's basketball team captured most of the honors in the 1975-1976 season. Clarence Mason, William Griffey, and Mike Patterson were selected to the all-western division honorable mention team. Clarence Mason was also selected to the all-region team and Mike Patterson to the all-region honorable mention team. Coach Richard Moore was again selected as Co-Coach-of-the-Year. Both the women's basketball team, under first-year Coach Larry Gay Reagan, and the tennis team participated in the Region VII tournaments.

The 1976-1977 season brought 25 victories for the baseball team and participation by the women's basketball team in the Region VII tournament. William Griffey (men's basketball) was selected all-conference honorable mention; Linda Perry (women's basketball) was selected to the all-division, all-conference, and all-tournament teams. Teresa Gammons (women's basketball) was selected to the all-division and all-conference teams; Richard Daniels (baseball) made the all-division, all-conference, and all-region teams; and Charlie Payne (baseball) was selected to the all-division team. Tennis was discontinued as an intercollegiate sport.

In 1977-1978, the men's basketball team was under first-year Coach Howard Jackson. The baseball team and the women's basketball team had a number of outstanding players who reaped numerous honors. Diane Cummings, Linda Perry, and Jere Sneed (women's basketball) made the all-division team, and Perry was also selected to the all-conference team; Jim Ethridge, Neal Toms, Greg Hammer, and Stan Ryan (baseball) were selected to the all-division team; Hammer was also selected to the all-conference team and was awarded a baseball grant to University of Tennessee-Knoxville; and Stan Ryan was also selected to the all-conference team and was voted the Most Valuable Player in the western division of the TJCAA.

The 1978-1979 basketball season was concluded with the men's team ranked in the top 10 in the nation on defense and the women's team earning a berth in the Region VII play-off. The 1978-1979 baseball team finished the 1979 season with a 21-19 record for second place in the western division of TJCAA and as a result competed in the Tennessee state play-offs. Steve Moffat, Jimmy Whitaker, and Gary Williams earned spots on the all-western division team, and Williams also was selected to the all-Region VII team, was chosen Most Valuable Player in Tennessee, and was signed to a baseball scholarship with Memphis State University. Baseball Coach Tom Kirby received Coach-of-the-Year honors in the western division of the TJCAA.

In the first year of operation, the college designated 12 noon to 1:00 p.m. on Tuesdays and Thursdays, when no classes were scheduled, to permit free time for intramural sports, committee meetings, and leisure time for the students and faculty. During these times, organized intramural competition in basketball, softball, flag football, archery, tennis, table tennis, horseshoe pitching, volleyball, chess, free-throw shooting, and a variety of other sports have been offered.

As a commuter college, Vol State found it necessary to experiment with a variety of time schedules and numerous offerings in

Aerial view of campus. *Photograph courtesy Volunteer State Community College.*

activities to generate student participation in intramural sports. This process of elimination brought the college back to the original scheduling pattern and resulted in a limited number of sports in which the students expressed an interest and willingness to participate, namely coeducational volleyball and softball and men's and women's basketball. These sports were each played in a round-robin tournament format and resulted in 324 participants in 1978-1979.

In July of 1975, Vol State College was notified by the American Revolution Bicentennial Administration that it had been designated a bicentennial campus. Work toward this designation had begun early in 1975 and the campus bicentennial committee, chaired by Tom Gray, had devised year-long, meaningful programs in three theme areas: Heritage '76, Festival—U.S.A., and Horizons '76.

Folk Festival U.S.A. was planned for total community involvement and was designed to demonstrate American ingenuity and know-how. Simple but almost extinct crafts and artistry were demonstrated and displayed for young and old. *Bicentennial Lectures* consisted of a series of six lectures offered by Vol State faculty beginning October of 1975 and ending May of 1976. Presented were the "The American Revolution and American Ideology," by John Bell; "Diplomacy and the American Revolution," by Robert M. Ruff; "Religion in the American Revolution," by Richard Herrmann; "Blacks in the American Revolution," by Patricia Lebkuecher; "Tennessee in the American Revolution," by Fred Moore; and "Art, Music, and Literature in the American Revolution," by Neil Wright. *Bicentennial Youth Debates* were coordinated by the Vol State bicentennial committee and District XXIX and were held on the American Issue Forums' monthly topics.

On November 5, 1975, the college planted and dedicated a purple leaf plum tree in front of the auditorium building in memory of those early Americans who put into action their hopes and dreams and who bequeathed to posterity a freedom heretofore unknown. With this ceremony, Walter Durham, a member of the Tennessee American Revolution Bicentennial Commission, awarded Vol State its bicentennial flag and certificate, which came as a result of the college's designation as a bicentennial campus. The event also marked the fifth anniversary of the college and a commitment for the future to the fundamental issues upon which our country was founded. Respondents who also assisted Durham in the tree planting were Professor Richard Herrmann, Joe Loftin of the SGA, and President Ramer.

Through the years, the college has greatly benefited from the experience and wise counsel of citizens and professional personnel of affiliate agencies who have served ably and gratuitously on technology and liaison committees. Likewise, to promote closer working relationships between the college and its total service area and to cultivate support from its various constituencies, the president established in 1977 the college advisory and development council. Charter members appointed were James Bailey, Melvin Briley, Dan Calgy, Noble Caudill, Barry Cecil, Bud Coley, Walter Durham, John Malone, E. G. Mattox, Don Pierce, William Puryear, Maxine Sadler, Mack Stabler, Jr., Johnny Wade, and Ellen Wemyss. This group of representative citizen-civic leaders continues to render valuable aid toward enabling the college to serve better its communities and the state.

Left to right: Dean N. E. Bradley; Dean R. Wade Powers; Dr. John Mallette, U. T. at Nashville; Reverend Alfred Bennett, Old Beech Cumberland Presbyterian Church; Chancellor Roy S. Nicks, graduation speaker; President Hal Ramer; and Dean Bill Hillard following commencement in June of 1977. *Photograph courtesy Volunteer State Community College.*

At its charter commencement on June 9, 1973, the first three graduates of the college, among a total of 57, were Pamela Judy Doss, associate of arts-general, cum laude; James Owen Alexander, associate of science-business and commerce; and Marsha Diane Gregory, certificate of proficiency-teacher aide technology. Special citations also were conferred upon J. H. Warf and T. Wesley Pickel at the commencement program, during which the respective campus buildings officially named in their honor were dedicated. In the seven commencements through June of 1979, the college has awarded a total of 1183 associate degrees and 115 certificates. The one-thousandth associate degree, a notable milestone, was received on June 9, 1979, by Anita Olivier Francis, cum laude; a framed citation was also presented to her in recognition of this significant event.

Distinguished speakers featured at each of the seven graduation programs were as follows: Cecil C. Humphreys, chancellor, State Board of Regents (1973); Wray Buchanan, vice-chancellor, State Board of Regents (1974); Walter Durham, Gallatin businessman and historian (1975); Johnella Martin, educator and member of the State Board of Regents (1976); Roy S. Nicks, chancellor, State Board of Regents (1977); Jim Sasser, United States senator (1978); and Steve Cobb, Fulbright scholar and representative in the Tennessee General Assembly (1979).

Throughout its brief history, the college has enjoyed excellent support and encouragement from its various constituencies—the public, the State Legislature, the state administration, governing boards (the State Board of Education, and, since July 1, 1972, the State Board of Regents) and their officers and staffs, affiliated institutions, accrediting and coordinating agencies, the print and broadcast media, and, infinitely, from campus personnel.

That which forms the honored and salient past is to be cherished, recalled, and built upon. Volunteer State Community College embraces the future with enthusiasm. It is unalterably committed to and delivers its programs and services under the concepts, "education as if people matter," and "it's never too late to go to college!" In essence, that is the community college philosophy as it has emerged in the uniquely American experience of higher learning. Its endorsement by the state and citizens of the nation is resounding.

8

ROANE STATE COMMUNITY COLLEGE
by Cuyler A. Dunbar

The creation of Roane State Community College came early in 1969. In July Commissioner J. Howard Warf and other State Department of Education officials visited proposed sites for the college to be located in Roane County. After studies were made, a central location on Patton Lane was chosen as the site of the institution, which was to serve a 15-county area.

Dr. Cuyler A. Dunbar, then dean of students at Columbia State, was selected the first president in May of 1970. In the late summer, temporary offices were opened on Ruritan Road in South Harriman, while final architectural plans for the construction of a permanent facility were being drawn up. Bids were opened in August of 1970, and the low bid was approximately $700,000 higher than funds appropriated for the construction. Subsequently, a decision was made by State Department of Education officials and college administrative personnel to hold classes in temporary quarters during the fall of 1971. Bidding for the construction project was opened again in June of 1971 and a satisfactory bid—one within the amount of funds available—was finally received. Construction was initiated in July of 1971, but serious problems in the foundation were encountered; change orders were executed in the contract thus allowing for additional concrete supporting caissons to be poured under the building.

The second employee at the college was Fay Ray, Dr. Dunbar's secretary. The two were soon joined by Dr. Ronald McFaddin, dean of instruction; Dr. Donald S. Van Fleet, dean of student personnel services; and Paul Ellis, business manager. During the summer of

1970, a team of doctoral students from Auburn University's junior college leadership program assisted in the organizational and educational development of the new college. The team included two early employees of the college: Dr. Harold L. Underwood, division chairman of math and sciences (who became dean of instruction in 1972), and Carroll Marsalis, division chairman of technology (who became associate dean of career and continuing education in 1976). Also employed during the first year were these faculty members and administrators: Louise R. Greene, director of admissions and records; Dr. Anne Minter, instructor in the math-science division (now chairperson of this division); Dr. Nancy Fisher, chairperson of the humanities division; Jim Kring, instructor in biology; William Murray, instructor in math-science; Linda Simmons, instructor in history; G. A. Swanson, instructor in business; Ruth Richardson, instructor in secretarial science; Curtis Whalen, director of public relations; Dr. C. P. Keim, director of community and field services; Mildred Dillon, guidance counselor; Dr. Robert Jennings, instructor in electronics; and Phil Allen, instructor in physical education. In a 1971 statement to the press, Dr. Dunbar commented on the college's having attracted such a high caliber of personnel: "The opportunity to participate in the founding of a new college and the charting of its course has certain appeal to many educators." It is interesting to note that 11 of the original 19 members of the faculty and staff of RSCC have remained at the college during its eight-year history. The Southern Association of Colleges and Schools established correspondent status for Roane State in December of 1970.

Roane State admitted its first students and offered its first classes in September of 1971. The facilities were temporary and included an elementary school building with seven classrooms, a small cafeteria and kitchen area (used for the library, the bookstore, and science labs), and one office; two house trailers used for several offices; a small house for faculty offices; rented space from the training and technologies program at Oak Ridge; and various other locations in the Harriman area.

Most of the courses offered during the first year of operation were freshman-level courses in the associate of arts and associate of science transfer programs and the associate of science technology programs. Transfer programs offered at this time included those in art, art education, business and commerce, business education,

President Cuyler A. Dunbar. *Photograph courtesy Roane State Community College.*

Dr. Delorise Barnes conducts a class of shorthand students. *Photograph courtesy Roane State Community College.*

elementary education, health, physical education and recreation, mathematics, physical science, music, music education, predentistry, prelaw, premedical technology, premedicine, prepharmacy, and secondary education. The first career education programs offered were business occupations technology (general clerical and secretarial science), computer science technology, electronics technology, and general business administration. More than 35 credit courses were offered for the fall quarter of 1971. Non-credit community services courses also were offered in such areas as general education development (GED) preparation, guitar, art, bridge, and blueprint reading.

The college's open-door admissions and administrative policies, its low fees, and its aggressive scholarship and financial aid programs, along with a variety of academic programs, attracted students from Roane and surrounding counties. The students were both traditional and non-traditional—exemplary clientele of a new community college. Three hundred twenty-three students enrolled in credit classes during the fall quarter. In addition to classes meeting in the college's temporary facilities in Harriman, others were offered during the 1971-1972 academic year at Oak Ridge and at Brushy Mountain State Prison in Petros. Courses offered at Brushy Mountain were unique because they were for inmates. The Tennessee Jaycees were responsible for paying the inmates' registration fees for business administration and psychology classes offered at the prison.

The number of people working at the college had grown to 23 full-time faculty members and administrative officers and 17 other full-time employees. Twenty-six part-time faculty members and seven other part-time and temporary employees were also on the payroll. The high caliber of faculty members associated with RSCC was evident from their educational backgrounds: eight of the 23 full-time faculty held doctoral degrees; 13 had master's degrees. Roane State first participated in the governor's summer youth program in the summer of 1971. Activities were held in nine area centers, and the program reached more than 1000 young people during its first year. Offering supervised recreation for all school-age young persons, it operated for the eighth time during the summer of 1978.

Roane State grew rapidly during its second year of operation. Non-credit activity, measured by the average number of instructional hours per quarter, rose from 1433 during 1971-1972 to 2010 during 1972-1973, an increase of 40 percent. At the same time, the credit program, measured by full-time equated (FTE) students, also experienced considerable growth. The average FTE student enrollment per quarter rose from 251.3 during 1971-1972 to 444 during 1972-1973, an increase of 77 percent. Enrollment in credit classes for the fall quarter of 1972 jumped a full 146 percent over that of the college's initial fall quarter.

During 1972-1973, RSCC continued to hold the bulk of its classes in the Fairmont building, the former elementary school which it had leased as a temporary facility. However, due to rapid growth in student enrollment, a need for more facilities was obvious. The community responded to the college's plight, and new class locations were developed at such dissimilar sites as South Harriman Baptist Church, Margrave Elementary School, Tri-City Lanes, Suzanne's School of Ballet, Emory Heights Elementary School, and Harriman High School. The move toward a healthy mixture of both on- and off-campus classes was well-rooted in the college's beginning.

Roane State's rapid growth and attendant space problems, as well as its need for expanded labs, library, student services, faculty and administrative offices, and community services, directed everyone's attention to the time when RSCC could move into its new facility. Originally it was hoped that the move to the permanent facility on Patton Lane could occur during early 1973, but that was not to be the case. Continual construction problems—the most serious of which was the need to reinforce the foundation with extra 15- to 90-foot deep concrete caissons and a "floating" concrete base under a part of the building—caused delay after delay and meant that the new facility could not be completed during the 1972-1973 academic year.

Off campus, Roane State continued expanding its offerings in the Oak Ridge area; under the Intergovernmental Cooperation Act of 1968, it made use of Union Carbide's Y-12 facility and also utilized several of the local fire halls. Because of its success here, plans were made to increase programming in Oak Ridge and several other counties adjacent to Roane during the following year. Expanding to meet the needs of students, business, industry, and community, Roane State added several new programs for 1972-1973, including associate degree programs in accounting technology, fire science technology, hotel-motel-restaurant management, management and supervision technology, and technology transfer. One-year certificates in electronics technology and in general clerical also were to be awarded.

"Firsts" recorded during 1972-1973 included Roane State's beginning a two-year ROTC program and intercollegiate men's basketball, baseball, and golf programs. Two other important events in RSCC's short history also occurred during 1973: The process which leads from candidate status for accreditation to full accreditation was begun, and during June commencement exercises, Roane State's first graduating class, 39 students, received degrees.

RSCC's community services and credit programs continued to grow during the college's third year of existence. In community services the average number of instructional hours per quarter rose 23 percent; in credit programs, the growth was even greater, with the average FTE student enrollment rising 77 percent. RSCC continued to expand its offerings during 1973-1974, adding degree programs in dietetic technology, medical records, and recreation management.

During the fall quarter of 1973, RSCC moved into its new facility. However, college growth forced the development of other new locations for classes—especially in areas outside of Roane County. The college began offering classes in such diverse locations as First United Methodist Church in Oak Ridge, Oak Ridge Police Lodge, Oak Ridge Hospital, Ozone, Lenoir City High School, and Central High School in Wartburg. The expansion of off-campus classes allowed RSCC to begin effectively serving five counties in its service area.

In sports, intercollegiate tennis and women's basketball joined men's basketball, golf, and baseball in 1973-1974. Roane State also graduated its first prepharmacy student, Angela Cross, who was immediately accepted at the University of Tennessee Medical Unit; Jerry Lemons became the first student to have his work published in the *College Poetry Review;* and Joy Liggett (who joined the RSCC faculty in 1978) became Roane State's first student to receive an upper division scholarship from the college entrance examination board.

Two words best characterize the evolution of Roane State Community College in academic years 1974-1975 and 1975-1976—*student explosion.* The dramatic and challenging 60 percent growth in credit head count during 1974-1975 was followed by a 62 percent boom the following year. Every employee of the college and many members of its community were simultaneously pleased and wary of the effects of such enrollment increases. Perhaps the biggest challenge facing the administration of the college during those two years was how to maintain the quality of programs on fewer dollars per pupil.

Certainly 1974 through 1976 were years in which Roane State was beginning to realize the vast potential for educational service that had not been anticipated in earlier growth projections. The college had been expected to rank among the lower three community colleges in terms of student numbers when compared to many of the state's more urban campuses. However, by the end of the 1975-1976 academic year, it was evident that demands for community college programs in the RSCC service area would far exceed expectations. The fall quarter of 1975 credit head count was 2394 and was showing every sign of continuing to increase in subsequent years.

Other kinds of growth were also taking place in 1974-1975. The college received from the state its first million dollar appropriation—an increase not nearly as proportionately large as the number of students. Full-time faculty and administrators increased from 60 in 1973-1974 to 68 in 1974-1975. As with many colleges facing enrollment growth, the employment of greater numbers of part-time faculty may have been a saving grace. Roane State was fortunate to be able to call on many highly skilled and well-qualified citizens in the community to teach the burgeoning numbers of students. This was especially true of rapidly emerging programs in the technically-oriented career education division which, by the end of the 1975-1976 year, enrolled about one-half of the college's students. Several part-time faculty members were regularly employed at the Oak Ridge facilities of the Union Carbide Corporation and at what was then the Energy Research and Development Administration (ERDA, now the Department of Energy). These and other part-time instructors played a significant role in meeting the challenges of dynamic student body growth without necessitating a proportionate growth in revenues. Another interesting characteristic of the faculty and administration was its youth. Eighty-four percent of all full-time faculty and administrators were under the age of 40—representing yet another challenge to youthful President Cuyler Dunbar and Dean of Instruction Harold Underwood.

In 1974-1975, curricula at the college expanded to include a certificate program in police science and criminology, which later was to become an associate degree program. Also added were engineering technologies programs, including chemical, civil, electrical, and nuclear options. Previously existing divisions expanded their offerings to meet the needs and demands of students. Perhaps the most significant addition to the curriculum was developmental studies. Courses in this division were established because many students were coming to the college with insufficient backgrounds in basic areas such as math, reading, and writing. Developmental studies courses have helped prepare many students for the rigors of college-level work.

A continuing problem, the need for space became critical in 1974-1975. The career education division enrolled about 50 percent of the student body, but the campus facility only afforded it about 13 percent of the available space. Efforts to construct the technologies building, which was planned to house this division, continued, and during the 1975-1976 school year the building project was approved and funded.

Other expansions during 1974-1975 were evident in the college's library and computer center. Library holdings were increased by 52 percent, causing the beginning of crowded conditions in that facility.

A computer was installed which opened the way for new services in academic and administrative computing. Faculty in-service training that year concentrated on possible uses of the computer for computer-assisted instruction and computer-managed instruction. So popular did the use of the computer become that by the end of the first year, the faculty had begun to use it in classes such as chemistry, history, developmental studies, English, biology, education, mathematics and reading. In December of 1974, the Southern Association of Colleges and School's Commission on Colleges recognized excellence at Roane State by granting it full accreditation. Roane State thus entered a new phase in its development as an accredited institution of higher learning.

Community services under Dr. Paul Goldberg also became a rapidly expanding area. The enrollment in non-credit offerings grew 64.3 percent in 1974-1975. Classes were offered for the first time in neighboring Loudon County. The office of community services was successful in getting three projects funded by external sources, including Title I of the Higher Education Act of 1965 and the Tennessee Committee for the Humanities.

An aggressive program to enroll veterans was begun, and during the first year the program more than doubled the previous veteran population of students. More space was needed for the veterans program office, for student couseling and testing, and for expansion of the school's general education development (GED) program for persons desiring a high school equivalency certificate.

Among several faculty honors, which included a growing list of publications, was an outstanding achievement by Dr. Anne Minter, chairperson of the math-science division. She was selected by the Manufacturing Chemists Association to receive the Southern Regional Award for 1975. In recognition of her total contribution to chemical education, Dr. Minter, one of four recipients, was presented a citation, a medal, and an honorarium during the 1975 RSCC graduation exercises.

The college's tennis team also brought recognition to the school for an outstanding season. In 1974-1975, the Raider squad compiled a 15-1 record, the best record in the conference and in the state. They won second place in the TJCAA Tournament, third place in Region VII competition, and went to the national tournament.

During the academic year 1975-1976, growth in the number of

off-campus offerings continued, and, on campus, plans proceeded for building additional facilities. One group of building plans, referred to as Campus Expansion Phase II, was coming off the architectural drawing boards and included a new library learning resources center, a maintenance and storage facility, and a central heating plant. Phase II also called for some long-needed renovations. Book acquisitions for the expanding curricula had outgrown the capacity of the present library, and student study and reading space was becoming more and more crowded as enrollment increased. Warehouse facilities for the building and grounds department also were filled.

Off-campus expansion in 1975-1976 saw classes being taught at sites such as Oak Ridge, Rhea County, Jacksboro, West Knoxville, Wartburg, and three belonging to the Tennessee Valley Authority. The college indeed had begun to take its progams to the people—a trend that would increase in subsequent years. There was a growing institutional commitment to all its service area, which includes 15, many rurally isolated, counties.

During 1974-1976, Roane State's impact on the local area was felt more and more. One hundred four students graduated in the spring of 1975; many of them went into skilled jobs in the area, while others went on to pursue four-year programs at nearby universities. The college payroll continued to increase and contributed greatly to softening the blow of the 1974 recession in the Roane County area. The college was opening its doors to the community and slowly was becoming a cultural center for the area. Many concerts were held at the college in 1975-1976, such as ones by the Roane Choral Society, the Knoxville Symphony, the Duke Ellington Orchestra, the Amazing Rhythm Aces, and Chet Atkins. More evidence of community support can be seen from the tremendous jump in participation in community service programming—up 122 percent based on student in-class hours. Roane State was beginning, by the end of 1976, to fulfill its role as a cultural and educational leader for its multi-county area.

Staff achievements that year included recognition of Financial Aid Director Curtis Whalen as Outstanding Financial Aid Administrator in Tennessee for 1975-1976 and of Yoonchung Kim, art instructor, whose works were included in the Tennessee Bicentennial Exhibition. An administrative services component was added to the organizational chart, and Dr. Fred H. Martin, then RSCC's director of institutional research, was named its dean. The division consolidated many of the academic support and administrative service functions in the college and accepted responsibility for planning future growth. During the period of 1974-1976, Roane State had learned that its future could be as challenging and unpredictable as its past.

In its sixth year of operation, Roane State experienced continued growth in both on- and off-campus enrollment in academic programs, physical facilities, and a variety of other areas. A six percent increase in enrollment during the fall quarter of 1976 brought more than 3000 students into contact with the credit and non-credit programs at RSCC; the total head count for the fall reached 3133 students, including 2537 who enrolled in credit courses and 576 students who enrolled in non-credit courses and workshops. More than one-fifth of these students were served off-campus, reflecting the college's commitment and efforts to meet community needs.

During the previous summer (1976), an agreement to lease space for classes was reached with the First United Methodist Church of Oak Ridge. The additional space made it possible to expand the number of class offerings and to increase the variety of courses offered at this location. During the fall of 1976, more than 30 different classes, some with several sections, were taught at the church during the day and evening, bringing the total number of classes taught to 47. Approximately 350 students were enrolled for at least one class at the church during the fall.

A variety of non-credit classes, from "slimnastics" to cake decorating to backpacking, were offered throughout the year. In addition, special workshops were also conducted: in-service training workshops for Roane County teachers, working with the elderly workshops, assertion training workshops, and job hunting seminars.

Four new academic programs were approved during the year, and Roane State received approval for a degree program in coal mining technology. The first of its kind in the state, the program was designed to provide students with proper educational and technical training for securing and maintaining managerial positions within the coal mining industry. Approval of two new options in early childhood education and in special education gave RSCC students eight majors from which to choose within the education division. An associate degree program in radiologic technology also was approved, and classes were offered for the first time during the fall quarter at the Cumberland Medical Center in Crossville.

Rapid growth in enrollment and subsequent growth in programs for meeting student needs and demands necessitated growth in the college's physical facilities. The first phase of expansion at RSCC came in January of 1977 with the groundbreaking for the technologies building, which was to house the career education division. Architectural plans for the 40,000 square foot facility included 13 laboratories, five general classrooms, two demonstration areas, and space for 37 offices, making it one of the most highly technical and unique facilities on any community college campus. Specialized study areas with typewriters, computer terminals, calculators, and other equipment also were included in the new facility so that students could prepare homework assignments without tying up classroom space. The $1.9 million project also called for built-in equipment, an organic chemistry lab renovation section, and a parking lot.

From its beginning, Roane State has assumed a unique position in energy technologies because of its location near Oak Ridge and its proximity to most of the Tennessee Valley Authority power-generating activities. The college has been called upon by the Energy Research and Development Administration, Union Carbide Nuclear Division, and TVA to develop and implement many non-traditional programs relating to the scientific field. In the fall of 1976, Roane State was one of four schools in the nation selected to coordinate a nuclear technology workshop for a national conference on energy technology training in Atlanta. Conference sponsors, ERDA and the American Association of Community and Junior Colleges, chose Roane State for the project. Their selection was indicative of the college's important role in the development and implementation of energy-related technology programs. In addition to the nuclear workshop which RSCC coordinated, seminars covering technology training in coal mining, petroleum, and solar energy were also conducted during the three-day conference.

This year was one in which there were several "firsts" for RSCC students. They were enfranchised by the Miss Tennessee Pageant Organization to conduct a local Miss America preliminary pageant. In the first official pageant held at the college, Donna Crass of Harriman was crowned Miss Roane State of 1977 and represented RSCC

Bryan Eubank demonstrates operation of a terminal during a computer programming seminar conducted for high school juniors in the
summer of 1976. *Left to right, standing:* Wesley S. Corley, Dagny Vigan-
der, and Bill Collier. *Photograph courtesy Roane State Community College.*

in the Miss Tennessee Pageant that June. For the first time, a Roane
State team was ranked in the National Junior College Athletic Association. The Raiderettes finished their basketball season with a
23-3 record and were ranked fifth in the nation among junior college teams. Randy Schubert, a member of the Raider tennis squad,
brought special recognition to the RSCC athletic programs when he
won the singles division tennis crown for both the TJCAA and Region VII of the NJCAA and went on to play in the national tournament.

During the summer of 1976, two activities were added to programs available for youth in the RSCC service area. The first annual
girls' basketball camp brought more than 90 girls in grades 7
through 12 to the campus to study fundamentals of basketball and to
participate in special game and league play. Twenty high school
juniors participated in the college's first computer programming
seminar, receiving an introduction to the basics of computer programming and to the many and varied uses of the computer. Both
programs have continued, and their enrollments have increased.

At the end of the 1976-1977 academic year, diplomas were
awarded to 150 students who completed associate degree require-

ments. Thirty RSCC students named earlier in the year to Who's Who Among Students in American Junior Colleges for 1976-1977 also were recognized during the commencement ceremony.

The college's seventh year of operation saw a credit head count of 2807 students for the fall quarter of 1977, an 11 percent increase over the fall of 1976. Approximately 760 students were enrolled in non-credit courses and workshops during the quarter. This brought the total to more than 3600 students served by both credit and non-credit activities during the fall.

Plans were being made for additional expansion. In June of 1977, an agreement between the Oak Ridge Hospital of the Methodist Church and Roane State was reached whereby the college would lease a portion of the hospital's former nursing home for use as a classroom facility. After approval by the governing boards of both institutions and renovation of the nursing home building, the college was able to move from the space leased from the First United Methodist Church to its new facility. In the larger building, RSCC was able to offer a greater range of academic programs, more courses (both day and evening), and a wider variety of courses to serve students in the Oak Ridge area more effectively. In addition to classrooms and laboratories, the facility, known as Roane State-Oak Ridge, had space for a student lounge and faculty and administrative offices. Space also was available so that representatives from various main-campus offices, such as financial aid, veterans' affairs, counseling, and cooperative education and placement, could be accessible on a rotating basis in Oak Ridge.

In addition to the expansion which the new building made possible in Oak Ridge for the fall quarter of 1977, Roane State classes were also offered for the first time in Fentress County. During the following spring quarter (1978), Roane State offered classes in Scott County for the first time, bringing to eight the total number of counties in which the college was offering off-campus classes. Plans also were made to add Blount County and Clinton to the growing list beginning in the fall of 1978.

In addition to non-credit classes offered during the year, a variety of activities were offered in cooperation with various community groups and agencies. Among them were a basketball coaching clinic and workshops on cardiopulmonary resuscitation, houseplants, women's assertiveness training, law and women, holiday crime, teenage pregnancy, employment security, and one for the elderly entitled "Rebirth of Worth." These special workshops are indicative of RSCC's continuing efforts to work with representatives of educational, governmental, industrial, and business organizations to plan special activities which are of benefit to their organization and the community.

New academic programs in mini-microcomputer service technology, respiratory therapy technology, and medical laboratory technology were approved for implementation in 1978-1979. RSCC's new mini-microcomputer program, the third of its kind in the country and the first for the Southeast United States, is intended to provide students with training to secure stable and economically substantial positions as computer service technicians in this highly technical industry. Respiratory therapy and medical laboratory programs will join medical records technology, radiologic technology, and dietetic technology programs as options available to students interested in the allied health field.

The groundbreaking ceremony for the college's Campus Expansion Phase II project was held in June of 1978. Included in this second building project are plans for the library-learning resources center to house the college's library, media center, and laboratories for developmental studies and reading and for provision of rooms for conferences and testing, as well as several areas with connections for television monitors and computer terminals. Also included in the project plans are a new maintenance building-central heating plant, which will make the college's conversion to a coal-based operation possible.

During 1977-1978, Roane State undertook an institutional self study, a step toward acquiring reaffirmation of accreditation by the Southern Association of Colleges and Schools. Members of the faculty, staff, administration, and student body, as well as community members, participated in a wide variety of activities involved in the self study which, when completed, would be followed during the fall of 1978 by a visit from a Southern Association committee.

The college faculty increased in 1977 in an effort to keep pace with tremendous growth in other areas at the college. Of the 131 instructors at the college that year, 64 were employed full-time and 67 part-time. Twenty-three, or 18 percent, had doctoral degrees, while 92, or 70 percent, had master's degrees. Three administrative positions were created and filled: an associate dean of career and continuing education to supervise the college's career education programs and to administer the college's off-campus operations; a coordinator of off-campus instruction to supervise daily operations of the off-campus program; and an administrator for Roane State-Oak Ridge to supervise all college operations in Oak Ridge. All three were also to serve as a liaison between various communities and the college in the development of educational services and programs.

In November the college received national recognition for its computer services when it was selected one of 106 outstanding examples of educational institutions throughout the United States to use computers for teaching and learning effectively. The institutions, including elementary and secondary schools, community colleges, four-year colleges, and universities, were recommended resources for other educational institutions seeking advice and guidance on academic computing. Roane State was recognized for excellence in three areas: computer science or data processing curricula; spectrum of application; and outreach. This project, which was sponsored by the National Science Foundation, was conducted by the Human Resource Research Organization.

Since beginning its operation in June of 1977, the college's community child center has played an important role in the community and at the college. In addition to providing a stimulating educational environment for the 30 children enrolled there, the center has provided a supplement to classroom instruction for early childhood and special education majors. Two courses in which a local newspaper served as the "textbook" for the class were offered as were, during the fall, a police science class via *The Oak Ridger* and, in the spring, "Popular Culture: Mirror of American Life"—a social science elective through *The Oak Ridger* and *The Roane County News*.

The seminar has always been an adaptable instructional tool at Roane State, but one of the college's most unique seminars, initiated in the summer of 1977, has been the social science division's annual field trip to the American Southwest. This two-week field trip has proven successful because of its combination of academic work and learning experiences in several of the social science areas.

The Roane State Players' winter production of *Barefoot in the Park* was the first dinner theatre performance for Roane County; a general performance was also presented. Due to the success of this initial

Ralph Nader addresses largest audience for an academic event in the school's history. *Photograph courtesy Roane State Community College.*

dinner theatre, a spring production of *A Funny Thing Happened On The Way To The Forum* was presented in both dinner theatre and general performance.

Consumer advocate Ralph Nader became the first nationally known speaker to visit Roane State. In April, during a special afternoon session, he participated in a social science seminar, "Consumer Protection and Business Structure," and then gave a special public lecture on "Corporate Responsibility and Consumer Protection" during a night session. More than 1500 people attended the evening lecture, which probably attracted the largest audience for an academic-related event in the school's history. In addition to Nader, a special series of speakers visited the campus for Winter Thaw-Out, which was organized around a theme of energy and the environment.

The athletic department also saw a couple of "firsts" during the year. The first college basketball tournament held at RSCC was on Thanksgiving weekend. The Raiderettes were hosts for City and County Bank's "Superstar Classic," which featured four teams ranked among the top ten squads in the country during the previous year. Plans also were announced for the incorporation of a women's tennis team into the athletic programs already available at the college. The Raider tennis team had another "first" when Randy

Schubert again won the TJCAA and Region VII number-one singles championships—the first time in the history of the conference and the region that a player had won back-to-back number-one singles titles.

During commencement exercises in June of 1978, the associate degree was awarded to 182 students, the college's largest graduating class. Forty-two of these graduates were recognized as being among the country's most outstanding campus leaders for their inclusion in Who's Who.

The eighth year of college operation was characterized by continued growth in enrollment, academic programs, physical facilities, and funding. Fall of 1978 saw student enrollment grow to 3223 credit head count and 1751 FTE; a milestone was marked as more females than males enrolled for the first time. The increasing emphasis on off-campus instructional delivery was evident in that 39 percent of the student credit hours were generated away from the main campus in the 11 counties served by RSCC. The credit and non-credit offerings taken together served more than 4000 students during the fall quarter. Faculty size grew proportionally to 148 members.

RSCC's efforts, particularly in Oak Ridge, continued to grow; almost 1100 students enrolled for classes during the fall of 1978, necessitating additional renovations in the leased facility. Meanwhile a team of consultants hired by the Tennessee Higher Education Commission studied the need for a permanent branch campus facility for Roane State in Oak Ridge.

A key event of the year was the reaccreditation visit by a SACS committee in October. The four-day visit was a critical part of the college's continued commitment to quality education and culminated the previous year's five-year self-study process. Several new academic programs reflected the college's increasing involvement in the allied health career field. A dietetics technology program was implemented as were newly approved programs in respiratory therapy, medical lab technology, and mini-microcomputer technology.

The first comprehensive institutional five-year plan was completed to guide the institution toward the future, with a combined college-community committee responsible for its development. Areas covered included academic programs, staffing, affirmative ac-

View of campus buildings. *Photograph courtesy Roane State Community College.*

tion, physical facilities, computer services, library-audiovisual services, and budget.

RSCC's three-story technologies building was occupied in December, housing the college's expanding career education programs and personnel. Progress also was made on the $3.4 million Campus Expansion Phase II project with plans for partial conversion from dependence on gas and oil to coal for heating to take place by year's end. Completion of Campus Expansion Phase II would alleviate Roane State's serious needs for library and maintenance space, greatly improving college services to both students and the community.

The second annual two-week interdisciplinary field trip to the American Southwest was a highlight of summer activities, and three plays were presented by the Roane State Players—*Mousetrap, The Fantasticks,* and *Harvey.* A small singing and dancing troupe, the Roane State Cabaret, was formed for entertaining on special occasions. In October a noted art department faculty member, Anne Powers Bouldin, held a one-person show in Knoxville. In February RSCC served as host for the Tennessee Intercollegiate Forensics Tournament; Ron Howell, the first tournament president elected from a community college, was an RSCC faculty member. Another faculty honor came when Kathy Jones, a member of the education division, was elected southeastern representative to the NEA Higher Education Council. Scott Pugh, a sophomore student from Rockwood, was appointed to serve as a student member of a State Board of Regents committee.

A new athletic program, women's tennis, was initiated in addition to the five programs already ongoing. The women's basketball team won their second annual superstar classic in November, while the men's basketball team was host to and finished third in their first Christmas tournament. RSCC also was host for the NJCAA Region VII women's basketball tournament in February and March.

Academic programming for the future will continue to revolve around service area demands of the continually shifting job market. Areas of major concern with respect to academic program plans include the following:

1. Based on the lead provided by the Department of Energy's Oak Ridge facilities, it is anticipated that a considerable amount of re-training and upgrading will be needed as alternate sources of energy are researched and implemented. The implementation of such programs will require the delivery of more classes to federal property sites. Consequently, more cooperative arrangements (such as the ones provided for in the Inter-Governmental Act) with federal agencies and government contractors will be demanded. Efforts along these lines have already taken place as personnel at Roane State have met with officials at Oak Ridge Associated Universities for the purpose of beginning such programs.

2. Roane State will be asked to provide educational-training components for several new public service programs in the region, including those of law enforcement agencies, fire departments, banks, and recreation. Many of these programs will stem from Roane State-TVA efforts in the past and from TVA's charge to become a model laboratory for social, economic, and environmental change in the nation.

3. Roane State will become the center for coal mine training programs in Tennessee, the thrust of which will involve training of associate degree students in coal mining as well as the upgrading of workers already in the field. The Roane State coal mining program will involve the training of several hundred people in both surface and deep mining operations. The Roane State mining ef-

fort will involve cooperative arrangements with the Tennessee Valley Authority, U.S. Soil Conservation Agency, Department of Energy, U.S. Mining and Safety Administration, U.S. Department of the Interior, Tennessee Department of Labor, and the Tennessee Conservation Department.

4. An increased emphasis will be placed on allied health programs. Along with allied health programs already approved, new curricula will be proposed for development and implementation. The thrust of these programs will be toward the delivery of health services to the rural areas of the college's service area.

5. Roane State will become more heavily involved in educational programs at the prisons in the region. Based on activities already begun at Brushy Mountain State Prison, Roane State will offer comprehensive educational programs for staff and inmates there and at the new regional facilities in Morgan and Bledsoe counties when completed. These efforts will involve cooperative arrangements with local prison officials and the Tennessee Department of Corrections.

The college's five-year plan projects new programs in banking and insurance, corrections, and nursing during 1979-1980, with others to follow as demands surface. Another section of the plan deals with campus development. At the completion of Campus Expansion Phase II, RSCC will have buildings possessing most of the square footage needed for future growth. Deficiencies will still exist in functional space, however, in, for example, art, music, physical education, offices, and parking. A humanities building-auditorium (possibly expanded into a jointly funded community arts center) is tentatively projected for completion by 1982, with a possibility of a technologies building addition by 1984. A permanent building for Roane State in Oak Ridge continues to be a possibility, with current projections set for occupancy by 1982.

A significant event scheduled for 1979 is the hoped for reaccreditation by SACS in December for a 10-year period. Individual program accreditation in career programs also will be sought, in addition to the specialized accreditation already received in medical records and radiologic technology.

Many opportunities and challenges are available to and will confront Roane State Community College in coming years. The institution is at a crossroad in its history in that, with the initial development stage behind it, the second phase of service and growth lies ahead. The challenges and opportunities of the community it serves cannot be divorced from those of the institution itself.

9

SHELBY STATE
COMMUNITY COLLEGE
by Jess H. Parrish
and Donald M. Mikula

While Shelby State did not begin to serve students until September of 1972, the institution in a real sense is a child of the 1960s. Indeed, the earliest beginnings of the college would have to be considered the mid-1960s when the community college program of Tennessee was planned. Initial action specific to Shelby State began in June of 1969 when J. Howard Warf, state education commissioner, announced that three new colleges would be established in the state, one of these in Shelby County.

Shelby State also is a child of controversy. The decade of the 1960s was one of national controversy: the Vietnam War was at its peak, student activism and student protests were taking place across the nation, and practically every college and university experienced backlash from these protests. Much of higher education was falling from grace. At the same time, there was what appeared to be a public contradiction—while higher education was being criticized generally, the times also were ripe for establishing community colleges. At one juncture, it was said that community colleges were opening nationwide at the rate of one per week. Such schools were comprehensive in nature, and the urban trend was toward the multi-campus, comprehensive community college.

Shelby State was originally planned as the only comprehensive, multi-campus community college in Tennessee. But from its beginning, a lack of understanding was evident among various groups and individuals as to the value and purpose of the proposed school. There was scant understanding not only of the direction the institution should take, but also a lack of understanding of the basic need for a community college in Memphis and Shelby County. One often heard the question, "Why another college?" Other schools—a university of some 20,000 students, a thriving state technical institute, and numerous vocational institutions—had already made their mark on the community. Thus the challenge of educating area citizens as to the nature of a truly comprehensive, multi-campus community college loomed large on the horizon of the 1970s, and this challenge has greatly affected the building and destiny of the college.

The most crucial task in educating the public as to the correct role and scope of a community college surfaced in the selection of building sites. During this process many mistakes were made—mistakes not so much in philosophical perspective but in terms of a language which seemed to be popular among certain leaders in the state. Perhaps the greatest mistake, as far as terminology was concerned, was that some officials were quoted in the media as saying that there would be a "main" college campus along with several "satellite" locations. The concept of satellite operations frightened some people, whereas others felt that such locations would function as something less than the so-called main body of the campus. This unfortunate terminology has retarded the growth of the college and set back the construction of more than one campus for Shelby State, perhaps for as many as 10 or more years.

With the naming of President Jess H. Parrish in the early summer of 1970, efforts were made to publicize correct versions of both the concept and philosophy of a multi-campus institution, one school with equally important campuses placed in strategic parts of the city and the county. Shelby State was conceived and originally designed to serve all of Memphis and Shelby County by way of a unique system of educational delivery, one based on the idea of several state-owned facilities but with many educational opportunities being made available to students through the facilities of churches, community centers, business establishments, and governmental agencies. While this educational philosophy was espoused by college officials, it was complicated by a growing controversy among lay people and local elected officials over the campus sites to be selected.

The usual requirement of 100 acres of land and $250,000 of local participation contributed much to the controversy. Unfortu-

President Jess H. Parrish. *Photograph courtesy Shelby State Community College.*

nately the original legislation which made community colleges possible in Tennessee did not lend itself particularly to the development of a multi-campus institution. Moreover, it became increasingly obvious to many persons in Memphis that a 100-acre site would be impossible in the mid-city area, yet the mid-city area certainly needed the benefits of a community college. Thus an essential factor in the controversy which grew out of the late 1960s and flowered in the early 1970s had to do with the fact that only one site—the one on which an east campus was planned—was large enough to house certain kinds of facilities. This meant that a larger share of state dollars would be allocated to that location. Of five million dollars, a slightly larger portion would have been budgeted to build the suburban campus.

The philosophy behind the development of a somewhat larger east campus was that certain kinds of operations, those not affecting any educational programs, could be placed where there was adequate space. These operations included a central admissions office, certain kinds of administrative spaces, and perhaps maintenance facilities. At the time, Shelby State had a firm commitment for only 2.6 acres in the mid-town location. That commitment later grew to 17 acres, but only after the college was well into its operational stages.

While the controversies and infighting over need and site selection were underway, various proposed solutions to the problem were humorous. It was suggested, for example, that the college ought to build on Mud Island or that air space over an interstate highway could be utilized. While many ideas were not out of the question, some did not need to be considered because there was in fact adequate space to construct both an inner-city campus and a suburban campus. When officials affiliated with the city and the county agreed that the county would donate 100 acres to the college on the Penal Farm site, situated in east Memphis across the Wolf River, it also was agreed that the city could make a site available in the mid-city area, known at that time as the Beale Street Urban Renewal I and II projects. This appeared to be an acceptable solution and, had it not been for growing discontent and further suspicions within the black community and second thoughts among many persons about the need to develop Penal Farm land into more commerce and asphalt, that solution perhaps would have saved the college from inheriting what seemed to be insurmountable obstacles in the way of achieving racial balances and the offering of full collegiate services to more than one geographic group of area citizens.

Before any construction was begun, Shelby State was made a part of the statewide litigation relative to the desegregation and merger of two middle Tennessee universities, and decisions affecting this case have turned out to be especially poignant to the current status of the college. The first official action to block the construction of two campus sites for Shelby State Community College came on August 1, 1972, when the court was petitioned to intervene in the desegregation plan involving Tennessee State University and the University of Tennessee at Nashville. The college eventually was enjoined from building on two sites at the same time. When it became evident that Shelby State could not open in its own facilities, a struggle to open the college—anywhere and in temporary quarters—resulted in further delays. At first it was thought that the college might begin operation in the fall of 1971. This possibility was supported by Governor Winfield Dunn, but the timing of such a move carried too many obstacles. Shelby State was destined to begin classes no earlier than the fall of 1972.

As plans proceeded to open Shelby State in temporary facilities, many sites were considered. After much discussion and deliberation, it was decided that Shelby State's best opportunity to open for full-service classes would be in temporary quarters at 4101 Park Avenue on the site of the old Veterans Hospital, now owned by Memphis State University. An agreement was reached with Dr. Cecil C. Humphreys, president of the university, which allowed the college to operate in a 30-year-old hospital ward and in one small building which had been a morgue. During the following year, a portable building, made available by the Memphis Board of Education, was added to the complex.

Shelby State's first day of classes occurred on September 12, 1972. During the registration process, accomplished in three days of scramble, nearly 1000, mostly first-generation, first-year college students enrolled in approximately 200 different class periods. The excitement and confusion of that first day long will be remembered by the original faculty and staff. In two converted buildings of approximately 25,000 square feet were 39 faculty members and more than 1000 students, wall-to-wall. The old morgue, with only two rooms and one office, was used as the music building, but this meant that from the first day of classes there was the sound of music at Shelby State.

The local news media covered the opening of Shelby State with the usual interviews with students and staff. Notable quotes ranged from "the rooms are a little crowded," and that was putting it mildly, to proclamations concerning the virtues of a school which for the first time in the history of higher education in Memphis and Shelby County was "low cost" in an "open-door" atmosphere.

It was realized from the beginning that Shelby State could not and ought not be confined to one place of operation. Therefore, measures were taken immediately to bring education to the people. Accordingly the division of continuing education and community services has been a key component of the instructional program since the college opened. At first this division was to function in the same manner as the regular academic divisions, but it was to work as an operationally separate unit in order to emphasize instruction for "adult" learners. The division was to facilitate personal development, cultural enrichment, occupational upgrading, and other kinds of "non-traditional" education which would serve the needs of adults.

The first chairman of this division, Troy Simpson, Jr., was appointed on September 1, 1972, and served as the only administrative person in the division for one year. Limited but intense efforts in the winter, spring, summer, and fall of 1973 resulted in 313 residents being served through enrichment-type courses. During the fall quarter of 1973, a continuing education coordinator, Linda Brasfield, was employed to assist with the development of short-course, CEU activities. Shortly afterward, the division began to make real strides as it moved from being a fledgling entity into a full-blown program of studies operating on a par with the other academic units of the college.

The academic year 1974-1975 can be described as "the year of great expansion" for continuing education and community services. The division was redefined and changed into an area of emphasis reflecting intra-divisional involvement versus inter-divisional and autonomous operation. Mrs. Brasfield resigned, but two additional professional coordinators were employed, Marsha Jenkins and Jeannette Gunter, and the chairman was assigned the responsibility of effecting courses and programs which cut across every area of concern at the college. The significant expansion of staff, together with the addition of Ken Eaton during the summer of 1975, led the way for the development of three specific offices: community services; continuing education short courses; and conferences and institutes.

During the fiscal year 1977-1978, the area of continuing education and community services touched the lives of nearly 6500 persons in Shelby County. The program currently offers more than 200 short courses, more than 40 conference-type workshops and clinics, numerous special programs as a result of the acquisition of government and foundation funds, and a wide array of social, public, and community services. Perhaps the best example of how Shelby State has generated interest in cultural activities was with its creation of a symphonic orchestra in the spring of 1977. Under the direction of Nobuo Takahashi, the community orchestra premiered at the Orpheum Theatre to the delight of more than a thousand listeners. The orchestra itself was composed of students, townspeople, and a sprinkling of professionals—a healthy mix of Memphians, young and old.

The reality of providing off-campus credit courses in higher education by way of the community college materialized in the fall of 1973. One year after classes began at the Park Avenue site, three other locations were chosen for credit activities away from the Park Avenue campus. Simultaneous with this move was the opening of regular classes at another "campus" located at the old Gragg Junior High School in northeast Memphis. The three teaching centers were situated in south Memphis at the Whitehaven Community Center, in southeast Memphis at the Asbury United Methodist Church, and in north Memphis at the Frayser Christian Church. Since that time, a fourth major teaching site has been developed in Millington at the Naval Air Station.

The following year, off-campus teaching sites were developed to such an extent that by February of 1975 more than 60 classes per quarter were being taught at numerous locations throughout the county. This brought about the creation of a division of field services and the employment of a director of off-campus operations, Dr. Clyde Smith, Jr.

Currently, the division provides off-campus credit courses at more than 40 teaching locations, in addition to offerings made possible by way of the press and radio. A review of fall quarter offerings for 1978 shows a division head count of more than 1500 students, approximately 15 percent of the total number of FTE students who attend the college. The major teaching centers hold more than 100 credit courses with an average class size of 18 students. Other significant teaching locations have included the bulk mail center of the U. S. Post Office, the Federal Correctional Institute, the Fayette County Vocational Center at Somerville, and the Neshoba Center in Germantown. A highly successful early admissions program has been conducted at four high schools in the county. Classes have also been held at the Arlington Development Hospital and the Shelby County Government Office Building, and a rehabilitation program has been offered at the U. S. Navy Correction Center. During academic year 1978-1979, a business math course has been provided to area citizens through *The Commercial Appeal,* enrolling more than 100 students for credit, with several other students electing to take the course for equivalent continuing education units. During the spring quarter of 1979, United States history will be taught by radio over the local PBS affiliate, and telecourses are being investigated carefully for implementation during the fall quarter of 1979.

Over the years the basic academic thrusts of the college—the instructional units being headed first by Dr. Don Mikula and most recently by Dr. Karen Bowyer, with assistance from Dr. Doug Tuech—have been central to the role and scope of the institution, with specific philosophies of purpose attached to developmental, transfer, and career studies. Unique modes of instructional delivery have been emphasized in order to promote schools as "places to learn" according to the actual needs of students. In this regard, instructional development, directed in the media center by Jim Baxter and Lyall Sherred, has received strong audio-visual support and engaged modern approaches to curriculum design. Challenges therein have been crucial to the structure of what otherwise would be regarded as merely "traditional" college courses. Mathematics, for example, has been taught on a computer-managed basis for the past five years. Overall, few if any courses are treated in routine fashion at Shelby State, and student evaluations of the effectiveness of collegiate offerings at the college are almost always glowing with praise. Members of the faculty have gained a reputation for being quite innovative, and they are hard workers.

Students at work in advanced audio-visual technology. *Photograph courtesy Shelby State Community College.*

The development of the curriculum at Shelby State has been evidenced by adaptation to the realities of the marketplace. When the college opened in 1972, the curriculum blueprint, as expressed in the first *Bulletin,* was one of anticipation based on what was offered at similar urban colleges and on what seemed to be right for the Memphis area. Since that time the curriculum has been modified in accordance with the expressed needs of the students and the demands of the job market.

Throughout the existence of Shelby State, a large percentage of the students have come to the college with academic deficiencies. As a result, the present developmental studies program at Shelby State has evolved through a series of changes parallel with the growth of the total instructional program. Originally there were plans for a center for guided and developmental studies which was to include non-credit remedial courses in all of the general education disciplines. For a variety of reasons, however, the center concept was discarded in favor of a more creative and integrated approach to developmental studies. Through the efforts of the respective division chairpersons Dr. Herbert Temple and Dr. Ron Smith, the mathematics and freshman composition courses have been individualized so that each student can begin and progress according to his or her own level of academic achievement. Only the reading and study-skills courses have been retained in the curriculum as discrete, non-credit offerings. Funds from an advanced institutional development program (AIDP), by way of the U. S. Office of Education, have been allocated for a pilot program of basic skills to begin in September of 1979. It will further integrate the development of communications and computation abilities.

While some substantive changes have occurred in career areas of study, the transfer programs and the academic support functions have remained either close to the original concept of a broad-based core curriculum, or they have grown according to predetermined plans. Most standard transfer programs were included in the first *Bulletin,* and none have been added to the general curriculum. Some transfer programs, such as geology and urban studies, did not prove to be fundable, feasible, or attractive to a sufficient number of students, and such programs have been dropped. In addition, all transfer programs in education have been consolidated into basic curriculum plans adaptable to alternative programs of study for elementary and secondary education majors.

Shelby State was established with no separate vocational-technical division; rather a decision was made to conduct career studies, along with transfer studies, within the structure of the regular academic divisions and departments of the college. This relatively new technique in occupational programming has worked well in most instances. The greatest positive value of this approach to career education has been that the usual stigma attached to career programs—the notion that they are for the slow learners or students otherwise unfit for "real" college work—has practically been eliminated at Shelby State. Because of a lack of input from the employment community when the first set of career programs was developed, several of the original 23 associate degree programs have been deleted from subsequent bulletins. As the school has grown, career advisory committees have become an important aspect of academic planning, and ongoing program operations have changed according to need. The advisory committees are composed of potential employers of graduates, including persons who are employed at the same level of work that graduates of the various programs might be expected to enter. Each of the current career programs operates now under advice of committee members who meet on a quarterly basis. Each career program which functions at Shelby State under the auspices of Norm Ervin provides respective students with sponsored experiential learning assignments. The specific types of assignments vary with each program, some of them offering cooperative education or other kinds of field work, a clinical experience, or a practicum. The practical experience segment of the career programs is required in some cases and optional in others, with the trend being toward requirement.

In the business area, programs in secretarial science, accounting, and business management have attracted increasing numbers of students, and a new frontier for the whole region of the Mid-South was opened recently with the development of a unique program in postal management. An emphasis on public service has been shown by the growth of exceptional programs in police science and corrections technology, conducted by Bill Wannamaker, and the patient persistence of personnel in the area of early childhood education came to fruition in 1978 with the opening of a model day care center, managed by Brenda Taylor. The rapid expansion of such popular new programs as merchandising and family services, directed by Sue Field and supported by Dr. Yvonne Hooks, also has been encouraging.

The prestige of Shelby State in the medical community has been enhanced by the high quality of programs in nutrition and dietetics, X-ray and medical laboratory technology, and excellent new programs in emergency medicine, orthotics/prosthetics, physical therapy, and histotechnology. The program in emergency medical technology enrolls a large number of city firemen each quarter, while the orthotics/prosthetics program is interesting and important insofar as it is regional in emphasis and limited to 10 outstanding students a year. The allied health division at the college is unique in that Dr. Pete Rosato, III, its chairperson, is on joint appointment with Shelby State and the University of Tennessee Center for the Health Sciences. This arrangement permits interrelationships of facilities and staff to take place between the college and the university.

New and developing academic programs are evidence of the fact that Shelby State personnel attempt to meet the expressed demands of the community. The general curriculum of the college is espe-

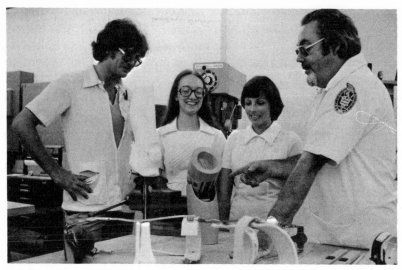

A class in orthotics/prosthetics technology in progress. *Photograph courtesy Shelby State Community College.*

cially geared to producing either well-trained paraprofessional or well-prepared university transfer students who have received a strong general education core, along with specialized training and developmental assistance according to personal needs.

An important ingredient of any college is the library—how it works, where it is located, its scheme of colors, its size and shape, and its personnel. It is impossible, of course, to provide a library instantly; that is, building a collection of books and related audio-visual media requires a number of years. Two giant steps were taken at Shelby State toward accomplishing the impossible: (1) a library of 20,000 volumes was purchased from Siena College, a four-year Catholic girls' school which discontinued operation at the time Shelby State opened, and (2) an agreement was reached with the Memphis and Shelby County Public Library and Information System whereby each branch library in the system would become a Shelby State library. The outstanding advantage of this agreement to administer Shelby State libraries under contract is that students can check materials out at any library location in the city and county and return them to any Shelby State library; conversely, students can check materials out at a Shelby State library and return them to any branch library in the system to have them forwarded to their assigned locations within 24 hours. In effect, Shelby State became heir overnight to a million-volume library of books and other media. During the first two years of Shelby State's existence, the agreement with the Memphis and Shelby County Public Library and Information System was important for purposes of accreditation. The first library facility was housed in only 600 square feet at the Park Avenue campus and could not accommodate even the Siena collection. Another Shelby State branch in the system opened at the Gragg campus during the fall quarter of 1973 occupying about 1200 square feet of space. Relief was not really felt until March of 1975 when the Park Avenue operation moved to the mid-town campus; however, there it remained in temporary quarters until December of 1976 when it moved to a permanent Phase II location, occupying a total of 11,198 square feet.

Services for students at Shelby State, begun when a few extra chairs were moved into the long hallways of the Park Avenue campus, have expanded to include benefits of a professional staff and the addition of comprehensive programs to meet the demands of a wide array of student interests. Counseling and advisory services are currently under the direction of Rachel Miles. Federal funds have provided a program of study skills designed for academic survival; it has been valuable for students at both the mid-town and Gragg campuses and operates under the tutelage of Debbie Northcross. Placement services, relative to employment opportunities for students, are the responsibility of Lonnie Latham. A full complement of activity programs, coordinated by Celeste Gipson, is available to all students.

Each year students and staff have experienced several "firsts" at the college: the first drama production, *Antigone,* in the portable building behind the old hospital ward on the Park Avenue campus during the winter quarter of 1973; the publication of the first issue of the student newspaper, *The Insider,* in November of 1973; the establishment of the first honor society, the Alpha Alpha Beta chapter of Phi Theta Kappa, in January of 1974; the recognition of Phi Beta Lambda, a national organization for students enrolled in business programs, in November of 1974; the chartering of the first student organization, the She Bonettes Hostess Society, on November 10, 1972; the creation of the Shelby State Music Society in March of 1974; the establishment of a bio-science club in April of 1973 and the veterans club in April of 1975; the arrival of several associations, including the student dietetic association in May of 1978, the Tennessee Correctional Association in March of 1977, and the Tennessee Home Economics Association in January of 1979; the founding of the human key society in October of 1976; and the production of the first play in the new theatre at the mid-town campus, *Raisin in the Sun,* directed in May of 1978 by Anastasia Herin. Officers of the initial student government association were elected and installed during the spring quarter of 1978.

The office of student development was established at Shelby State in January of 1973, with Charles Sueing assigned director. His first duty was that of chief recruiter for the college, but he later doubled as director of the Park Avenue campus. The major task of the office of student development initially was to extend the position of dean of students, held by Dr. Don Lamb, to include campus operations. Dr. Lamb, along with the other deans and the president, maintained central administrative offices at 3540 Summer Avenue.

In 1973 a center for student services was formed and staffed by a director, Lillian Hammond, eight persons who were employed to provide additional counseling/advising services, a coordinator of job placement services, and officers assigned to oversee veterans' affairs at the various locations of the college. Grant funds made possible a special services tutorial program which was added to the center in 1974. Later a coordinator of counseling services was appointed, and the counseling staff increased to eight professionals. In 1977 Ms. Hammond moved to central administrative offices, and Terry Johns was appointed director of the center for student services as a reorganization of duties made room for two new components. Basic institutional development program (BIDP) funds resulted in the establishment of offices of testing and placement, and student services were increased to include the Gragg campus and major teaching centers in Millington, Frayser, and Southeast Memphis. Staff affiliated with the center increased to a total of 24 persons. The counseling office was restructured to include three professionals and six paraprofessional academic advisors. In 1978 the replacement of the BIDP grant by the AID program allowed for expansion of the career information laboratory. It became a separate facility, no longer sharing space with the special services tutorial laboratory. The AIDP grant provided for the expansion of the center in 1979;

the employment of two more academic advisors increased involvement of staff in personal/career counseling, and a counselor was added at the diagnostic laboratory to support the testing program. Full services to students had grown to include two campuses—at mid-town and the Gragg site—three of the teaching centers, and liaison with both the cooperative studies program and the essential skills program.

The office of admissions and records was created three months prior to the opening of Shelby State, with full-time operations beginning in June of 1972. Dr. Morgan Richardson was appointed director. Admissions policies and procedures were generally worked out by the dean of students, the director of admissions and records, and the dean of instruction. An admissions committee was organized later in the year, and members of the administrative council passed approved policies on to the Tennessee State Board of Regents for final review and resolution. In order to accommodate the press of off-campus needs, admissions functions were carried on by the administrative assistants at the various centers. In the fall of 1973, the Gragg campus came under full-service status and the office of the director of admissions and records was moved to that location. However, central admissions and records folders were maintained at the Park Avenue campus—an arrangement that continued until the spring of 1975 when the first building at the mid-town campus was opened to students. Services at the Gragg campus continued with the help of the campus director there, aided also by a direct phone line to the mid-town offices.

Registration procedures at Shelby State changed significantly in the fall of 1977 when the old "card-pulling" systems, which had been inherited from Memphis State operations, was replaced with an on-line system. The processes of registration thus were made more accessible to the teaching centers through "call in" or actual computer terminal input at respective locations. The Gragg campus makes use of a fairly self-sufficient registration system due to the presence of an on-site printing terminal. The mechanics of registration continue year-round at Shelby State, without beginning or end, due to so-called "short quarters." Bringing the traditional quarter to only nine and one-half weeks of study, by way of 60- and 90-minute classes, the academic calendar at the college reflects an attempt at flexibility and creative change inasmuch as the period between the fall quarter,

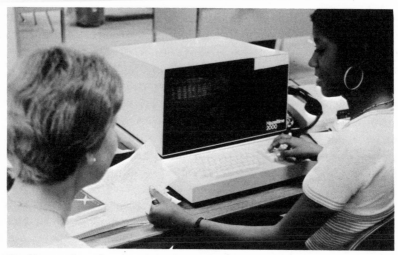

On-line registration in operation. *Photograph courtesy Shelby State Community College.*

which ends just before the usual Thanksgiving break, and the winter quarter, which begins early in January, makes room for a three-week intersession. The idea behind the intersession was that, while some community college students may need to work during the whole month of December, others may need to retake a crucial course or two under even more intense learning formats than the short quarter requires, prior to registering for their second or fifth quarters of study. For a variety of reasons, the idea has not been entirely successful; a better calendar, an alternative suitable to everyone at the college, has yet to be proposed, however.

Athletic programs at Shelby State have had to make the best of a variety of off-campus situations, mostly in old and sometimes in abandoned facilities. With scarcely enough room to house the faculty and staff during the first year of classes, the problem of space for physical education activities was paramount. The first-year problem was solved in part by way of an agreement which permitted Shelby State students to utilize the Mason YMCA. Students were transported on scheduled bus runs to and from the Y, which was located near the Park Avenue campus, enabling the college to offer such classes as swimming, badminton, and physical exercises.

On the intercollegiate level, Shelby State staff forged ahead with plans to engage in league play, and participation in the Tennessee

Junior College Athletic Association began with the first basketball season in 1972-1973. John Townsend, athletic director and department head for health, physical education and recreation, employed two coaches, Joe Proctor for basketball and Joe Platt for baseball. For four years, the two coaches helped each other as assistants, and, in spite of negative odds, Shelby State has had only one losing season in either of these major sports. The teams have often been title contenders, a stellar year being 1976-1977 when the men's basketball team won the Region VII championship and participated in the National Junior College Athletic Association Tournament in Hutchinson, Kansas.

Shelby State baseball teams have had to practice wherever they could find an empty field, and official games have been played on numerous baseball diamonds throughout Memphis—at Memphis State University, Christian Brothers College, community centers, Gagliano Field, and Blues Stadium. This condition exists not only for baseball, but for golf and tennis as well. During the college's first year, the basketball team played in the gymnasium of Airways Junior High School. When the Gragg campus opened, an adequate gymnasium on the same grounds was rented as a part of the arrangement with the Memphis Board of Education. The first basketball game in Shelby State's own gymnasium was not played until 1978.

A committee of students and staff was formed in October of 1972 to select a school mascot. It was felt that the college ought to symbolize its spirit of community and its "belonging" to Memphis. The Saluqi is one of the oldest of purebred dogs in the world, dating to the early history of Egypt. After learning that only one other school in the nation—Southern Illinois University—had adopted this sleek, greyhound-type of animal as its mascot, Dr. Parrish visited the university to view the Saluqi. He returned to Tennessee with two of the dogs and keeps them at the president's residence. On occasion, Sal and Oogie are brought to Shelby State games, and their presence on such occasions reminds everyone that the Saluqi hails from a sensitive and regal heritage.

Highlighting Shelby State's athletic program in academic year 1977-1978, was the introduction of women's basketball to intercollegiate competition. In 1978-1979, under the direction of Anita Malone, the women lost only two games, were ranked nationally throughout the year, and won the Tennessee Junior College Athletic Conference.

The outstanding thing to be said about facilities at Shelby State, or the lack of them, is that few buildings are rented or designed for singular use by any one department or division. The fact that legislative appropriations come to the college in amounts which fund only one or two buildings at a time has necessitated continual shifts in room use. Also, Shelby State has often utilized temporary quarters of some kind or other in order to accommodate full-service functions. The physical arrangements for staff at central administrative offices have undergone extensive modifications, and, over a period of six years, the Siena library books, along with other materials, have been moved into three different locations.

Maintenance personnel at the college often are either tearing something down or renovating an old or outdated facility. The allied health annex, located at 889 Linden Avenue, has undergone an extensive conversion from a regular office building to space suitable for X-ray technology, classes in physical therapy, and other types of laboratory situations. Musical offerings at the mid-town campus once were conducted entirely within the walls of an old automobile agency located at 1011 Union Avenue, and the maintenance staff was housed in what was referred to as "the Jolly Green Giant," a large cement building located on the corner of Linden Avenue and Walnut Street. Otherwise known as the Fischer property, that huge bulk of steel and concrete also housed the career and cooperative studies staff, continuing education and community services personnel, field services, and other offices prior to being demolished in the summer of 1978 in order to make room for the new allied health building. In the meanwhile, two other buildings, dating from the early decades of this century, were being renovated in order to house the art faculty and the maintenance crews.

The history of Shelby State is a history of leases. Beginning with the Park Avenue campus, leased for one dollar a year from Memphis State University, Shelby State has been forced to rent numerous buildings, none of which were especially suited to college needs. In almost every case, however, favors have been rendered to the college by its lessors who, in view of the special aims of Shelby State, often totally reconstructed unit interiors. The college has had lease arrangements with more than a dozen agencies.

Construction at the mid-town campus began in May of 1973; occupancy of the first building occurred in March of 1975. Innova-

Views of the mid-town campus. *Photographs courtesy Shelby State Community College.*

tion was once again in vogue at the college due to the fact that the unique process of utilizing pre-laid brick panels on the exterior facade enabled Shelby State to speed construction and open for classes at the mid-town campus much earlier than anticipated. In addition to regular classrooms and certain designated spaces for the natural sciences, business and commerce, secretarial sciences and mathematics, as well as offices for admissions and records personnel, veterans' affairs, and staff affiliated with financial aid, space was made available later for the dean of instruction. Phase I, encompassing 60,000 square feet, was built at a cost of $2,150,000. Throughout the early stages of planning campus design and until the mid-town units were well past any danger of losing continuity, Dr. Calvin Street, a fine gentleman and scholar on loan from Memphis State University, worked half-time as special assistant to the president; he also served as liaison with state and local architects, with engineering officials at the State Board of Regents, and with personnel on construction sites.

Construction on four interconnected buildings related to Phase II, creatively referred to as buildings A, B, C, and E, was begun in September of 1974. Occupancy of the 132,000 square feet in the four units occurred in December of 1976 at a cost of $6,967,000. Building A was designed to house the anticipated nursing program, the nutrition and dietetics program, and the family and consumer studies program; building B became the home of instructional development and media, student services, the mid-town library, the dean of students, and the department of general education; building C made room for the cafeteria, the bookstore, and the department of student activities; and building E was occupied by staff in three academic departments: speech and theater, humanities, English and the social sciences. Construction of buildings D and F began in March and November of 1976. Each unit added more than 50,000 square feet of usable space to the mid-town campus at a total cost of $6,246,000. Building D, including the gymnasium, other athletic facilities, and a new theater, was designed to accommodate the departments of health, physical education and recreation, and music; building F, fronting on historic Beale Street, included the day care center—a campus showplace—and an expansive area of open space for conducting the essential skills program. South of Phase II and across Linden Avenue, construction of the new allied health building followed demolition of the Fischer building in August of 1978. Scheduled for completion in August of 1979, at a cost of $1,782,000, the allied health building would share the site with two renovation projects.

In spite of inadequate facilities, overcrowding of students and

Campus intramurals. *Photograph courtesy Shelby State Community College.*

staff, and limited funds, accreditation by the Southern Association of Colleges and Schools was achieved on schedule in December of 1974 at the Dallas meeting of the association, and Shelby State's reaffirmation of accreditation, complete with an elaborate self study, began in April of 1977 under the direction of Dr. Dot Saunders. The accreditation visit relative to this process occurred in March of 1979. The study showed that Shelby State was indeed "many places to learn," complemented by a truly creative and innovative faculty. Also evident was the college's maintenance of a frank, open, and dedicated staff.

Due to inadequate facilities and limited funds, enrollment was actually restricted at Shelby State during the fall quarters of 1973, 1974, and 1975. The exact effects of these restrictions cannot be fully determined, but it can be said safely that they have taken a significant toll on overall growth of the college and that they will continue to affect that growth in years to come. Whether Shelby State can move on to acceptable racial balances and continued growth in other parts of the Memphis area remains something of an open question. If so, it will take the commitment from throughout the state of all concerned: the legislature, higher education commission, State Board of Regents, and local leadership agents at every level of community affairs.

It is clear that Shelby State has grown from its small start and the efforts of one man. For several months in late 1970, President Parrish was known to say, "Hello, I am the head of a school that does not exist. And my office is located in the trunk of my car." To these inauspicious beginnings, Dr. Parrish added a secretary, Patty Byrd, for many years an employee at Memphis State University. For almost one year, they were a two-person staff of a not-yet college. In June of 1971, Dr. Mikula joined them in the new Summer Avenue offices of central administration, and shortly thereafter George Walker was employed to help prepare the initial college publications. By January of 1972, other members of the staff began to fill the administrative gaps. Seven years later, at the beginning of academic year 1978-1979, Shelby State had a total of 644 employees, and the first faculty of 39 individuals had grown to a total of 161 professionals. Another 225 instructors served the college on a part-time basis. Clerical and support staff numbered 166 full-time persons who assisted about 50 administrators and 40 department heads and division chairpersons. Shelby State now serves the interests of more than 15,000 persons each year.

CHATTANOOGA STATE TECHNICAL COMMUNITY COLLEGE
by Charles W. Branch

Social demands and commitment of resources have made the community college a reality. Chattanooga State Technical Community College is establishing a tradition of community services, vocational-technical education, college transfer education, and student services. The time has come for Chattanooga State to become a more active agent in developing its identity as an educational force.

Public-supported higher education in Chattanooga, a city which ranks 12th nationally in manufacturing employment as a percentage of the total population, carries a dramatic history. The growth and development of Chattanooga State represent the will and determination of citizens to provide essential educational services for the community.

Chattanooga State Technical Community College originally operated as Chattanooga State Technical Institute, a two-year, coeducational, college-level institution, established by the legislature of the state of Tennessee in 1963. As a result of the General Education Act of 1963, the Tennessee State Board of Vocational Education (House Bill Number 633) included in its plan for higher education the following mandate:

> A regional technical school shall be established by the State Board for Vocational Education in such location or locations as it may deem necessary to provide technical training, and said regional technical school shall function as a two-year terminal training center for the purpose of (a) training engineering technicians for industry, and (b) preparing the student to earn a living

as a Technician or Technical worker in the field of production, distribution, or service.

Chattanooga State Technical Institute was established as the first technical institute in the state, as well as the first public institution of postsecondary education in the Chattanooga area. The final report of the legislative council committee in December of 1958 reported that Clarence Kolwyck drafted the initial memorandum for the Hamilton County delegation in January of 1959. With support from citizens of the Chattanooga area and after several aborted attempts to establish a technical institute in the area, House Bill Number 633 was passed and signed by Governor Frank G. Clement, on May 22, 1963, and was to take effect on July 1, 1963. Located at Fourth and Chestnut streets in downtown Chattanooga, the institute began offering regular programs of study in September of 1965.

The institute's formative years were not without growing pains, but the challenge was accepted. Recorded in CSTI's 1967 yearbook, *The Falcon,* the words of the original director of the institute, Charles O. Whitehead, reflect a commitment to succeed; they were delivered in an address to the first 92 graduates: "Our history is very short, our precedents are few, our acceptance and recognition are practically non-existent. You have had, and will have, the major obligation of making our history, setting our precedents, and establishing our acceptance and reputation."

In 1967, the institute moved to its present site by the Tennessee River, and in December it received initial accreditation from the Southern Association of Colleges and Schools. In 1968 one million dollars in matching state and federal funds were received for further expansion. In announcing the funding, State Senator Don Moore, Jr., stated, "It's just the beginning of a much, much larger complex. It may become a part of a community college before it's over. Chattanooga is going to get a community college. I don't know exactly when, but we are going to get one and CSTI may become a part of it."

In October of 1969 Chattanooga State Technical Institute began preparing the institutional self study for the Southern Association of Colleges and Schools, the first step in the reaffirmation process. The institutional self study contained the following points as basic to the institute's purpose:

1. Our primary obligation is to prepare our students according

President Charles W. Branch. *Photograph courtesy Chattanooga State Technical Community College.*

Aerial view of Chattanooga State. *Photograph courtesy Chattanooga State Technical Community College.*

to their individual qualities, aptitudes, and interests. The individual student is further served with assurance that the training he receives is marketable. This assurance results from careful liaison to determine the changing needs of business, industry, and government agencies which this institution also acknowledges obligation to serve.

2. The curriculum and instruction are geared to produce technicians. We define a *technician* as a person who fills the gap between the professional engineer or scientist and the craftsman or vocational graduate. This requires the development of a math and science base beyond the vocational or trade level, with emphasis on application.

Reaffirmation was received in December of 1971; however, the self-study process continued and the future seemed to call forth old dreams and new visions. The self study had addressed a critical issue—the future—and indicators focused on an expanded mission, role, and scope for Chattanooga State.

The crucial question facing CSTI and the citizens of its service area was whether the institutional mission was too limited. National and regional trends, rapid technological changes, increases in population and movement, growth of a meritocracy, and demand for upward mobility and individualization challenged the adequacy of a limited technical educational mission. A ground swell of community interest and discussion facilitated an expanded mission for Chattanooga State Technical Institute.

Chattanooga area citizens, individually and through their representatives, expressed their intent to have a community college program in the Chattanooga service area. The result of local interest, Senate Joint Resolution Number 125 was introduced and passed by the 1972 session of the Tennessee General Assembly. It called for action:

> Be it Resolved... that the Tennessee Higher Education Commission, in cooperation with the State Department of Education, be directed to a study of the best ways of providing a community college program in the Chattanooga metropolitan area with the study to include, but not be limited to, the full range of occupational, college transfer, and community service programs....

During the summer of 1972, community hearings were held to determine program needs and to recommend the best way to provide community college programs in the area. After lengthy assessment studies and an examination of alternatives, the Tennessee Higher Education Commission gave support to expanding Chattanooga State Technical Institute into a comprehensive community college. This alternative was seen as a viable and pragmatic means of meeting a wide range of consumer needs within the context of a single institution, allowing students to transfer between programs easily and facilitating counseling and guidance for those unsure of career objectives.

On April 10, 1973, Senate Bill Number 361 of the Tennessee Legislature proposed that Chattanooga State Technical Institute become Chattanooga State Community College and transferred its operation from the Tennessee State Board of Education to the Tennessee State Board of Regents, effective July 1, 1973. Seventeen days later, as a result of local concern for the integrity of the technical component, Senate Bill Number 1010 changed the name of the institution to Chattanooga State Technical Community College. Among the state community colleges, Chattanooga State has the unique role and scope that incorporates the continued emphasis in the technical institute program. Section one of the latter bill reads:

> The name of Chattanooga State Community College is changed to Chattanooga State Technical Community College, with continuing responsibility for providing comprehensive one and two

year occupational, college parallel, continuing education, and community service programs, providing quality technical and scientific occupational programs, serving as a regional technical school to train engineering technicians or technical workers in the fields of production, distribution, or service.

The primary mission of Chattanooga State was expanded to offer more diversified and comprehensive programs to serve educational needs of a service area having a wide range of cultural, educational, and social experiences. As mandated by the legislation, Chattanooga State continued to provide high quality technical and scientific occupational programs, enabling students to earn a living in the fields of production, distribution, or service. The college was to offer comprehensive and flexible programs and delivery systems that provided knowledge, skills, and attitudes necessary for its students to enter technical and career areas; to transfer to other institutions of higher learning; to seek professional growth and development, personal enrichment, retraining in a current field; and to change occupational fields.

The institution's mission speaks out against fragmentation of education and for providing a comprehensive educational center which unites liberal arts with technical education. Dr. Charles W. Branch was appointed president in January of 1974 to implement this significant new mission. The college is committed to striking a balance among the aspirations, expectations, and hopes of its students and to continuing to seek resources for meeting these demands. Chattanooga State represents a unique educational model in Tennessee.

The college has a legislative mandate to provide programs to a primary service area which includes one urban county and four isolated, rural Appalachian counties. The population of the institutional service area has increased since the 1970 census period but has failed to draw closer to national economic averages as seen in Table I.

TABLE I
SERVICE AREA PROFILE

County	1977 Estimated Population	Median Income
Hamilton	264,700	$8,609
Marion	21,900	6,118
Sequatchie	7,200	6,111
Rhea	21,300	5,705
Bledsoe	8,100	4,738

Chattanooga State is a people's college, maintaining an open-door policy and comprehensive programs. This democratic philosophy promises universal postsecondary educational opportunity for all in the service area. The positive enrollment growth pattern Chattanooga State Technical Community College has maintained since it began operation in 1974 is, as shown in Table II, directly related to this opportunity.

TABLE II
FALL STUDENT CREDIT ENROLLMENT PROFILE

	Chattanooga State Technical Institute			Chattanooga State Technical Community College			
	1972-1973	1973-1974	1974-1975	1975-1976	1976-1977	1977-1978	1978-1979
Head count*	1,238	1,373	2,245	3,471	3,503	3,797	4,233
FTE**	758	780	1,373	2,327	2,349	2,407	2,632

*Head count is the total number of full- and part-time students.
**FTE is full-time equivalent students; 15 quarter credit hours equal one FTE.

Central to the mission of the college is the major tenet that a cross-section of the population would be recruited and served. Table III clearly indicates that the student population is comprehensive and reflective of the greater service area. All programs are open to all persons, regardless of race, color, religion, sex, national origin, or handicap. The Chattanooga State student population is further characterized by persons who have completed high school and desire to complete the first two years of a baccalaureate program prior to transferring to a senior institution; persons who are preparing for specific career or technical occupations which require two years of education beyond high school; persons who are presently employed full-time and desire to attend college on a part-time basis; persons who require mid-career technical redirection and/or retraining; persons who desire or need additional education for personal, economic, social, or other reasons; and those who are economically and/or culturally deprived.

TABLE III
FALL STUDENT DEMOGRAPHIC PROFILE, 1978

Enrollment	Male	1,961
	Female	2,272
Age	Under 15	22
	15-19	976
	20-24	1,260
	25-34	1,292
	35-64	672
	Over 64	11
Race	Black	687
	Caucasian	3,428
	Other	118
Employment Status	Unemployed	1,143
	1-20 hours	465
	21-30 hours	432
	31-40 hours	772
	40 or more hours	1,421
Income Levels (in dollars)	0- 4,999	508
	5,000- 9,999	1,566
	10,000-14,999	635
	15,000-24,999	804
	25,000-49,999	635
	50,000-over	85

The institution has successfully passed through a transitional period of expanded mission and increased community leadership. During the summer of 1978, Chattanooga State developed and implemented a comprehensive marketing plan to accomplish more effectively its objective of meeting community needs. To achieve its purpose, the college must communicate its programs and services to those who do not come to the institution because they are unaware of their access to college. Coordinated by the office of admissions and records, the plan is designed to involve all aspects of the institution and supporting community groups. To reach the general population, the college has implemented two innovative techniques: an annual report to the people and businesses in the greater Chattanooga area and an annual collegewide display at a major shopping center called "Campus-on-the-Mall." High school students are contacted through traditional methods and in unique ways as well. Workshops and seminars are provided on such topics as choosing a career, job locating, and interviewing. The joint enrollment program provides academically qualified high school seniors with an opportunity to take college credit courses during the regular school day at their high schools. The marketing plan also includes specific proposals for student retention. Faculty members identify students who are experiencing serious academic difficulty and send personal letters explaining the wide range of counseling services available at the college to each of them.

Chattanooga State places heavy emphasis on developing a career guidance and placement service for the student that typically pursues a technical career-oriented program. Listings of part-time and career job openings have almost doubled each year since they began in 1975. Beginning in the fall of 1976, students have participated in programs designed to develop expertise in marketing job skills. Through an established college-community-employer career placement network, Chattanooga State students are provided opportunities for employment interviews with campus representatives of prospective employers such as Tennessee Valley Authority, Argonne National Laboratories, Union Carbide, and Bell Labs. In 1977 a placement newsletter was developed to provide information to employers on prospective graduates.

Counseling services have expanded in direct proportion to growth in student enrollment. In addition to regular activities related to academic, personal, social, and career counseling, special programs have been designed for handicapped students and for students deficient in certain developmental learning skills. During 1977 a new course, psychology of personality, was developed as a part of the counseling and developmental guidance program. The course was designed to measure behavioral change in the areas of self concept, grade point average, class attendance, and attrition, and it includes activities related to transactional analysis, assertiveness training, life goals, and study skills development.

The institution has continually placed emphasis on its financial aid program for students. During the past three years, significant increases have occurred in available funds and student participation in the program:

TABLE IV
STUDENT FINANCIAL AID ASSISTANCE PROGRAM

	Number of Recipients	Total Amount Available
1975-1976	631	$278,510
1976-1977	825	440,676
1977-1978	974	468,349

A campus-based academic work scholarship program was implemented in 1977. This cooperative education program provides an opportunity for students to obtain practical work experience in a field directly related to their academic education.

An individualized instructional program for the hearing impaired was realized in the fall of 1974, with special provisions for differences in communication skills, interests, and aptitudes. Interpreters are provided for regularly scheduled courses. The program has provided direct supportive services to include individualized instruction from qualified instructors for the deaf; interpreters in the regular classroom to assist in note-taking; tutoring; advising and counseling; instruction in sign language; a collegiate Sertoma Club for the deaf, sponsored by the Highland Sertoma Club; and use of the TTY telephone. Additionally, a one-year preparatory program of development studies is provided to assist these students in making the transition to their career choices.

The 1974-1975 academic year marked the beginning of the college parallel program at Chattanooga State with an enrollment of approximately 150 students. Comprehensive transfer agreements have been developed with the University of Tennessee at Chattanooga, Tennessee Technological University in Cookeville, and the University of Tennessee at Knoxville. This course-by-course articulation guide enables each student to determine at the outset of his college experience the best course of study to follow. Students who enroll in college parallel or transfer programs have opportunities to receive academic educational experiences in 20 program areas within the arts and humanities and in 22 program areas in the sciences.

When Chattanooga State became a comprehensive community college, the open-door policy was fully implemented. A commitment was made in 1976 to develop and implement individualized courses for reading, fundamentals of grammar, math, and psychology of personality. The developmental studies program was designed to enable students with learning skill deficiencies to have an opportunity for upward mobility. Developmental study courses are competency-based, outcome oriented, and individually prescribed as a result of diagnostic assessments.

Significant growth, outlined below, has occurred in Business and Commerce, a viable part of the college:

TABLE V
DEVELOPMENT OF BUSINESS AND COMMERCE PROGRAMS

Associate Degree Programs	1973-1974	1974-1975	1975-1976	1976-1977	1977-1978	1978-1979
Accounting	X					
Computer Science	X					
Data Processing	X					
Management Information	X			O		
Secretarial Service	X					
Legal Option	X					
Medical Option	X					
Professional Option	X					
Insurance Option					X	
Advertising Arts			X			
Management			X			
General Management Option					X	
Insurance Administration Option					X	
Banking and Finance Option			X			
Forestry/Fisheries Option				X		
Hospital Option			X			O
Hotel-Motel Option			X			
Industrial Option			X			
Landscape and Turf Option				X		
Systems Option			X			O
Traffic and Transportation			X			
Aerospace Option			X			
Certificate Programs						
Accounting	X					
Computer Operator	X					
Advertising Arts			X			
General Clerical			X			
Management			X			
Secretarial Science			X			
Traffic and Transportations			X			

X=Program implemented
O=Program terminated

The secretarial science department was established in 1973, became fully individualized in 1976, and is now complemented by a newly designed word processing center which enables advanced secretarial science students to utilize the most advanced equipment in the field. The individualized instructional approach of the program allows students to enroll in several typing and/or shorthand classes concurrently. This instructional strategy enables flexibility in course scheduling.

Chattanooga State has become a national educational leader in the life and health sciences and currently maintains exemplary programs in radiology technology, orthopaedic physicians assistant, and dental hygiene. A complete outline of program development is provided below:

TABLE VI
DEVELOPMENT OF LIFE AND HEALTH SCIENCES PROGRAMS

Associate Degree Programs	1973-1974	1974-1975	1975-1976	1976-1977	1977-1978	1978-1979
Occupational Safety/Health	X			O		
Orthopaedic Physicians Assistant	X					
Allied Health Science						
Medical Records Option			X			
Mental Health Option				X		
Occupational Therapy Assistant Option				X		
Physical Therapist Assistant Option				X		
Dental Hygiene				X		
Radiologic Technology		X		X		

Certificate Programs						
General Medical Terminology		X				
Occupational Safety and Health		X				
Dental Assistant			X			

X = Program implemented
O = Program terminated

In January of 1979, an energized teaching laboratory, including a lecture-demonstration, an examination lab with a radiographic and cranographic unit, and a large modern darkroom designed for 35 students became available on campus. The program, accredited by the American Medical Association in 1974, has grown to a total capacity of 66 students. Hospital-clinical affiliation agreements are presently maintained with Erlanger Medical Center and Memorial Hospital. Additional affiliation agreements have been negotiated with the Bradley Memorial Hospital in Cleveland, Tennessee, and with Rhea County Medical Center in Dayton, Tennessee.

During the period of 1970-1971, planning was underway with Erlanger Medical Center and the area orthopaedic surgeons to conduct an orthopaedic physicians assistant program. The first class graduated in 1972. The program was one of six nationally which gained American Medical Association accreditation status.

With endorsement of the Tennessee Society of Orthopaedists, the program at Chattanooga State has continued and is one of the two remaining programs in the nation.

The college obtained approval to implement dental assistant and dental hygiene programs in 1974. The dental assistant program was transferred from the Chattanooga City School System and enrolled its first class of 30 students in September of 1974. In 1975 the dental assistant program obtained full accreditation status from the American Dental Association. In September of 1976, 15 students enrolled in dental hygiene for the first time. Provisional approval accreditation status was obtained for the dental hygiene program in 1978. Both programs place emphasis on clinical proficiency. A 19-chair clinical care facility and a technical laboratory support both the preventive dentistry services of hygiene students and chairside training for assistant students. Approximately 140 local dental practitioners provide dental restorative services in the college's dental clinic each year to enhance the training of assistant students. More than 70 practitioners also provide extensive clinical experience for assistant students in their private offices.

Through the joint enrollment program, college services were extended into the Hamilton County Department of Education school system during the 1978-1979 school year. Guidelines for admission to the program include classification as a high school senior, attainment of a high school grade point average of "B" or better, and recommendation by the high school principal and/or guidance counselor. Chattanooga State faculty provide five class hours of instruction per week, as well as tutorial sessions, counseling, and career guidance. The program is currently being offered on an experimental basis in four Hamilton County high schools: Red Bank, Central, East Ridge, and Soddy-Daisy.

From a library of 14,000 volumes in June of 1972, the instructional materials center has grown into a multi-faceted, multi-media center serving the entire college community. The new IMC houses a library that contains more than 26,000 volumes, classroom area for the individualized and self-paced developmental studies program, the college print shop, a photography darkroom, and the educational television studio. Facilities are being developed to house the proposed FM radio station upon its approval by the Federal Communications Commission.

Chattanooga State's instructional roots are in the technical area. The development of engineering technology programs is traced below:

TABLE VII
DEVELOPMENT OF ENGINEERING TECHNOLOGY PROGRAMS

Associate Degree Programs	1973-1974	1974-1975	1975-1976	1976-1977	1977-1978	1978-1979
Biomedical Engineering	X				O	
Civil Engineering	X					
Highway Option	X			O		
Structural Option	X			O		
Electrical/Electronics	X					
Biomedical Option				X		O
Communication Option				X		
Power Option	X					
Basic Instrumentation	X					
Environmental Technology				X		
Air Pollution	X			O		
Chemical Technology	X			O		
Electromechanical	X		O			
Mechanical Engineering	X					
Nuclear Technology	X					
Certificate Programs						
Concrete Laboratory Practices	X		O			
Construction Supervision			X			
Cross-Connection Control	X			O		
Industrial Processing	X			O		
Natural Gas	X					
Nondestructive Testing	X					
Reinforced Concrete Design	X					
Structural Steel Design	X					
Structural Steel Detailing	X					
Surveying	X					

X=Program implemented
O=Program terminated

NOTE: The highway and structural options combined into a general civil engineering technology program; the biomedical engineering program converted to an option under electrical/electronics; and air pollution and chemical technologies merged to create an environmental program.

In keeping with national trends and government regulations, an environmental science program has been provided since 1970. A federal grant was obtained to provide necessary equipment and professional expertise. Through an Environmental Protection Agency contract, Chattanooga State operated a 10-station air sampling network in the service area.

Instructional Materials Center. *Photograph courtesy Chattanooga State Technical Community College.*

Chattanooga State initiated programs within the areas of public service, education, and behavioral sciences in 1974. Significant growth has occurred, particularly in support areas such as psychology, sociology, and education. During the past five years, a major effort has been undertaken to expand continuing education and community services through non-credit, short-term classes, specialized seminars, and workshops. The continuing education division is actively engaged in the development of programs which will further advance services to the community. Growth of services can be seen by data provided in Table VIII:

TABLE VIII
CONTINUING EDUCATION ENROLLMENT DATA

	1974-1975	1975-1976	1976-1977	1977-1978
Number of Students	1,520	1,890	3,508	5,906
Continuing Education Offerings	148	117	159	316
Management Upgrade Offerings	—	19	52	117

In 1976 Chattanooga State instituted a new outreach program by providing first-line and middle-management development training services to Chattanooga's large and expanding economic sector. Job skill improvement and specific job training services have been provided for such companies or agencies as E. I. duPont de-Nemours, Memorial Hospital, TVA, City of Chattanooga, and the Tennessee Department of Public Health.

The community services program has become vital to the Chattanooga area. Since 1976 activities have been extended to numerous social, civic, and local interest groups. Workshops have been held on community education for the elderly, and enrichment lectures have been presented to Senior Neighbors, Incorporated. In 1977 a 24-member advisory committee, composed of community leaders representing various professional, business, and industrial interests was established to provide assistance in identifying community needs.

The child development demonstration center officially opened in the fall of 1978 and is intended to serve as a practicum site and resource laboratory for Chattanooga State's early childhood education majors, as well as a continuing education center for people working in day care centers and kindergartens. The center provides an open classroom learning environment that is child-centered. Children, ages four and five, attend either half- or full-day sessions, five days a week. A unique contribution is its utilization of many existing facilities and programs within the college (audio-visual, dental clinic, etc.), creating an effectively symbiotic relationship between instructional programs and the center.

The college has provided leadership in continuing education activities for the deaf. The program is a cost-sharing effort with Gallaudet College, the legislatively designated college for the deaf, located in Washington, D. C. Major program objectives provide for courses and activities that are of interest to deaf adults and mainstream deaf adults in various courses and activities.

As a member of ACCTion, a 122-member private and public two-year college consortium organized to assist developing institutions of higher learning, Chattanooga State has been able to strengthen its instructional and administrative staff through workshops, seminars, and exemplary visitations. These staff development experiences represent means of providing technically educated and trained personnel with formal exposure to instructional and evaluative techniques for facilitating learning outcomes. Outcomes of the staff development program include implementation of developmental reading and math courses; development of computer-assisted instruction; design of a joint enrollment program, where secondary senior students take college credit courses within the secondary physical facility; and revision of all course syllabi.

During 1978 five-year comprehensive planning guidelines were established which were based on an expanded mission, role, and scope statement; they were designed to provide a management by objectives system. All available student, staff, and facilities data was formulated into inventories which were interfaced with planning goals. Professional staff, faculty, and support personnel participated in drafting the initial planning document.

To provide better means for institutional planning, effective communications, and decision-making procedures and to facilitate more decentralized planning and governance, a collegewide reorganization was completed in 1978. It provided the means to consolidate five instructional divisions into three and to departmentalize all major program units within divisions. Newly created departments provide additional means for staff leadership and management opportunities, especially for women and minorities. During 1978, two positions were created and filled, making operational the offices of special projects and institutional research and planning. The office of special projects coordinates the exploration of both financial and human resources available to the college. The office of institutional research and planning coordinates long-range planning and research for various reports and projects.

During the spring of 1975, Chattanooga State conducted a comprehensive workforce analysis of existing employment conditions; specific attention was given to the number of women and minorities employed, to comparison of average annual salary by job classification, and to availability of personnel within the service area. In the summer of 1975, the affirmative action equal employment opportunity office and a standing college committee were established; specific goals were developed, and policies and procedures were adopted to implement the program, which is monitored on a semi-annual basis.

The vitality of Chattanooga State is directly correlated to the personnel who provide college services. A faculty—numbering 81, with 11 percent holding doctorate degrees and more than 70 percent master's degrees or above—provides a background ideal for a

Bobby C. Smith, dean of students, addresses class. *Photograph courtesy Chattanooga State Technical Community College.*

comprehensive college parallel-technical education program. Faculty with diverse non-academic experiences, such as community social work, Apollo project management, oil company engineering, naval architecture, and dental administration, work cooperatively with academically oriented faculty to provide an instructional strategy relevant to meeting the needs of a community college student population. A complementary component is represented by management and professional non-faculty personnel who provide expertise drawn from such diverse environments as university teaching, research and development, curriculum centers, public community services, national advisory councils, regional academic accreditation associations, educational consultant agencies, and national educational workshop or seminar leadership. The faculty and administrative staff are supported by technical and clerical personnel, many of whom have completed educational programs at Chattanooga State.

A major strength of Chattanooga State is its ability to manage financial resources available from its several funding sources. Primary financial activities include acquiring funds on a timely and adequate basis and providing for their safekeeping, collecting and maintaining accurate records, and effectively utilizing available funds to meet the goals and objectives of the organization. Financial management at Chattanooga State encompasses long-range and short-range attributes which are analyzed and revised each year. The long-range dimension includes the campus master physical facility plan, the five-year capital outlay plan, and the five-year operating budget. The annual fiscal year budget process translates college objectives into a financial planning document. The annual operating budget preparation incorporates two management tools, management by objectives and zero-based budgeting, and the process incorporates a merit review and evaluation of each employee at the college.

Chattanooga State developed and implemented a master plan for the orderly growth of the college in 1976. Inherent in the campus master plan was provision that all buildings be located above the 100-year flood level elevation and that additional parking facilities be built above the 30-year flood level elevation. In addition, the campus master plan impacted to coordinate underground facilities—such as heating and air-conditioning supply lines, water and sewage lines, storm drains, and electric power distribution—in an orderly configuration.

During 1973-1974 expansion provided an addition to the cafeteria and a temporary area for student recreational activities. Laboratories for the dental auxiliary programs and the expanded secretarial science program also were completed. An unusual visual landmark called "The Bubble" was erected in 1974. The air-supported structure served as the physical education and intercollegiate facility until it was replaced by the modern building used now.

The student and community affairs center was completed in 1978. It houses student recreational areas, offices of student services personnel, classrooms and faculty offices, conference rooms, and the campus bookstore. During this same year, the allied health

Physical education facility that replaced "The Bubble." *Photograph courtesy Chattanooga State Technical Community College.*

wing was constructed to accommodate an energized lab for radiologic technology classrooms, and the child development demonstration center. Six professionally styled tennis courts and a baseball diamond became centers of athletic activity in the fall of 1978. The new athletic building incorporates a multiplicity of functions in its design and expands the capabilities of Chattanooga State. The facility contains varsity athletic, physical education, recreational leadership, and music facilities and has a seating capacity of more than 1800.

The music complex includes a tiered band and chorus room and individual practice rooms for piano and other instruments. Laboratory space is also provided for arts and crafts activities. The central energy plant was completed in December of 1978 and houses an 11 million BTU coal-fired boiler, which was designed to virtually eliminate the college's dependence on gas or oil fuels. The conversion from gas to coal as a primary energy system was governed by the state of Tennessee's policy decision affecting newly constructed facilities. Improved campus accessibility, enforcement of one-way traffic flow to complement the pedestrian mall, and provision for adequate parking spaces have been other major accomplishments.

Chattanooga State Technical Community College is at the stage

Student Services Center. *Photograph courtesy Chattanooga State Technical Community College.*

of evolution historically where the need exists to concentrate on a planned process of development in finding an optimum balance between the demands and needs of the community and the demands fostered by institutional goals. Breaking ground toward new horizons is the driving force permeating future expectations. The historic roots of Chattanooga State signal that a new day is dawning. For everything there is a season and a time. It is a season for growth and great expectation at Chattanooga State.

SUMMARY

*T*he development of Tennessee's community colleges during the founding and early years has, in full perspective, been affected by a number of major events and considerations. Such factors as governance, role and scope, and support have undergirded and significantly impacted the progress and direction of the entire community college program. Threaded throughout this crucial period and evident throughout the book, various common features have emerged that characterize the colleges as unique institutions within the realm of higher education in the state.

Perhaps of greatest significance to the community colleges' initial and continual progress is their governance by a statewide lay board with comparable responsibility for senior colleges and universities. Their association with a comprehensive system of four-year institutions was significant at first to the new two-year colleges' identity as higher education entities, not as extensions of local public school systems or as less-than-collegiate-level postsecondary schools. Under the State Board of Education, the community colleges benefited from centralized planning and staff support services; operational development became a reality in a remarkably brief period, and the colleges immediately became accustomed to system-oriented coordination, management, and policy considerations. For example, the colleges' common fee structure, quarter-term academic calendar, and financial reporting procedures were established early.

The creation in 1972 of the State University and Community College System of Tennessee by the General Assembly represented a dramatic event in the development of community colleges and coincided with the conclusion of their founding period. The stated purpose of the new system was to enhance the effectiveness of the higher education institutions formerly under the State Board of Education. As the new governing body, the State Board of Regents was charged with responsibility for enabling the member institutions to be more competitive and accountable for state support and establishing a system of higher education, which would provide direction necessary for the colleges and universities to fulfill their mission, goals, and objectives. This transition also represented a structural shift of the community colleges and universities from the executive to the legislative branch of state government, thus affording the institutions the same status and relative degree of autonomy long enjoyed by the University of Tennessee. Important to the success of the transition of the colleges and universities from the State Board of Education to the State Board of Regents was the transfer of four members from the old to the new governing board. The experience and expertise in lay governance of Dale F. Glover of Obion, James H. Jones, Jr. of Mt. Pleasant, J. Frank Taylor of Huntingdon, and Dr. Kenneth P. Ezell of Murfreesboro provided valuable leadership in the establishment of the new board's bylaws and original policies. Continuity in control was further enhanced with the statutory appointment of J. Howard Warf.

Under the direction of the State Board of Regents and Chancellors Cecil C. Humphries (1972-1975) and Roy S. Nicks (1975-present), community colleges and universities have operated as partners in a decentralized system of individual institutions. The Board of Regents has maintained fervent belief in delegated authority, institutional integrity, strong campus administration, and preservation of community-institutional relations. Community colleges have been guided toward the goal of full development by board policies and decisions which provide broad campus latitude and discretion in accordance with unique local considerations. As member institutions of the system, community colleges have steadily progressed with their original comprehensive purposes intact. The effective working relationships of the State Board of Regents and the system chancellors with the legislature and Governors Winfield Dunn (1971-1975), Ray Blanton (1975-1979), and Lamar Alexander (1979-present) have provided the colleges essential support to grow and pursue determined objectives through the close of the early years.

Unlike other institutions, the colleges' enabling legislation intentionally lacked specific authorization as to mission, program offerings, and limitations. Determination of the colleges' role and scope was vested in the governing board, and they evolved as particular higher education considerations, goals, and objectives became evident. In the beginning, only basic comprehensive constructs were adopted by the State Board of Education to provide central guidelines for program and service development. It was felt that fundamental directives were essential for developing solid curricula and programs while, at the same time, fostering response to local community needs.

As the individual colleges, as well as other public institutions, grew and became more involved in diversifying offerings, the desirability for more definite authorization became apparent. At the November 4, 1971, meeting of the State Board of Education, the first formal role and scope statement for the community colleges was adopted. Proposed by the college presidents, it represented in large part a summary of the board's previous actions and commitments to the comprehensive community college program. It emphasized the colleges' implicit relationships with the developing state technical institutions and expanding university programs and reaffirmed the colleges' original purpose and their basic prerogatives in providing university transfer and community-oriented programs and services. These broad objectives then were reflected in the Tennessee Higher Education Commission's first master plan, *Higher Education for Tennessee's Future,* issued in 1973, and were again recognized in a State Board of Regents study report of 1975.

It was not until 1977 that the colleges formulated individual role and scope statements of official bearing. Developed by campus faculty and staff, the colleges' statements, along with those of the universities, comprise the working elements of a comprehensive five-year plan directed by the board as a framework for system and institutional development through the early 1980s. Each of the colleges' statements, which were considered in the 1979 Tennessee Higher Education Commission master plan, identify particular areas of instruction and service the institutions intend to pursue based on needs assessment and given enrollment and resource requirement assumptions. For planning and policy purposes, the newly defined role and scope of the colleges, both individually and collectively, demonstrate that maturity has not lessened the commitment to meet the changing needs of community college education in Tennessee.

Academic program development at the colleges has involved steady progress toward comprehensive offerings in concert with community needs. General core curricula and programs were first established at each college while continuing education, public service, and non-credit and off-campus instruction also were developed. From the outset, curricular development has been the prerogative of campus faculty, with authority for degree program approval resting with the governing board and the higher education commission.

One of the first objectives was regional accreditation by the Southern Association of Colleges and Schools, and, without exception, the colleges earned this recognition in the minimum allowable time. With the encouragement of Chancellor Nicks, the colleges also have sought and secured program accreditation from most all applicable agencies as an evaluation measure of program quality and accountability. Through abilities and insights gained from experience, they have expanded initial core programs to meet the particular needs of their career-oriented clientele by having the specific directions of the vocational-technical programs directly correspond to the manpower needs of their service areas. At the close of 1978-1979, the colleges collectively offered some 86 different associate degree majors and 48 different one- and two-year certificate programs. The close association of the community colleges with one another and universities within the same system of governance.has enhanced their academic program development through articulation of course offerings, cooperative and joint programming, and academic policy decisions on a systematic basis. The community colleges' programming prerogatives regarding two-year associate degree offerings are likewise assured.

The community colleges, dedicated to more than the philosophy of open and equal access, have from the beginning provided exceptional student services in support and full complement of instructional programs and have exerted great emphasis on serving the extracurricular needs of diverse student clienteles. Academic programs, as well as academic counseling, developmental instructions, and career guidance services, are geared to the needs of commuter, non-traditional, working, and older students. In carrying the fundamental concepts of full access beyond the bounds of specific programs, community colleges have continually acted on the cutting edge of implementing various state and federal social policies. Student activities and campus policies have consistently demonstrated affirmative efforts in providing opportunities to all individuals; as a result, staffs and student bodies are truly representative of a cross-section of Tennessee's citizenry.

The development of physical facilities during the founding and early years has represented progress through the critical path of time, educational specifications, and available resources. By necessity, each college commenced operations in temporary housing— schools and other public buildings, churches, and private dwellings. From these often humble origins, the physical plants, second-to-none, emerged as outstanding educational facilities. Initial campus construction was supported through the prerequisite local contribution of $250,000 and state/federal matching funds. Federal funding under the 1963 Higher Education Facilities Act, principally, and the Appalachian Regional Commission provided some $10 million for construction of original buildings, with the first colleges receiving the bulk of available funds. The campuses, based on the State Board of Education prototype, were to consist of separate, free-standing facilities for classrooms and laboratories, the library, student services, physical education, administration, and plant operations. This model was followed with some modification; as programming diversified, variations in facility plans were necessary to accommodate special educational programs and to support functional needs.

Federal construction funds were depleted early, and the state provided capital improvement funding to complete the institutions' building programs. As of 1978-1979, the colleges had received a total of nearly $70 million in state capital outlay, with distribution and level of funding depending upon the priorities of the State Board of Regents and the availability of funds. As a group, the colleges have received an equitable share of state capital dollars over the years and full campus development at all colleges has consistently been a major objective of the Regents. While this objective remains unmet at some of the higher growth colleges, the formulation of campus master plans and long-range capital improvement plans will provide the means to ultimate achievement.

Since their inception, community colleges have proven to be fiscally responsible and accountable and have received operating support sufficient to implement and maintain quality programs. By intent, the colleges are almost totally dependent upon state funding. Low student fees generate modest revenues, and federal vocational education dollars provide nominal support, amounting to an aggregate total of less than $8.6 million for all of the colleges through 1978-1979. State operating appropriations allocated directly to the institutions from general fund revenues represent an average of 70 percent of the colleges' annual budgets. Through 1978-1979, they received a total exceeding $148.3 million in state support. As the colleges have developed, overall emphasis has been placed on external resource development. Campus foundations have been established to support particular activities and financial needs, and, on a modest yet increasing basis, individual institutions have secured additional assistance through various federal, state, and private grants and contracts.

Beyond the founding and early years, future development of the community colleges is imminent due to the availability of adequate support, effective resource management, and planned growth. Unlike many other types of institutions, the Tennessee community colleges have yet to realize full potential; there continue to be segments of the population unserved by higher education, and campus and program development remain to be fully achieved. Since their establishment, however, the rate of Tennessee high school graduates entering postsecondary education has grown to boldly challenge the national average, and approximately 15,000 community college graduates have entered the labor force as trained professionals or transferred to university baccalaureate programs.

Community college education represents the major growth area of higher education. The specialized community-emphasis programs each college has nurtured will be refined and more responsive to changes in student and local job market demands. The need for community college programs in geographical areas still unattended will be met through joint and cooperative institutional efforts and through well-defined off-campus services and branch campus operations.

Tennessee's community colleges are well-prepared to enter the 1980s as mature institutions. As a unified and vital dimension of the State University and Community College System of Tennessee, their individual roles and scopes are essential to the promise of all Tennessee higher education. Proven resilience and integrity will insure fulfillment of the belief that all citizens shall have the opportunity to pursue their educations to the maximum of their desires and abilities. The tremendous progress of Tennessee's community colleges in their founding and early years will remain a tribute to all Tennesseans, but especially to those who represented the state's dedication to the full investment of its human resources and to the accessibility of quality postsecondary education for lifelong learning opportunities.

APPENDIX A

STATE BOARD OF EDUCATION
August 9, 1963

Governor Frank G. Clement
  ex-officio
Ernest C. Ball
  Memphis
Thomas M. Divine
  Kingsport
John W. Finney
  Columbia
Dale F. Glover
  Obion
Edward L. Jennings
  Liberty
T. R. Keys
  Erwin

Mrs. B. A. McDermott
  Nashville
F. Thornton Strang
  Chattanooga
J. Frank Taylor
  Huntingdon
Harold D. West
  Nashville
James Williams
  Henderson
Mrs. Sam Wilson
  Loudon
J. Howard Warf
  Commissioner, Chairman

STATE BOARD OF EDUCATION
August 9, 1963 to June 30, 1972

Governor Frank G. Clement (term
ended 1966)
  ex-officio
Governor Buford Ellington (1967-1971)
  ex-officio
Governor Winfield Dunn (assumed
office 1971)
  ex-officio
Ernest C. Ball (retired 1969)
  Memphis
George H. Barnes (appointed 1970)
  Memphis
Thomas H. Divine*
  Kingsport
Kenneth P. Ezell (appointed 1971)**
  Murfreesboro
John W. Finney (deceased 1965)
  Columbia
John K. Folger (appointed 1968)
  ex-officio
  Executive Director, THEC
Dale F. Glover**
  Obion
H. Lynn Greer, Jr. (appointed 1971)
  Nashville
Edward L. Jennings*
  Liberty

James H. Jones, Jr. (appointed 1965)**
  Mt. Pleasant
Edwin H. Kennedy (1966-1970)
  Newport
T. R. Keys (deceased 1966)
  Erwin
Hugh T. McDade (appointed 1969)
  Alcoa
Mrs. B. A. McDermott (term ended
1971)
  Nashville
D. M. Spotwood (appointed
1967-deceased 1970)
  Pulaski
Mrs. C. Lentz Stevens (appointed 1971)
  Memphis
F. Thornton Strang*
  Chattanooga
J. Frank Taylor**
  Huntingdon
George W. Turner (1970-1971)
  Lewisburg
Harold D. West (retired 1967)
  Nashville
James Williams (term ended 1971)
  Henderson
Mrs. Sam Wilson (term ended 1967)
  Loudon

Chairman

J. Howard Warf (term ended 1971)**
  Commissioner

E. C. Stimbert (appointed 1971)
  Commissioner

*Appointed prior to 1963 and terms extend past 1972
**Appointed to State Board of Regents July 1, 1972

APPENDIX B

STATE BOARD OF REGENTS
July 1, 1972 (established) to July 1, 1979

Governor Winfield Dunn (term ended 1975)*
    ex-officio, Chairman
Governor Ray Blanton (1975-1979)
    ex-officio, Chairman
Governor Lamar Alexander (assumed office 1979)
    ex-officio, Chairman
Martin A. Abraham
    1977-1978 Student Regent
    Austin Peay State University
Gwen Awsumb (appointed 1979)
    Memphis
Charles N. Berry (term ended 1975)*
    Chattanooga
Claude C. Bond (appointed 1975)
    Chattanooga
G. Wayne Brown (appointed 1975)
    ex-officio
    Executive Director, THEC
Benjamin E. Carmichael (1972-1975)
    ex-officio
    Commissioner of Education
Edward A. Cox (appointed 1979)
    ex-officio
    Commissioner of Education
J. C. Eoff, Jr. (appointed 1976)
    Tullahoma
Kenneth P. Ezell**
    Murfreesboro
William W. Farris (appointed 1978)
    Memphis
John K. Folger (term ended 1975)*
    ex-officio
    Executive Director, THEC
Dale F. Glover**
    Obion
Jere Griggs (appointed 1979)
    ex-officio
    Commissioner of Agriculture
Dwight Henry
    1975-1976 Student Regent
    Tennessee Technological University
Sam H. Ingram (1975-1979)
    ex-officio
    Commissioner of Education

James H. Jones, Jr.**
    Mt. Pleasant
    Vice-Chairman (1976-   )
Ben S. Kimbrough (term ended 1976)*
    Clarksville
    Vice-Chairman (1972-1976)
George M. Klepper, Jr. (term ended 1979)*
    Memphis
Charles J. Liner (term ended 1977)*
    Athens
Johnella H. Martin**
    Nashville
C. Scott Mayfield (appointed 1977)
    Athens
Edwards S. Porter (1975-1979)
    ex-officio
    Commissioner of Agriculture
Patrick W. Prill
    1979-1980 Student Regent
    Memphis State University
Ella V. Ross**
    Johnson City
Van L. Riggins, Jr.
    1978-1979 Student Regent
    Austin Peay State University
Anthony A. Seaton
    1976-1977 Student Regent
    East Tennessee State University
E. C. Stimbert (1972)*
    ex-officio
    Commissioner of Education
J. Frank Taylor (term ended 1975)*
    Huntingdon
Guilford F. Thornton (term ended 1975)*
    ex-officio
    Commissioner of Agriculture
J. Howard Warf**
    statutory member
    past Commissioner of Education
David V. White**
    Knoxville
Clyde M. York (1979)
    ex-officio
    Commissioner of Agriculture

Chancellor

Cecil C. Humphreys (1972-1975)   Roy S. Nicks (1975-   )

*Charter member
**Charter member and terms extend past 1979

APPENDIX C

TENNESSEE COMMUNITY COLLEGES
SELECTED DATA FOR 1978-1979

ENROLLMENT, FALL OF 1978

Total Degree-Credit Head Count: 29,562

Full-Time:	11,744	39.7%	Caucasian:	23,757	80.4%
Part-Time:	17,818	60.3%	Black:	5,049	17.1%
			Other:	756	2.5%
Freshman:	20,763	70.2%	Under 18 to 24:	15,458	52.3%
Sophomore:	5,931	20.1%	25 and over:	13,835	47.7%
Special	2,868	9.7%	Average Age:		27.5 years
Male:	12,501	42.3%	In-State:	29,207	98.8%
Female:	17,061	57.7%	Out-of-State:	355	1.2%

Total Full-Time Equated: 17,284

STUDENT FEES

In-State Full-Time:	$ 84 per quarter
In-State Part-Time:	7 per credit hour
Out-of-State Full-Time:	312 per quarter
Out-of-State Part-Time:	26 per credit hour

FACULTY

Total Full-Time: 617

Professor:	10	Doctorate:	96
Associate Professor:	102	Master's+90 hours:	46
Assistant Professor:	259	Master's+45 hours:	66
Instructor:	246	Master's and other:	409

FINANCES

Total State Operating Appropriation: $27,577,400
Total Unrestricted Operating Expenditures and Transfers: $38,531,766

PHYSICAL PLANT

Total Plant Value: $92,628,846
Total Campus Size: 1,244 acres
Total Net Assignable Space: 1,411,403 square feet

APPENDIX D

DEGREE-CREDIT HEAD COUNT ENROLLMENT: FALL 1966 THROUGH FALL 1978

	Chattanooga State	Cleveland State	Columbia State	Dyersburg State	Jackson State	Motlow State	Roane State	Shelby State	Volunteer State	Walters State	Total
1966			393								393
1967		681	1,025		640						2,346
1968		1,368	1,125		1,436						3,929
1969		1,576	1,215	588	1,438	530					5,347
1970		1,909	1,331	626	1,341	748				389	6,344
1971		2,170	1,330	636	1,350	861	323		578	1,106	8,354
1972		2,167	1,326	754	1,329	862	703	1,059	1,198	1,357	10,755
1973		2,444	1,278	899	1,712	1,017	923	2,199	1,342	1,710	13,524
1974	2,245	2,576	1,366	1,046	1,834	980	1,476	3,287	1,667	1,927	18,404
1975	3,471	3,169	1,797	1,106	2,186	1,108	2,394	4,050	2,347	2,877	24,505
1976	3,503	3,067	1,728	960	2,099	1,373	2,537	4,677	2,519	2,752	25,215
1977	3,797	3,263	1,898	1,054	2,275	1,566	2,807	4,657	2,717	3,381	27,415
1978	4,233	3,415	2,161	1,042	2,503	1,954	3,223	4,939	2,682	3,410	29,562

Source: Tennessee Higher Education Commission Statistical Abstracts and Student Information System Reports

APPENDIX E

DEGREE-CREDIT FULL-TIME EQUATED ENROLLMENT: FALL 1966 THROUGH FALL 1978

	Chattanooga State	Cleveland State	Columbia State	Dyersburg State	Jackson State	Motlow State	Roane State	Shelby State	Volunteer State	Walters State	Total
1966			361								361
1967		555	761		506						1,822
1968		1,118	933		1,101						3,152
1969		1,186	1,061	301	1,034	400					3,982
1970		1,409	1,226	514	1,047	600				255	5,051
1971		1,506	1,201	564	1,050	685	235		446	745	6,432
1972		1,516	1,007	570	1,034	651	578	846	1,023	939	8,164
1973		1,658	903	614	1,082	738	729	1,552	1,067	1,130	9,473
1974	1,373	1,693	970	645	1,125	709	997	2,300	1,190	1,250	12,252
1975	2,327	2,059	1,218	764	1,478	815	1,527	3,057	1,683	1,949	16,877
1976	2,349	1,919	1,150	664	1,459	870	1,637	3,301	1,663	1,768	16,780
1977	2,411	1,910	1,165	665	1,437	973	1,661	3,135	1,657	1,794	16,808
1978	2,632	1,919	1,248	626	1,522	1,068	1,750	3,068	1,577	1,874	17,284

Note: From 1968, FTE computed by dividing total student credit hours by 15 (full-time load). Prior to 1968, FTE represented the number of full-time students (12 hours or more) plus total student credit hours divided by 12.

Source: Tennessee Higher Education Commission Reports and Student Information System Reports

APPENDIX F

Associate Degrees and Certificates Awarded: 1967-68 through 1978-79

	Chattanooga State	Cleveland State	Columbia State	Dyersburg State	Jackson State	Motlow State	Roane State	Shelby State	Volunteer State	Walters State	Total
1967-1968											
Associate Degrees			44								44
Certificates											
Total			44								44
1968-1969											
Associate Degrees		61	94		55						210
Certificates											
Total		61	94		55						210
1969-1970											
Associate Degrees		69	123		78						270
Certificates											
Total		69	123		78						270
1970-1971											
Associate Degrees		106	209	72	104	86					577
Certificates		6									6
Total		112	209	72	104	86					583
1971-1972											
Associate Degrees		203	296	110	127	112				56	904
Certificates		4									4
Total		207	296	110	127	112				56	908
1972-1973											
Associate Degrees		244	250	93	178	141	21		56	84	1,067
Certificates		8								4	12
Total		252	250	93	178	141	21		56	88	1,079
1973-1974											
Associate Degrees		225	206	106	144	149	71	25	129	148	1,203
Certificates		17	8			2	2				29
Total		242	214	106	144	151	73	25	129	148	1,232

	Chattanooga State	Cleveland State	Columbia State	Dyersburg State	Jackson State	Motlow State	Roane State	Shelby State	Volunteer State	Walters State	Total
1974-1975											
Associate Degrees		332	188	70	182	140	85	87	186	151	1,421
Certificates		8	3			1		1	17	4	34
Total		340	191	70	182	141	85	88	203	155	1,455
1975-1976											
Associate Degrees	177	354	221	91	211	167	104	154	220	226	1,925
Certificates	39	5	14			5			16	33	112
Total	216	359	235	91	211	172	104	154	236	259	2,037
1976-1977											
Associate Degrees	201	274	229	95	214	150	152	198	211	329	2,053
Certificates	43	20	18			9			22	8	120
Total	244	294	247	95	214	159	152	198	233	337	2,173
1977-1978											
Associate Degrees	201	361	199	79	273	159	183	230	206	277	2,168
Certificates	52	11	4			2	2	4	27	8	110
Total	253	372	203	79	273	161	185	234	233	285	2,278
1978-1979											
Associate Degrees	253	341	213	90	273	162	167	229	183	288	2,199
Certificates	57	10	24		22	2	2	11	30	17	175
Total	310	351	237	90	295	164	169	240	213	305	2,374

Source: 1966-1967 through 1972-1973, State Board of Education Annual Statistical Reports
1973-1974 through 1978-1979, State Board of Regents Annual Reports

APPENDIX G

State Operating Appropriations: 1966-1967 through 1978-1979

	Chattanooga State	Cleveland State	Columbia State	Dyersburg State	Jackson State	Motlow State	Roane State	Shelby State	Volunteer State	Walters State	Total
1966-1967		$ 50,000	$ 400,000		$ 50,000						$ 500,000
1967-1968		400,000	750,000		400,000						1,550,000
1968-1969		755,000	975,000	$ 75,000	755,000	$ 75,000					2,635,000
1969-1970		1,054,000	1,025,000	483,000	1,054,000	483,000				$ 72,000	4,171,000
1970-1971		1,181,000	1,054,000	712,000	1,135,000	760,000	$ 71,000	$ 95,000	$ 71,000	475,000	5,554,000
1971-1972		1,592,000	1,327,000	757,000	1,189,000	804,000	536,000	146,000	585,000	706,000	7,642,000
1972-1973		1,814,000	1,322,000	790,000	1,297,000	932,000	740,000	1,283,000	1,022,000	1,022,000	10,222,000
1973-1974		1,846,000	1,289,000	790,000	1,297,000	932,000	938,000	1,824,000	1,576,000	1,219,000	11,711,000
1974-1975	$1,672,000	1,923,000	1,271,000	849,000	1,391,000	988,000	1,120,000	2,688,500	1,530,000	1,353,000	14,785,500
1975-1976	1,829,000	2,076,000	1,382,000	920,000	1,512,000	1,054,000	1,198,000	2,856,000	1,646,000	1,495,000	15,968,000
1976-1977	3,102,000	2,588,000	1,801,000	1,059,000	1,864,000	1,177,000	2,050,000	3,867,000	2,046,000	2,325,000	21,879,000
1977-1978	3,227,000	2,681,000	1,863,000	1,059,000	1,989,000	1,466,000	2,185,000	5,040,000	2,269,000	2,402,000	24,181,000
1978-1979	3,676,500	3,070,600	2,135,600	1,141,600	2,279,000	1,843,400	2,693,700	5,330,000	2,728,800	2,678,200	27,577,400

Source: Institutional, Tennessee Higher Education Commission, and State Board of Regents Reports

APPENDIX H

Total Unrestricted Operating Expenditures and Transfers: 1966-1967 through 1978-1979

	Chattanooga State	Cleveland State	Columbia State	Dyersburg State	Jackson State	Motlow State	Roane State	Shelby State	Volunteer State	Walters State	Total
1966-1967			$ 589,701								$ 589,701
1967-1968		$ 638,534	1,122,003		$ 635,453						2,395,990
1968-1969		1,156,317	1,303,875	$ 36,649	1,180,375	$ 36,901					3,714,117
1969-1970		1,389,888	1,477,577	604,826	1,471,864	560,813				$ 59,754	5,564,722
1970-1971		1,644,355	1,470,527	932,409	1,600,924	857,966	$ 63,682	$ 43,181	$ 59,697	570,268	7,243,009
1971-1972		1,956,203	1,895,107	1,029,887	1,640,632	979,019	496,365	155,646	728,200	977,956	9,859,015
1972-1973		2,313,429	1,810,453	1,088,195	1,899,906	1,170,025	891,730	1,373,822	1,504,896	1,392,264	18,444,720
1973-1974		2,493,650	1,772,819	1,095,038	1,786,117	1,221,525	1,329,254	2,344,229	1,957,615	1,593,918	15,594,165
1974-1975	$2,298,427	2,921,477	1,925,017	1,210,754	2,050,330	1,457,525	1,744,569	3,530,909	2,362,730	1,952,904	21,454,642
1975-1976	2,748,024	3,578,206	2,136,616	1,374,124	2,385,023	1,679,239	2,006,163	4,517,534	2,541,745	2,336,496	25,303,170
1976-1977	4,019,183	3,480,781	2,712,873	1,357,743	2,680,461	1,806,817	2,676,173	5,708,536	3,054,745	3,329,534	30,826,846
1977-1978	4,838,199	3,689,820	2,622,311	1,569,430	2,921,122	2,226,704	3,239,658	6,372,048	3,209,770	3,490,819	34,179,881
1978-1979	5,752,573	4,259,634	2,961,553	1,466,267	3,162,252	2,598,884	3,800,666	7,010,245	3,679,365	3,840,327	38,531,766

Source: 1968-1969 through 1972-1973, Institutional Annual Financial Reports
1967-1968 and 1973-1974 through 1978-1979, State of Tennessee Annual Financial Reports

APPENDIX I

State Capital Outlay: 1965-1967 through 1978-1979

	Chattanooga State	Cleveland State	Columbia State	Dyersburg State	Jackson State	Motlow State	Roane State	Shelby State	Volunteer State	Walters State	Total
1965-1967		$1,246,000	$1,333,333		$1,375,000						$ 3,954,333
1967-1969		750,000	600,000	$1,449,000	600,000	$1,449,000				$1,100,000	5,948,000
1969-1971		465,000	425,000	100,000	460,000	250,000	$2,000,000		$3,000,000		6,700,000
1971-1972		250,000		70,000		50,000	150,000	$5,000,000	275,000	150,000	5,945,000
1972-1973		131,000			225,000	400,000		3,000,000	1,000,000	1,000,000	5,756,000
1973-1974		150,000					95,000		333,000	155,000	733,000
1974-1975								420,000	9,000	160,000	589,000
1975-1976	$1,935,000		150,000	25,000		24,000	266,000	3,546,000	39,000		5,985,000
1976-1977	2,240,000						2,445,000	3,870,000	1,470,000	2,218,000	12,243,000
1977-1978	3,667,000					141,000	3,530,000	1,782,000		68,000	9,188,000
1978-1979	100,000		18,000		40,000		25,000		3,255,000	2,990,000	6,428,000

Note: Prior to 1971-1972, Appropriations on Biennial Basis
Source: Tennessee General Assembly Appropriation Bills

INDEX